TERROR

and everyday life

TERROR
and everyday life

Singular Moments in the History of the Horror Film

Jonathan Lake Crane

SAGE PUBLICATIONS
International Educational and Professional Publisher
Thousand Oaks   London   New Delhi

For information address:

 SAGE Publications, Inc.
2455 Teller Road
Thousand Oaks, California 91320

SAGE Publications Ltd.
6 Bonhill Street
London EC2A 4PU
United Kingdom

SAGE Publications India Pvt. Ltd.
M-32 Market
Greater Kailash I
New Delhi 110 048 India

Printed in the United States of America

Library of Congress Cataloging-in-Publication Data

Crane, Jonathan Lake, 1959-
    Terror and everyday life : singular moments in the history of the horror film / Jonathan Lake Crane.
        p. cm.
    Includes bibliographical references and index.
    ISBN 0-8039-5848-X. — ISBN 0-8039-5849-8 (pbk.)
    1. Horror films—History and criticism. I. Title.
PN1995.9.H6C72   1994
791.43'616—dc20   94-29949
                                                                  CIP

94 95 96 97 98 10 9 8 7 6 5 4 3 2 1

Sage Production Editor: Yvonne Könneker

Sage Copy Editor: Joyce Kuhn

CONTENTS

PREFACE

This work carries with it a serious bias. The reader will find that I hold in question much of the popular and academic work done on the meaning of horror in film. This slant arises from a dual dissatisfaction with psychoanalytic film theory and with mainstream critics who see contemporary cinematic violence as nothing more than simple blood lust on the part of today's audience.

The bulk of academic research on the horror film has looked to Freud and his heirs for direction. In reading through the criticism of the genre, one is likely to find a limited set of interpretive possibilities that too often refers the meaning of scary tales back to repressed instinct. There is more to screen violence than thwarted libidinal desire or some other variation of psychic upheaval. I hope that my readings across the history of the horror film will prove useful to those not entirely convinced that the unconscious unilaterally determines the meaning of terror.

If academic research in horror is problematic, so too is mainstream wisdom concerning the horror film. According to critics who operate outside the campus (who all seem to have their own television show), horror films have reached an unprecedented low. For mainstream critics, today's horror films are moronic efforts designed to sate sadistic and illegitimate appetites.

These concerns are nothing new. Anyone marginally acquainted with the history of American popular culture knows we are periodically subject to hysterical pronouncements over what we are doing to ourselves and our children for entertainment. What is different at present is that the stakes are higher.

Low culture—the entertainment of the young, minorities, the working class, or the disenfranchised—is under serious fire. The critics of the mainstream have decided we should be protected from "illicit" cultural objects. Whether it's a Body Count tape, the new Slayer CD, or a horror film that Blockbuster Video will no longer carry matters little. Excessive culture (productions which speak too loudly) is being banned, outlawed, or otherwise made unavailable to the many who want it.

Case in point: The last rock 'n' roll show I attended ended with the heavy metal parody band GWAR (who claim to be barbaric cannibals from outer space stranded on Earth) being arrested for their on-stage antics. What got GWAR in trouble was a sarcastic skit in which the band humiliated and dismembered a hanging judge who wanted to ban "satanic" rock. For this act, the group was arrested by police who surreptitiously filmed both the show and the audience. GWAR was fined and prohibited from performing in North Carolina. The venue where they played (at the time the only bar in town that booked radical bands and allowed kids under 18 entrance) was permanently closed for hosting an obscene performance.

These sorts of attacks on illegitimate entertainment are becoming all too frequent as mainstream critics persuasively argue the case that no good can come from watching performances that are too bloody, too real, or too vicious. Present-day horror films, if one believes the public guardians, stimulate the desire for real bloodshed as they enthrall witless audiences. As a fan of the horror film, I find this argument both libelous and fraught with formidable hazards for anyone who believes in free speech and the ability of popular culture to reflect serious concerns. In opposition to critics who would save us from ourselves, I have tried to elaborate some of the good reasons fans have for relishing ultraviolence.

Prefaces generally end with an acknowledgment of debt, and while my debts cannot be discharged in the space of a few sentences, I would like to make public a list of those to whom I owe a great deal. For her patience, abiding support, and helpful comments on the manuscript, I wish to thank my wife, Barbara. Without her considerable aid, this project would have been infinitely more difficult. I also want to thank her for actually watching, against her better judgment, some of these films with me. Many friends enabled me to write this book, but I must give particular thanks to Lou Ann Lamb, Sara Pitzer, Bishwarup Sen, John Nerone, Ivy Glennon, Phil Gordon, and Lynn Gordon.

I am also lucky to have had the assistance of two fine editors at Sage, Sophy Craze and Joyce Kuhn, who have made this a better work. Yvonne Könneker, in Books Production, was also an invaluable aide as the book went to press.

I am especially grateful to James Carey, Joanne Case, Norman Denzin, David Gaydos, Robert Jones, Cary Nelson, and Lawrence Grossberg. These exemplary teachers and scholars were a source of inspiration and guidance. I hope they see something of themselves in the text.

Finally, this book is for my father—Richard Otis Crane. He showed me how to write it.

1. TERROR AND EVERYDAY LIFE

Everybody is a book of blood.
        —Clive Barker (1984)

If our world is a dangerous place (and who could deny it?), then what of the darkened cinemas and entertainment centers in which we share bloodied impressions of everyday life?[1] Millions of fans now consider any horror film absent unprecedented scenes of graphic mayhem a waste of precious leisure time. Exploding heads spewing forth brain tissue, meathooks baited with twitching corpses, and the slow-motion arc of a costumed maniac's axe cleaving delicate flesh are now hallmarks of worthy entertainment.

Living in a violent time has not diminished our taste for blood. Instead of seeking relief from a surfeit of violence, many of us have opted to celebrate entertainment that makes a virtue of attempting to surpass any crazed act of real everyday slaughter. We cherish the gory piecework of Hollywood slashers and have made them media luminaries for their exemplary efforts.[2] In so doing, in canonizing horror films and ranking serial killers among the entertainment elite, have we made the perilous environment that lies just beyond the coursing marquee lights and pale glow of the video monitor an even more dangerous space?

Violent pastimes are nothing new, but there has never been anything quite as violent and massively popular as the contemporary horror film.

AUTHOR'S NOTE: A version of this chapter originally appeared as an article, "Terror in Everyday Life," in *Communication*, 1988, Vol. 10, Summer, pp. 367-382. Copyright © 1988 by Gordon & Breach, Newark, NJ. Used with permission.

1

Reborn over the past two decades, with a novel and startling emphasis on ultraviolence, the horror film has entered a revolutionary new epoch.[3] Horror films, and the many mainstream movies that have followed the horror film's lead, are now best measured by how well they deliver pain. In the celebrated films of Sam Raimi, Tobe Hooper, David Cronenberg, Sean Cunningham, George Romero, Steve Miner, Wes Craven (where stars like Jason, Freddy, Dr. Giggles, zombie hordes, and countless mass murderers play), torment takes center stage. As Carol J. Clover (1992) notes, "To the extent that a movie succeeds in 'hurting' its viewers . . . it is good horror; to the extent that it fails, it is bad horror" (p. 229). And of course, the best way to hurt viewers is to attack, as viciously as possible, the poor souls whose bad luck has placed them in a slasher's sights.

In this extraordinary shift, older forms of horrific imagery and storytelling have vanished. Horror films that rely on the hallowed legends of the past, spiced with just a hint of spurious violence, are gone. Spooky tales stressing the importance of group solidarity in the face of evil have also been driven from the cineplex. And films that assayed the meaning of dread, dwelling deep into the mysterious psychology of madness and evil, while eschewing vulgar and bloody spectacle, have faded from view as well. Only those with a nostalgic bent, who yearn for the return of dated tales, are interested in films that celebrate the indomitable power of community while gingerly avoiding unnecessary bloodshed.[4] In their place, we have films that reject the stories and stylistic devices of older horror tales in preference for inordinately simple narratives that seem to exist solely to showcase the latest leap forward in stomach-churning special effects.

This dramatic turn has not gone unremarked. Not everyone is altogether pleased by the direction taken by the new horror film. Critics are almost singularly unanimous in their concern over the hazardous content of the contemporary horror film. Gene Siskel and Roger Ebert (the flagship brothers of mainstream film criticism), teams of social scientists, many feminists, and those who diligently monitor popular culture (the PTA, the Parent's Music Resource Center, evangelists, newspersons, columnists, etc.) have all raised similar alarms about what we are doing to ourselves by indulging in the blood sport of contemporary cinematic shock (Donnerstein, Linz, & Penrod, 1987; Dworkin, 1981; Ebert, 1969, 1981; Gore, 1987; Monaco, 1980; Plagens, Miller, Foote, & Yoffe, 1991; Prawer, 1980; Ventura, 1990).[5]

For these dismayed authorities, the most alarming aspect of the contemporary horror film, far more frightening than even the bloodiest on-screen assault, is the existence of an audience of millions that craves gore. Of course, the film industry has been duly criticized for pandering to the decadent taste of the masses by supplying the market with a seemingly endless series of shockers, but it is the mute audience that has borne the brunt of attacks against contemporary horror, as it is they who heartily absorb vast quantities of carnage and bloodletting. Even horror aficionados, like Chas. Balun (1987), author of *The Gore Score*, a fan's guide to the best in ultraviolent horror, know the "horror audience would sit through just about **anything** to see a graphic knife wound or a splashy decapitation" (unpaginated). One can understand the profit motive in quenching spurious appetites; it is a bit harder to empathize with sadistic junkies who take glorious delight in vicious slaughter.[6]

Enjoying endless reels of gratuitous ultraviolence is taken by critics of recent shockers to mean that not only do woefully impressionable viewers endorse the heinous acts committed by countless avaricious psychos but that these same thugs are also ready to reenact their favorite moments of movie mayhem in public. Today's horror film, as Robin Wood (1987) sees it, "invites a dangerous identification (either sadistic or masochistic or both simultaneously) with punishment" (p. 82). Roger Ebert (1981) takes this line even further, arguing that influencing horror fans is

> a simple matter of construction. These films [are] not about their villains. They [are] about the *acts* of the villains. Dismayed, I realized that the visual strategy of these films displaced the villain from his traditional place within the film—and moved him into the audience. . . . The lust to kill and rape becomes the true subject of the movies. And the lust is not placed on the screen, where it can be attached to the killer-character; it is placed in the audience. The missing character in so many of these films can be found in the audience; we are all invited to be him, and some (such as my white-haired neighbor) gladly accept the role. (p. 56)[7]

Along these lines, either you identify with the slasher—you'd like to have a razor-sharp, foot-long machete in hand as well—or you identify with the worthless victim whose spectacular dismemberment becomes the death you too merit. If one does not actually go so far as to mimic the mayhem oneself (identifying with the killer), then audience members will applaud another's right to commit film-inspired atrocities (because the hapless dead deserved to die).[8]

These unenviable viewing positions don't leave the audience much room to maneuver. Either you wish you had the power to carve up a score of unsuspecting victims or you envy the dead. The only way to prove yourself immune from the noxious influence of these dangerous films is to do as Ebert and Wood have done: You must denounce them. Given their argument, acknowledging that you are a latter-day horror fan is tantamount to announcing that you too are a monster.

The longevity of the slasher cycle and its complete displacement of all earlier styles of horror film, in combination with its appeal to a mass audience, might indeed testify to an appalling lack of taste among an entire generation of filmgoers, but it might also represent something more than a lamentable drop in popular standards. When distressed critics write off today's horror fans as a horde of potential serial killers they might feel better, having had the opportunity to reaffirm the sound moral foundation which underlies their aesthetic sensibilities, but left abandoned is the difficult question of why do people enjoy such sadistic swill? A more measured evaluation of the new horror is necessary if we hope to explain why so many of us have found a diet of boundless violence so deliciously satisfying. In the end, even if the new horror is nothing more than de Sade disguised behind a goalie's mask, we must still ask, how did it become so damnably popular?

Unquestionably, contemporary horror films are infinitely more violent than their predecessors in the genre; yet these films and their abominable fans are not treated as pariahs by mainstream reviewers and many scholarly cineastes merely because modern horror films contain extraordinarily violent displays. For degreed critics, the basis for horror's present-day opprobrious status lies beyond an academic squeamishness to engage grotesquely violent texts. Film scholars have, after all, found something good to say about bloody films like *Casualties of War* (1989) and *Lethal Weapon* (1987) (Fiorillo, 1987; McKinney, 1993). Similarly, critics whose audience is not narrowly confined to fellow scholars have given a hearty thumbs up to films structured around violent set pieces (Canby, 1990; James, 1990; Maslin, 1990a).

It is not violence per se that renders the contemporary horror film a distasteful read. It is the nihilistic context in which this violence occurs that makes the horror film irredeemable. Violence in the contemporary shocker is never redemptive, revelatory, logical, or climactic (it does not resolve conflicts). An unlettered viewer who comes to the theater with the expectation that bloodshed will serve a traditional narrative function is likely to leave the film wondering why any healthy individual would willingly choose to consort with such atavistic tripe.

Although violence in the slasher film makes little conventional sense, it does offer a vivid visual approximation of what it feels like to live in an inordinately dangerous world—a world, which, like the purposeless scenes of graphic mayhem randomly scattered through the slasher film, has also stopped making sense.

Extraordinarily negative productions, according to J. G. Ballard, the British master of dystopic fiction, allow audiences to "confront the terrifying void of a patently meaningless universe by challenging it at its own game, to remake zero by provoking it in every conceivable way" (quoted in Wagar, 1982, p. 175). Although Ballard is talking about contemporary works of grim science fiction, this contest of excessive provocation is most commonly found in the contemporary horror film. Horror is not the only nihilistic center of cultural production today, but it is certainly the arena with the sharpest teeth. If the present-day work of horror generally follows Ballard's lead, then it is important to assay the appalling depths to which these "terminal visions" will descend (Wagar, 1982, p. xi).[9]

A very wide and disparate group of critical commentaries have marked our days as the end times. These doomsday proclamations can be located within any sector of cultural production. From the frenzied bully pulpits of the fundamentalist far right, in the now defunct, jaundiced pages of *The Saturday Review,* to the harangues of Marcuse and other similarly aligned leftists, resound the mournful cries that this age is condemned because it cannot imagine, and thus create, a **meaningful** future. For these dispirited commentators, we live in the desperate closing hours of the age of *Homo hydrogenesis* (Ballard, quoted in Wagar, 1982, p. 123).

For *Homo hydrogenesis,* eschatology no longer belongs solely to those who passionately proselytize for mystical bands and established religions. We inhabit a world in which the future has vanished before everyday signs of the last things. These signs, billboards loudly proclaiming our imminent erasure, are openly available to all; no one is illiterate or otherwise incapable of recognizing these tokens of quotidian damnation.[10]

Living amid these cruel signs that herald our extinction has had a corrosive effect on our ability to imagine tomorrow as a better time and tomorrow's world as a safer place.[11] When the world seems clearly beyond repair, we are only capable of private amusement, narcissistic whimsy, and mass despair. For this reason, religious philosopher Jacques Maritain condemns "the modern mind [as] intrinsically evil" (quoted in

Wagar, 1982, p. xii). It is pernicious and vile because it will not imagine a future.

The future belongs to nothing and no one. The only possible future is one lived by resigned individuals whose sole link to one another is the sure knowledge that we are all equally damned. It is not coincidental that our "strongest communities" (strong in the sense that they share a seemingly indivisible belief system) are those enclaves that are fiercely committed to leaving the Earth in an upcoming worldwide conflagration (Lifton & Strozier, 1990). The world may have to be destroyed before we have anything in common.

For those who do not and cannot share an indivisible system of belief, "all statements of what is good, beautiful, true, and real [become] matters of private or social [not societal] preference; moreover . . . all words, numbers, logics, grammars and sciences are games" (Wagar, 1982, p. xi). The appearance of a infinite multitude of solopsistic language games, making sense to none but the initiated few, confirms the disappearance of the future. As shared languages, common to many, collapse into untranslatable private dialects, communities shatter into isolated and evanescent cliques.[12] When no durable consensus can be reached on anything that matters, as there is no common tongue to make us one, future time and possible histories are vitiated.

As an eschatological force, science is indistinguishable from religious practice. The end times are heralded by a diverse set of calamitous phenomena: the population explosion, the greenhouse effect, leaky toxic dumps, acid rain, poisoned seas, cancerous holes in the ozone, global deforestation and subsequent global desertification, continental famine, and the furious extinction of the world's animal and plant life (Conservation Foundation, 1987; Kassiola, 1990; Kemp, 1990; Tobin, 1990).[13]

All such straits serve as transitory markers (there is always another more pressing crisis looming on the horizon) of a necessary terminus. Our only collective knowledge, shared beliefs that brook little possibility of serious disagreement, is that we are dressed, in the culinary and sartorial senses, in what H. Bruce Farnsworth called "chic bleak" (quoted in Wagar, 1982, p. 3). We may quibble about the means but the end seems certain.[14]

This world, tomorrow's world, and individual fate cannot be mastered through knowledge, goodwill, or good works. Backs are resolutely turned on unrealized hopes, rational thought and any other pipedream of enduring, or even momentary, progress. Pessimism transcends ideological boundaries as ideology becomes the foundation for different bitter flavors of catastrophic prediction. Each year bereft of meaningful advancement or collective enrichment is just another "year of living stupidly" (O'Rourke, 1985, p. 91).

In the end, perhaps, the sanest course of action is to go mad and retire from hope. Lewis Thomas (1983), in a horrific exploration of what it must be like to mature as the world self-destructs, has written, "What I cannot imagine, what I cannot put up with, the thought that keeps grinding its way into my mind . . . is what it would be like to be young. How do the young stand it? How can they keep their sanity? If I were very young, sixteen or seventeen years old, I think I would begin, perhaps very slowly and imperceptibly, to go crazy" (p. 167).

The madness that Thomas contemplates, as a reasonable coping mechanism, is a consequence of having to participate, if only as an unwilling spectator, in an arms race that will almost inevitably end with one of the contestants crossing the finish line. No matter how much we hate this useless, ridiculous exercise, we must endure the spectacle and await the endgame.[15]

In addition to living with the very real possibility of destruction on a global scale, our franchised streets of commerce, supermarkets, and drugstores are plastered with once innocuous brand names that now recall brutal massacres—not small pleasant consumer satisfactions. A mild headache can be a death sentence, for the next Tylenol® you take may contain an undesirable portion of cyanide. Feel like a little snack to tide you over until supper? Enjoy a chilito at Taco Bell® or drop into McDonald's® for some fries—and perish as a lonely sniper empties his Uzi. If going out for fast food or even getting on the freeway that leads to the drive-through is potentially deadly, then watching *The Mummy* (1932) or *The Wasp Woman* (1959) is a waste of time—if you had hoped to find the experience pleasantly frightening.[16]

There are, however, visions of the horrible available, images that can pleasurably reawaken the horrific possibilities of atomic apocalypse or a trip to the local convenience mart. Only these scabrous images can approximate the speed and vigor of death's inflation, an immense expansion made possible by the dizzyingly rapid devaluation of all life. Only the contemporary horror film comes close to the terror of everyday life.

The horrific constructs available do not offer any possibilities beyond that of being able to confront terror. The engagement with such images is neither cathartic nor reassuring; it simply demonstrates that one's sight, if nothing else, still clearly registers the world. **Watching a horror film is a reality check;** it is the entertainment equivalent of checking CNN's *Headline News* for the latest tragedy or scanning monotonously bleak headlines over black coffee and an apple danish.[17]

Given these oppressive conditions, it is impossible to end a horror film with any plausible orientation to the future. The dawn is not brightest after the storm. The future is just an immediate sequel to this evening's insanity (video at 11).[18] The nihilism, as common wisdom, of the contemporary horror film is a function of overt codes that explicitly deny the possibility of knowledge or collective action producing a remotely viable future. Contemporary shockers speak articulately of everyday terror, but they cannot imagine a tomorrow without tremendous fear, a fear that modifies both the future and its imagination.[19] For the horror film, and everyday life, today is the last day of anybody's life.

Our town, the everyday present, is where menace is given substance. Monsters thrive along Main Street and Elm Street U.S.A. It is on these avenues, common to all of the public, where terror implacably strikes. The great man's laboratory, the gothic castle, the ruined mansion, and the pharaoh's sacred tomb have been dismissed from the screen. The Universal (Studio) age of spooky thrills is cheap fodder for late-night and weekend television. When these creature features are telecast, they are usually burlesqued by a horror host who vapidly, but correctly, jokes about how tired and silly Dracula and the Wolfman have become.

Today, it is the omnipotent serial killer, ravenous zombie hordes, and bodies in sustained visceral revolution invading middle-class havens of leisure and domesticity who embody horror. These truly repellent creatures do not come from outside our nebulous social networks; they do not arrive in our suburbs fresh from the remote Carpathian Mountains; they are not created by an exotic necromancer or by well-intentioned scientists who err as ambitious humans will. They are us, and we never know when we will act as monsters.

Atomic fictions also fail to deliver chills. The giant ant (or any of the other beasts in the immense nuclear menagerie) of the 1950s horror and science fiction cinema, which served as an emblem of "the new" for the emergent nuclear age, is now a bellwether in spectacularly inept special effects direction. Perhaps, we can scare up some faint measure of appreciation for the colossal beasts in *It Came From Beneath the Sea* (1955), *The Beast From 20,000 Fathoms* (1953), and *Godzilla, King of the Monsters* (1956) by treating them as objects of winsome drive-in nostalgia, but as far as representing a threat they are big and impotent.[20]

Today's monsters no longer cast an impossibly vast shadow over our land, trashing precious cities and insignificant citizens as they stomp their way through an unlucky metroplex. Immense property destruction, the fearsome mark of the atomic beast's power (think of Godzilla trampling various model Japanese cities), is more properly suited to big-budget summer comedies and feel-good action pictures featuring buddy bonding and pyrotechnic excess in equal measure. City blocks tumbling down in clouds of dust and flying debris as droll heroes dash for cover is material that demands a cheap laugh (in the words of SCTV, "that sure blowed up good") and not a tingle down the spine.[21]

Having forgone sabotage on an epic scale, in lieu of taking the blade to tender human flesh our monsters have returned to human dimensions. In eschewing dinosaur proportions, the contemporary monster has not, however, readopted the look common to all monsters prior to the invention of the atomic bomb. The climactic moment when the monster's ruined face is revealed, as in *The Phantom of the Opera* (1925) and *The Bride of Frankenstein* (1935), holds no privileged place in recent horror tales.

Once upon a time,

> all the resources of the costume and make-up department [were] mobilised precisely to give the monster an appearance and an appearance that will not only terrify, but will also give it credence. . . . Moreover, it is no accident that the most 'spectacular' and intricate—the most arresting—mobilisation of 'trucage' [special effects] centres so frequently either on the initial appearance of the monster or on its ultimate destruction. (Neale, 1980, p. 45)

The audience no longer needs the benefit of special effects to better imagine the face of the monstrous (Maslin, 1990b). We know the world is peopled with monsters whose faces come from a random assortment of high school yearbooks, driver's licenses, and bathroom mirrors. We are, however, in need of all the help that special effects teams like Industrial Light and Magic and other fantasy factories can furnish to capture not the look of the monstrous but the effect the monstrous has on us.

Special effects are now mobilized around human evisceration not only to terrify the audience but also to give credence to the fact that to be human is to suffer spectacular abominations. The only **object** of terror is the body; consequently, special effects are now concentrated on flaying the flesh off the body. All other aspects of everyday life have been totally terrorized; the body is just the last in a long line of useless objects to suffer inordinate violence.[22] As one more meaningless slate, some may find it objectionable that the body is now greasy with blood. While their shrill objections are understandable, their unwitting shock is not.

The central operation of present-day horror films, the inexorable splintering of the flesh, is abetted by some standard codes that help organize our demise. To begin locating the codes around which the dominant strand in contemporary horror is constructed, it is necessary to briefly examine representative works that have defined the field. *Night of the Living Dead* (1968) and *Halloween* (1978) are extremely popular films that strongly exhibit three primary codes around which many of the most memorable horror films produced over the past 20 years revolve.[23] These central axes, about which horror now makes itself known, are as follows: All collective action will fail; knowledge and experience have no value when one is engaged with the horrible; and the destruction of the menace (should it occur) carries no guarantee that the future will be safe.

Anyone with even the slightest familiarity with today's horror films knows that the most popular monsters at present are those who never die and star in multiple sequels. Sequels are made not only because the audience for a horror film is preconstituted, the product presold; they are also made because that which returns again and again provides the audience with the greatest pleasure. The return of the monster, confirming audience expectations about the impossibility of narrative resolution, also operates in terms of a second code. As audience members, our familiarity with the deadly habits of the menace further condemns those protagonists who struggle to learn how to defeat the enemy.[24] Audience foreknowledge works in a curious fashion; it does not lead to a simple sadistic delight in the predetermined fates of those on the screen, even though we are generally not preoccupied with the survival rate of those cast against the monster. Rather, it pleasurably confirms the impossibility of gaining any parcel of knowledge that is efficacious when one is confronted with the unknown. What the audience knows, like that which the protagonist eventually acquires, has no value. The audience may scream instructions at the screen, but the protagonists cannot be helped. Unlike what the protagonist learns, audience knowledge carries a degree of pleasure with the pain that knowledge is not remotely instrumental. For we, at least, know what's coming.

In earlier horror eras, the monster could be conquered with science, engineering, and a group effort guided by good men.[25] Until *Night of the Living Dead* appeared in drive-ins around the country, the majority of monsters were enemies who helped men gain confidence in their ability to control and understand the world. They also helped men not to forget that their greatest strength came when they stood as one against the Beast. You can defeat Frankenstein's monster with fire and a mob of angry citizens. Dracula can be dispatched with relative ease if one is familiar with the well-preserved lore of vampires. The original Thing can be destroyed by courageous men who know what's right. Guns loaded with silver bullets can decimate a snarling Wolfman; however, science, technology, engineering, and community effort will not repel an attack of slow-moving, flesh-eating zombies even though a hard blow to the skull puts them out of action.

The opening scene of *Night of the Living Dead* begins in a cemetery. Earlier horror films overcoded the cemetery as one of the definitive sites of horror. As the film begins, the graveyard is not a place of horror; rather, it is a spot of mundane bother. Johnny and his kindly sister have to spend an entire day driving out to their father's grave site to satisfy their mother's wish that the departed loved one be remembered with a plastic floral memorial. Barbara feels the task is a worthy one, but Johnny cannot muster any respect for the dead or their memory. He makes a number of sacrilegious remarks and begins to tease Barbara with an amateur Boris Karloff imitation. This weak imitation had previously caused Johnny's grandfather to condemn him to hell for mocking Barbara on hallowed ground. As the taunts continue, a drunk caretaker, or what looks like a drunk caretaker, looms closer to the couple. Johnny continues to pester Barbara, telling her in his awful Boris voice, "He's coming to get you." When Barbara nears the lumbering man she is clumsily attacked. Johnny tries to help his sister, but he cracks his head and dies when the queer adversary tosses him onto a tombstone. Barbara flees to a nearby farmhouse.

At this point, a number of codes emerge, codes that will become more apparent as the film continues. We expect Johnny to be punished for his disrespect of the dead, but we do not expect Barbara to be harmed. She is oppositionally positioned against the mean-spirited, wise-cracking Johnny as a good-hearted respecter of persons. We later learn she was going to apologize to the man who killed Johnny as she was upset that he might have overheard Johnny's crass remarks.

Johnny's death initially marks *Night of the Living Dead* as operating within the traditional moral landscape of older horror traditions. If Johnny blasphemes, then Johnny should and will die; however, Johnny's suffering is very limited when compared to that which Barbara must endure. She has to weather a relentless siege in the farmhouse until the zombies finally overrun the flimsy sanctuary. When the zombies enter, it is Johnny who pulls a terrified Barbara (caught while coming to the aid of another victim) into the mass of hungry flesh-eaters. Ironically, just as Johnny perished trying to help Barbara, Barbara dies an agonizing death because she tried to help another.

Altruism of any sort is no longer rewarded in the horror film. Most slasher and gore films kill off even the most heroic and self-sacrificing protagonists. If the monster should be bested, then, at the moment of apparent triumph, the protagonist must, to survive, become more violent, more savage, than the ostensible monster.[26] Even worse than the enmity that filmmakers feel for their characters, including the bravest and most intrepid souls, is the ill will that audiences feel for the ostensible heroes and heroines. The good oftentimes exasperate the crowd because they refuse to accept the plain truth that the world is a perilous place. The good are always the last to know of the danger about them, and once finally awakened to the presence of the menace, they strive to defeat the monster with entirely inappropriate means, having an uncalled-for faith in the efficacy of effort. Unwitting victims who believe they can help themselves and others are almost as abhorrent as the menace because both creatures are alien to ordinary humanity. The good then receive no special dispensation; they will be endlessly tormented with the cowardly, the weak, and the wise.

There is one other constellation of codes that the first attack introduces to the audience. When Johnny pesters Barbara with his Boris Karloff imitation—Karloff played Frankenstein's monster and countless mad doctors—he is also mocking older traditions in horror cinema. In some circles, Karloff is hailed as **the** interpretive master of horror (Glut, 1973). For some, his acting created portraits of twisted spirits with such pathos as to be worthy of accolades reserved for more legitimate theatrical endeavors. Along with Lon Chaney, Boris Karloff gave American films a cultural cachet they had never before possessed. Johnny's bit signals an end to nostalgic veneration for earlier horror presentations. The emotions that Karloff evoked, as well as the way in which he used special effects and makeup, belong to a dead tradition. Karloff is forgettable; his presence is invoked purely as comic device.

Along with Karloff's demotion comes the first presentation of the film's menace. The man who besets Barbara and Johnny is originally seen as a mildly comic drunk hobbling about the otherwise deserted cemetery. Johnny picks him as a figure of horror because he is so ludicrous as a figure of danger. Even after the zombie attacks the couple, the audience cannot be sure of who or what he is. His clothes are dusty and he doesn't carry himself in a threatening manner—he staggers and reels. The zombie does not make menacing noises or gestures and does not appear particularly strong. Johnny dies because he trips after being shoved by the zombie. At this point, the zombie appears to be an angry indigent on a bender or a mental patient who is no longer faithfully taking his usual dose of Thorazine. Just as Johnny and Barbara cannot fathom what the enemy wants, the audience cannot know the attacker wants to eat the couple. We can only assume he desires their money or her body for more ordinary acts of violence.

As individual cannibals, the zombies are not terribly dangerous. One character in the film when asked "Do they move slowly?" replies earnestly, "Yeah, they're dead, they're all messed up." To kill the awkward brutes, "Beat 'em or burn 'em. They go up pretty easy." It is only when a group of zombies gather together that one is in serious danger. The zombies overcome humans through sheer numbers. Although they do have some rudimentary tool-using capabilities, as they pound rocks against resistant objects in their path, they are basically defenseless when alone. They constitute a menace only when they outnumber human beings. Here, majority rule determines a life-form's success.

Although the majority rules in *Night of the Living Dead*, most other revered social conventions disintegrate under the zombie assault. As noted earlier, collective action comes to nothing; there is no siege mentality at work here, no successful repelling of the menace as the group becomes one. The farmhouse, where Barbara is cloistered with three other men, two women, and an injured little girl, functions as a space in which the only domestic conventions obeyed concern tending to one's private property with scrupulous care. Endless bickering, futile escape plans, cowardly insults, selfish priorities, and vapid dialogue (should love be mentioned) dominate the claustrophobic interior action. The virility with which the temporary survivors go at one another is further distinguished by the relative lack of malevolence with which the zombies try to capture and consume their venal prey.

The social fabric will not hold when faced with contemporary monsters. Husband and wife exist in the most uneasy of blessed unions.

Children kill doting parents. If a couple exchange tender sentiments, usually in the most clichéd fashion, they will expire in the near future. What was true for Barbara is true for all the good. Altruism, respect for others, and valiant acts will have the same nil effect on material circumstances as those actions that are motivated by baser desires and feelings. No actions are validated by success in *Night of the Living Dead*.

Compare these group projects with Wagar's (1982) description of social life after an apocalypse in the novel *On the Beach:* "The confrontation with death generates an intimacy of spirit among the last men and women that would otherwise never have emerged, an intimacy of wholeness and goodness unattainable in the everyday present" (p. 74). Camaraderie of this sort is unthinkable in recent horror films. In no way can a confrontation with death be said to generate the slightest hint of group unity. In a very short time—*On the Beach* was released as a film in 1959—we have become nearly incapable of producing believable portraits of group support in the face of catastrophe. Teamwork is an anachronism.

The supreme expression of contemporary nihilism revolves around the figure of the last survivor, the black male, Ben. Ben lives through a night of zombie attacks by hiding in the farmhouse cellar—a location that was vehemently defended as an ideal haven by the most cowardly victim among the group—only to be shot as a zombie by a jovial cracker posse.

After Ben is mistakenly executed, live-action photography is replaced with scanned newspaper photographs. These bits of grainy disaster candids follow the disposal of Ben's corpse. The body is pierced with meathooks (possibly the most graphic image of the entire film), dragged across the ground, tossed onto an unlit pyre, and then consumed by flames. It would be impossible for the audience to miss the ironic pit that engulfs Ben. The rescue squad produces the images that most potently demonstrate the vulnerability of the human body. Ben's strong presence vanishes instantly with his ridiculous and unnecessary death. He is shot, a silhouetted target framed within a window, from a distance of a couple of hundred yards by his erstwhile saviours who think he is just another ravenous zombie. He dies—a carnival duck dropped by a pellet gun.

Ben's story and remembrances of the other victims vanish when the rescue squad reach the farmhouse. The role of surviving narrator, voice of experience and wisdom, is erased. All that remains of his encounter with the monsters are some objective documentary newspaper photographs, pictures that apparently represent the truth of Ben's stupid demise. If any memory of Ben's last days survive, they will be based on these images. His valiant struggle is lost as his body is treated like zombie waste. He perishes as a nonhuman.[27]

Ten years after *Night of the Living Dead* appeared, *Halloween* (1978) reached American movie houses and drive-ins. Like *Night of the Living Dead, Halloween* was enormously popular with a wide group of audiences. If one looks at the ratio between ticket receipts and the cost of production, these films are among the most economically successful American films ever produced (Meyers, 1983).

Aside from *Halloween*'s massive popularity, there are additional reasons to discuss its construction. *Halloween* initiated the onslaught of slasher films that has dominated the horror market since 1978. There is now a slasher film for every major and minor rite celebrated in the United States. *My Bloody Valentine* (1981), *Silent Night, Deadly Night, Part 4: Initiation* (1990), *Mother's Day* (1980), *Graduation Day* (1981), *Prom Night* (1983), and so on owe a considerable debt to *Halloween*. *Halloween* not only strengthened the codes generated in *Night of the Living Dead,* it also entrenched the horrible deep into the mundane present.

After *Halloween,* contemporary horror films have been most effective when they are based within instantly recognizable locales during simple celebrations that once had signified the welcome renewal of shared bonds. In a largely secular society, terror has no need to abuse the sacred; it is enough to make even the most minor of holidays a potential massacre. Blowing up the world may be scary, but a birthday party or romantic St. Valentine's Day dinner that arouses a maniac is truly terrifying.[28]

As the opening credits for *Halloween* roll, a small blinking jack o' lantern, located on the far left of the screen, gradually moves forward to occupy half the screen. Until it becomes quite large, the carved pumpkin seems a simple iconic stand-in for the film's title. As the pumpkin looms large, a slit connecting the nose and mouth holes becomes visible, a neat incision that can only signify the killer's malevolence and mode of execution. Yet the cut is too clean for a deranged murderer whose weapon of choice is a keen blade. This signature belongs to a butcher and an imp. If the killer, Michael Meyers, made the mark, he is not only vicious, he also likes to play. The rest of the film makes clear that Michael is not the only one who enjoys playing cruel games.

Cruelty among the characters defines the everyday. Daily life is lived out between assorted insults and dirty snubs. The killer only plays a far more serious, less language-based version of common practice. At some point every character, except the female lead, refuses to acknowledge the humanity of his or her playmates, friends, clientele, and lovers. Each is guilty of practicing, and delighting in, little barbarities. These games seem to provide the only amusement in an otherwise gray existence.

We learn just how good Michael is at serious fun when Laurie, the female lead played by Jamie Lee Curtis, discovers her friends have been murdered. The murder site has been arranged by Michael, now more psychotic window-dresser than serial murderer, to double as a scene from a Kiwanis funhouse fund-raiser on Halloween. One victim is positioned, arms open, atop a bed with a tombstone standing above her head. As Laurie backs away from the arrangement on the bed, she bumps into a closet door that flies open to reveal another dead companion swinging upside down through the doorway. Immediately after the body ceases to sway, the door to the linen closet creeps open to expose yet another dead familiar. Michael has proved himself a subtle master of the delicate art of one-upmanship.

Later, as Laurie battles Michael, he twice plays dead when Laurie sticks him with a knitting needle and an unwound coat hanger. For his final trick, Michael gulls us and we believe, if only for a fatuous instant, that monsters can be vanquished. *Halloween* ends with Michael being shot several times at point-blank range, falling 15 feet, playing dead once again, and then vanishing. The end credits roll over the space Michael's corpse should inhabit. Like all contemporary monsters, he'll be back.

In *Halloween*, collective action has no effective role in fighting the menace. In fact, there is no collective effort in the film as the characters do not worry about a missing person's absence when it is time for a rendezvous. That absence gives errant protagonists and one indomitable antagonist time and space to follow individual desires. Knowledge and experience are also null and void in *Halloween*. The doctor who spent 15 years treating Michael, presumably learning something of his deadly habits, tracks him down only in the last minute of the film. This lapse is not created to raise tension levels in the audience. We know (except for the brief time we fail to trust our instincts) that the hapless doctor hasn't a chance—no amount of clinical experience will change his luck when it comes to finding Michael.

Finally, as the film ends, there is a series of shots that are absolutely incomprehensible if you do not realize that the future has collapsed into the everyday. These shots show an empty stairwell from the upstairs story, a living room couch, a closed window, the stairs from the living room, a house front, a neighbor's house, and the killer's old home. These images contain no people. They are not shot artfully. They look like the throwaway shots one takes when making sure the film is advancing in the camera after putting in a new roll of 24-shot Kodacolor. These shots (banality incarnate) do however, link menace with the mundanity of everyday existence. All the inconsequential moments and spaces of everyday life have been imbued with death. The future is a time to dread.

> Dreams waft upwards in the darkness to join the mirages of silver light. They are not quite real, the things that happen on the screen; they stay in some wide, troubled domain meant for the poor, for dreams and for dead men. You have to hurry to stuff yourself with these dreams, so as to get through the life which is waiting for you outside, once you've left the theatre, so as to last a few more days of this strife with men and things. You choose among these dreams those that will warm your heart most. For me, I must admit, it was the dirty ones that did. (Celine, 1960, p. 201)

To understand how we came to this gloomy conclusion, wherein Celine becomes just another pessimistic commentator on everyday existence, we need to begin with a critique of horror genre criticism. Most horror criticism is unable to move from a transcendental base, thus leaving critics unable to read contemporary films as a guide to ordinary experience and unable to understand where and how the horror film has now left behind past modes of presentation and adopted revolutionary styles of excessive communication.

Notes

1. "In New York City alone," according to Peter Marcuse (1992), "490,000 households [are] residing in areas of abandonment, where neighborhood conditions are such that no one feels 'at home' there during the daylight hours, certainly not after dark" (p. 88).

We are probably right not to feel "at home" anywhere given the fact that "about 20 percent of all homicides today have no apparent motive, [whereas] in 1966 only 6 percent of all homicides were motiveless. Many of the currently unsolved homicides are believed to have been perpetrated by serial murderers" (Holmes & DeBurger, 1985, p. 29).

According to the FBI, there are additional reasons to be nervous, given the "explosive escalation in the number and severity of violent crimes from 1965 to 1990" committed by youthful offenders (Marriot, 1992, p. E6; copyright © 1992 by The New York Times Company. Reprinted by permission). Outside the home we are no safer, as the places where we work have also become sites of extreme danger (see, e.g., O'Boyle, 1992).

Finally, in a wonderfully titled column, "When Chaos Gets the Green Light," Bob Greene (1992) examines the urban phenomenon of drivers who ignore red lights as a sensible safety precaution. Bringing the car to a dead stop is a driving mistake because a car at rest is a vehicle that is easily fallen upon by city predators (p. T5). For Greene, it would seem we must act like criminals if we desire safe passage through the world.

2. In early 1992, Eclipse Books released *Serial Killers and Mass Murderers*, a set of 55 trading cards with portraits of the killers on the front of the cards and a biography of the serial butcher and the nature of his or her crimes on the back. A comic book version of the Jeffrey Dahmer crimes came out at the same time and immediately sold out its initial press run.

Hollywood's annual celebration of the best in film also shows the high regard we have for the mass murderer. *The Silence of the Lambs* (1991), nothing more than an uptown slasher film, swept almost all the major Oscars® in spring 1992.

3. You do not even have to watch horror films to be aware of the significant changes undergone in the genre of late. When Darryl Talley of the ill-fated Buffalo Bills compared his team to Jason prior to the 1994 Superbowl, almost everyone, horror fan or not, knew what he meant. The Bills were as welcome at the Superbowl as Jason is when he inevitably reappears. And like Jason, the Buffalo Bills never die.

If the meaning of Jason and his ilk did not make common sense, then they would never be mentioned in the most clichéd and plain speech of all—the sports soundbite.

4. See any issue of *Filmfax,* a nostalgia/movie magazine that writes adoringly about Boris Karloff, horror films made prior to the 1960s, the Marx Brothers, early television stars, 1950s sci-fi, and other pop relics. The rhetoric of *Filmfax* is such that you inevitably feel like a moony antiquarian pining for a long-gone golden age by the time you are done reading it.

5. *Cosmopolitan,* a magazine not known for its interest in communication effects, counsels its readers against approaching single men in the horror aisle at the local videomart. The June 1992 issue warns that the man you see cruising the horror aisle "is a man with questionable feelings about women. Whether buried deep within him or overtly expressed in his words and actions, his misogynistic tendencies make him a man to avoid" (Lederman, 1992, p. 144).

6. The audience for horror films is not the only group to be regularly castigated for having criminal taste. Rap and heavy metal fans are also continually upbraided for making dangerously poor aesthetic judgments. See Weinstein (1991) and Nelson and Gonzales (1991) for close readings of the stigma associated with liking rap and heavy metal.

7. The case that Ebert and Wood make is based on the unproven assumption that when a camera takes the killer's point of view, which in contemporary horror films it almost inevitably does, we must, of necessity, adopt the killer's view as our own. As Andrew Tudor (1989) points out, the presumption that audience members always occupy the subjective position of the camera "grossly underestimates the complexity of the movie spectator's relation to the camera" (p. 201).

If the relationship between image and behavior is merely a simple matter of construction, surely some well-intentioned director would have happened upon a technique that renders the cinematic deeds of the pure unforgettably compelling. Why *The Texas Chainsaw Massacre* (1974) exercises a profoundly deleterious influence on viewers while *The Sound of Music* (1965) fails to have the opposite effect has never been adequately demonstrated. Why should insipidly graphic presentations of a sunny world composed of saccharine and light uniformly fail to drastically determine audience attitudes and behavior?

8. If this was not an operative assumption, would test subjects find themselves judging the respective culpability of a rapist and his victim after massive exposure to recent horror films (Donnerstein et al., 1987, pp. 123-133)?

9. Wagar (1982) uses the phrase "terminal visions" to denote literary fictions that explore the nature of human existence after a global catastrophe. The apocalyptic works that Wagar examined were, most often, considerably less pessimistic than the contemporary horror film. Wagar's fictions rarely found human praxis totally wanting; consequently, I use the term more narrowly and mean it to reference only those texts that find any attempt on the part of human actors to ameliorate a bad situation futile or, even worse, far more dangerous than simply doing nothing.

10. For example, according to MTV, the slogan of the decade, the words we lived by in the 1980s, was "Life sucks and then you die."

11. See Douglas Coupland's (1991, 1992) novels for his timely vision of what lies ahead in the coming dystopia. The beleaguered losers in Coupland's work are, all too understandably, painfully obsessed with their [no] future. These novels are also worth reading for the wonderful new vocabulary Coupland's characters invent to describe an age with no expectations.

12. A similar disintegration can be seen in the fragmentation of rock and roll. Greil Marcus (1992) notes that "the question of the death of rock comes up because 'rock 'n' roll'—as a cultural force rather than a catchphrase—no longer seems to mean anything. It no longer seems to speak in unknown tongues that turn into new and common languages" (p. 68).

Daniel Bell (1992), covering somewhat wider ground than Marcus, agrees, arguing that "we may be at the end of old ideologies and old history, but there are no unified sets of beliefs to take their place, only the splintering of cultures and political fragmentation. And that is the transition to the 21st century" (p. 17; copyright © 1992 by The New York Times Company. Reprinted by permission).

13. Even nature programming, most of which is aimed at children and families with kids, has been influenced by the changes in the horror film. An award-winning collection of tapes, *Trials of Life,* is advertised in exactly the same style used to promote horror films. Nature, according to the unseen narrator, is just another site of ceaseless violence, rife with exciting scenes of shocking cruelty.

If you only heard the commercial and didn't see the pictures of a shark chasing a scrambling tern or an adult seal crushing a pup in its jaws you would almost certainly assume the advertisement was for a newly released horror film with Nature reprising Jason's role.

14. See P. Kennedy (1993) for a well-researched and unspeakably depressing account of the world we are likely to inhabit in the 21st century.

15. As we celebrate the end of the cold war we must not assume that now, finally, we have achieved world safety. The technology that can kill us all still exists, and nuclear proliferation has not ceased but continues as many nations eagerly enter the arms chase, attempting to keep up with or, all to the better, outpace the field.

In Kidron and Smith's (1991) atlas, *The New State of War and Peace,* five countries— Britain, Russia, China, France, and the United States—claim to have nuclear weapons, while Israel and South Africa are likely to have the bomb, and India and Pakistan have the parts needed to assemble nuclear weapons. Countries with clear nuclear aspirations include Brazil, Argentina, Iran, Iraq, Libya, and Taiwan (pp. 60-61, 113-114).

It also seems likely that the new republics of the former Soviet Union are going to try to raise capital by offering nuclear warheads at crazy, low, low, bargain-basement prices.

16. Since 1989, cable access television in Los Angeles has run a weekly show called "Drive-by Agony." The show, hosted by Lorna Hawkins, a mother who lost two boys in drive-by shootings, is a forum for families to share their grief and talk about the lives of the departed. Ms. Hawkins was named "Person of the Week" by ABC News for developing the show.

17. Listen to the omnipresent drone of the radio that accompanies Lulu and her beau on their journey across America in David Lynch's *Wild at Heart* (1990). The only programming the protagonists can find is news bulletins delivered by on-air personalities who ape dyspeptic coroners.

18. Today's horror films are also excessively violent as an oppositional strategy to distinguish the genre from other violent programming, especially, television news and dramatic re-creations of true crime. The film industry must, if it is to turn a profit, manufacture a credible niche that marks off the territory belonging to horror films proper.

When the news became hyperviolent, horror films had to escalate the type of damage inflicted upon their supposed protagonists and dangerous villains. If filmmakers fail in this task and so-called reality programming exceeds the limits of **the genre of destruction**, a sizable portion of the audience would be lost. There is no point whatsoever in renting videos or heading off to the mall for films that are ludicrously tame in comparison with what suppurates from the television at any hour of viewing. This is not to say that horror films are exclusively determined, at present, by newsreel footage and docudrama, only that a genre known for shattering taboos must respond when previously unimaginable pictures of gore become part of a steady diet of information freely available at all times to anyone with a television.

An "interesting" attempt to explicitly bridge the gap between violent news programming and the gore film can be seen in *The Faces of Death* (1974, 1985, 1991, 1993) series. These films purport to show real, gruesome deaths, some of which are obviously faked, while a "Dr. Francis B. Gross" provides the shocking voiceover. Obviously, *The Faces of Death* is an updated version of the mondo film, but now films that celebrate the wild and weird things of this violent world must do so in explicit reference to the gore film.

19. During the late 1980s, the cool ironical, as well as colloquial, way to say the same thing was to sport a button or decorate your automobile with a bumper sticker featuring the tag line, "Sailing first-class on the Titanic."

20. Today, the closest living relatives to the atomic horror/sci-fi pictures of the 1950s are the Disney films *InnerSpace* (1987), *Honey, I Shrunk the Kids* (1988), and *Honey, I Blew Up the Kid* (1992). In these films, the horrors of gigantism, as in *The Amazing Colossal Man* (1957) and *Attack of the 50-Foot Woman* (1957), and miniaturization, best captured in *The Incredible Shrinking Man* (1957), are played strictly for laughs.

21. Epic destruction of property plays a central role in all the following comedies and action pictures: *Ghostbusters* (1984) and *Ghostbusters 2* (1989), *Die Hard* (1988) and *Die Hard 2: Die Harder* (1991), *The Blues Brothers* (1980), the *Lethal Weapon* series (1987, 1989, 1992), *Robocop* (1987) and *Robocop 2* (1990), and *The Terminator* (1984) and *Terminator 2: Judgment Day* (1991).

22. In a quantitative analysis of audience responses to the graphic horror film, Mary Beth Oliver (1993) notes that "while most studies acknowledge the extraordinary amount of violence contained within the slasher-film genre, few studies have examined the role that *patterns* of suffering and victimization may play in viewers' enjoyment" (p. 31).

One of the aims of this survey of the horror film is to work out the reasons why so many of us take such pleasure in watching others suffer under the blade of the slasher.

23. There are many films that have had some effect on the construction of the gore film. *Peeping Tom* (1959), *Psycho* (1960), any of the woefully inept, ultra-ultra-low-budget violence fests directed by Herschell Gordon Lewis, the gory Hammer productions of the late 1950s and 1960s, and even the ancient *Maniac* (1934) have all been cited as having some bearing on the direction of the latter-day horror film. Yet, even as we acknowledge the fact that superviolent horror films have many antecedents, the films that have most obviously exercised the greatest degree of influence on contemporary shockers are still *Night of the Living Dead* and *Halloween*.

24. At one time, the studio mavens who craft film titles, according to audience expectations, were planning to call one of the *Jaws* sequels *Jaws 3, People 0*. All contemporary films, at least implicitly, have similar titles. Fans go to these films knowing the monsters are ahead in the game.

25. Older genre entries nearly always featured men as the only gender capable of dealing with the monstrous. Women cowered in the background with scared children. Today's films are no longer as sexist when both men and women are equally ill-equipped to defeat the monster.

Although both sexes are weak in the face of death, it is also the case that, oftentimes, women are given special treatment in the shocker. They are, more often than not, singled out for notable disregard. According to Modleski (1986), women are more readily identified with the "specious good"; consequently, because they shoulder the burden of signifying spurious probity, females are singled out for particular abuse in the nihilistic horror film.

26. In *Men, Women, and Chainsaws: Gender in the Modern Horror Film,* Clover (1992) argues that the contemporary horror film does reward protagonists, especially females, who do battle with monsters. In her reading of the genre, Clover states that when "the Final Girl," or last survivor, destroys the monster, she also defeats some of the sexist stereotypes that the typical slasher film may appear to reinforce. Unfortunately, Clover neglects to mention that the victorious survivor is often the first to go in the sequel. In attempting to address how the contemporary horror film might just be sympathetic toward those who fight evil, especially when women are allied against the forces of Darkness, Clover "too easily valorizes heroic triumph" (Shaviro, 1993, p. 88).

27. See Dyer (1988) for a more developed reading of Ben's sorry end.

28. Even horror films with an occult theme, a subgenre not as popular as the slasher film, seem more concerned with demonstrating that Satan and his cohorts can be just as violent as killers who have not directly ascended from the pit of Hell. Now, the Devil must compete for our attention not with God but with serial assassins.

2. GENRE CRITICISM AND THE HORROR FILM

Dreams, indeed, are of astonishing force among all people of warm imaginations.

—Johann Gottfried von Herder (1784-1791/1968, p. 48)

Academic consideration of a film genre's current status, that is, the weighing of its present blend of cinematic codes and narrative conventions, is often predicated on the structuralist assumption that what we are seeing on the screen today is a carefully patterned re/presentation modeled after earlier efforts in the canon.[1] Endlessly revisiting the warehoused past, contemporary genre films are genetic heirs or blood kin to similar films that made it to the screen first. Over time, generation upon generation of retroactive films come to constitute a massive family tree in which every descendent bears a strong resemblance to its predecessors.

Given such a legacy, many critics commence their assessment of a genre's composition with the assumption that

> the essence of genre criticism is the construction of what, in contemporary critical jargon, might be called a macro- or supertext. The supertext (genre) claims to be an abstract of the most significant characteristics or family resemblances among many particular texts, which can accordingly be analyzed, evaluated, and otherwise related to each other by virtue of their connection with the supertext. (Cawelti, 1985, p. 56)[2]

Genre films are then best understood when considered members of an exclusive set of progeny all sharing a common genetic heritage.

Genre analysis, following this logic, is an exercise easily likened to compiling an exhaustive genealogical inventory, a task undertaken with the ultimate aim of identifying the parent or macrotext from which all genre films of a particular stripe are descended. The richest interpretation of a generic horror film is, consequently, that reading which comprehensively links the newly released horror pic to all other horror films by identifying the common imagery and aggregate themes that are passed from one film to another.

Unfortunately, when genres are treated like long chains of immutable codes, important historical shifts (or drastic genetic mutations) are treated as little more than minor variations, which have no significant bearing on the fundamental meaning or constitution of the genre in question. Oftentimes, when a critic looks too assiduously for an assortment of invariant characteristics across the history of a genre, significant differences among collectively grouped films are erased. As Neale (1980) notes in *Genre*, when critics tally up common conventions and call the sum a genre, such collective features "are rarely specified and analyzed in detail and in ways which recognize their specific autonomy and their role in the constitution of genre as an aesthetic category" (p. 10).[3]

Critics who conceive of genre as a stable repository of fixed codes sprung from a supertext are also hindered from marking distinct transformations in a genre because the effect of historical change upon film structure and content has been severely delimited. The influence of changing times upon generic films has been rigorously bracketed, according to Altman (1986), to "negate the notion of change and to imply the perpetual self-identity of each genre" (p. 34).[4] For this reason, "history has been conceptualized as nothing more than a discontinuous succession of discrete moments, each characterized by a different basic version of the genre" (p. 33).[5]

Horror is, without question, among film's most enduring genres; audiences in search of thrills have been able to find a chiller to attend since the turn of the century. Even the studio of film pioneer Thomas Edison produced a 16-minute version of the Frankenstein story in 1910. The remarkable longevity of a genre does not, however, guarantee that a near century's worth of fans have all been lining up for the same motion picture show.

The individual horror film is not an atemporal screen construct cloned from spooky stock footage. Horror films have changed significantly throughout the century, and the failure to see these changes because of a commitment to enduring value has made it impossible for certain critics to register important differences among radically divergent films.[6] Today's horror films do resemble one another to some degree, but they do not bear strong similarities to films produced 80 or even 40 years ago. Any similarity among horror films is a relatively short-lived affair.

The conventional notion of film genres having unbroken histories, a consequence of academic critics' adoption of structural modes of analysis, receives supplemental support in genre criticism specifically devoted to the horror film via the additional appropriation of psychoanalysis.[7] A psychoanalytically informed structuralism leads critics to theorize that not only are horror films shaped by a progenitive and inflexible "macrotext" but also that repetitive horror films satisfy an invariant audience desire for primal scenes of horrific imagery. Thus not only do the horror genre's hidebound founding texts prevent films from deviating too far from tradition but the audience is itself psychologically unsuited for drastic changes in the formula horror film.[8]

Freud, whose work, according to Carroll (1982), constitutes the lingua franca of horror genre criticism, asserts in "The Uncanny" that when we are frightened by a story or image, we are, in fact, really haunted by either repressed complexes acquired during a traumatic infancy (and infancy is a universally troubling state) or superstitious beliefs inherited from our "primitive forefathers" (p. 51; Freud, 1971, pp. 248-249).[9] Thus, when we encounter terrifying scenes on-screen or in the pages of the latest Stephen King blockbuster, what we are frightened of is "nothing new or alien, but something which is familiar and old-established in the mind and which has become alienated from it only through the process of repression" (Freud, 1971, p. 241). It would then seem, following Freud, that when audiences at the mall cineplex scream at Chucky's misdeeds in *Child's Play 3* (1991), they do so for the same reasons that penny arcade patrons were frightened when they watched a spooky film on a kinetoscope. Each audience would react in a similar fashion because both sets of spectators have experienced the same "process of repression."

Whatever repressed needs or dark desires these horrible films satisfy, one can be certain their composition lies outside the influence of everyday life and lesser, more timebound cultural imperatives. That is, the horror genre continually reworks unconscious complexes that are not responsive to local culture and the pandemic terrorism of everyday life. Again, according to Freud (1971), it seems as if each one of us has been through a phase of individual development corresponding to this animistic stage in primitive men, that none of us has passed through it without preserving certain residues and traces of it which are still capable of manifesting themselves and that everything which now strikes us as "uncanny" fulfills the condition of touching those residues of animistic mental activity within us and bringing them to expression. (pp. 240-241)

When audience members engage with a horror film they are not enjoying visions that respond to everyday fears; they are responding to atavistic terrors nearly as old as the reptilian brain.

In his award-winning *Dreadful Pleasures,* Twitchell (1985) provides the quintessential example of horror genre criticism:

When we look back over the past two centuries we see that certain images and sequences have plagued popular culture. Surely it must be important that these motifs won't go away. Surely it must be important that these nightmarish figments have become fantasies we all recognize. What we have experienced since the 1960s is a swelling of forms exploited in the films of the 1930s, which were in turn scenarios often based on novels of the 1890s, themselves the outgrowths of the "shilling shockers" which had evolved from the gothic novel. . . . Essentially modern works of artificial horror originated in the late eighteenth-century discovery that by inducing extreme feelings of dreadful pleasures, both print and illustration could arouse and exploit powerful feelings deep within the human spirit. Whatever first directed our attention toward the macabre, the mis-shapen, the barbarous, and the deformed, it has yet to be expunged. (p. 4)[10]

As Twitchell surveys the vast corpus of horrific imagery, note the ease with which he glides through the ages, across radically different audiences, media, and texts, finding the same frightening figures wherever he looks.

Twitchell goes on to give an explanation for horror, grounded in Freud, which finds that all images of scary fiends are generated by society to calm adolescent anxiety over sexual maturation. In effect, he broadens Freud's notion of the uncanny to include horror films as mythic responses to pubescent angst.[11] As sexual desire grows or, more accurately, ceases to be successfully repressed or sublimated, the adolescent finds him- or herself overwhelmed by some very powerful and very mystifying urges. Society answers this confusion with appropriate instruction in how to deal with nascent sexual desire via the mythic horror film.[12]

Evans (1984), working the same territory, also finds the cinematic monster a projection of ageless adolescent fears.[13] He, even more so than the average horror film critic, casts both the images on screen and the violent impulses surging within the newly sexualized teen in language at once embarrassingly romantic and unmercifully mythic. He begins to explain the workings of horror films and human beings by sighting a deep mystery:

> *As has ever been the case,* Dracula, Frankenstein, the Wolfman, King Kong and their peers remain shrouded in mystery. Why do they continue to live? Why do American adolescents keep Dracula and his companion monsters of the 1930s and early 1940s alive. . . . What is the monster formula's "secret of life"? Is this yet another of the things which "man was not meant to know?" (p. 53, emphasis added)

The fact is, adolescents do not keep these dated monsters alive. These once threatening creatures are for preadolescents who can't get past alert ticket vendors at R-rated films and find renting more timely fare at the neighborhood video store difficult without parental permission. In our time, Dracula sells achingly sweet chocolate cereal (Count Chocula®), and Frankenstein hawks artificially flavored strawberry cereal (Franken Berry®); such is the current flavor of these so-called timeless monsters (Daniels, 1975, p. 242).[14]

Also, what exactly is the rhetorical space and time continuum where "has ever been the case"? Even if such patently innocuous films were still scary (and they are not), even if they still attracted a large audience (and they do not), wouldn't it most likely be the case that people who continued to enjoy them today would have a somewhat different relation to these dated images than other audiences had 40 years ago?

Evans's (1984) obfuscatory rhetorical question "Is this yet another of the things man was not meant to know?" begs a mysterious answer. It is a question that calls forth a response as mystifying and arcane as the life-inducing electrical machinery of Dr. Frankenstein. The answer to horror's otherworldly attraction as one of the secrets of the ages "arises from the monster's overwhelming sense of alienation; totally an outcast, he painfully embodies the adolescent's nightmare of being hated and hunted by the society which he so desperately wishes to join" (p. 55). Alas,

> stirred from innocence and purity . . . by the full moon, which for millennia has variously symbolized chastity, change, and romance, the Wolfman

guiltily wakes to the mystery of horrible alterations in his body, his mind, and his physical desires—alterations which are completely at odds with the formal strictures of his society. The mysterious horrible, physical and psychological change is equally a feature of Frankenstein, of Dracula's victims, the Mummy and his bride, and countless other standard monster movie characters. (p. 54)

As long as we must all suffer the unavoidable transmogrification of puberty, monsters will prey among us.[15]

Once adrift in the agony of adolescence, our earliest fears are summarily reawakened when our bodies cease to be our own. We must have some explanation for the singularly peculiar experience of losing the able and unblemished flesh that so faithfully carried us through our halcyon childhood days. We are in keen want of some quick and ready answers; therefore, "we need myths when we need information, and because we need information when we are confused, fantasy structures are given by a society as maps—so to speak—by which a lost audience can find its way" (Twitchell, 1985, p. 87).[16] Thus society has seen fit, with some additional assistance from a beneficent movie industry, to give puzzled youngsters the spooky chiller.

Adolescence, an unquestionably turbulent stage in life marked by a daunting welter of psychological, sexual, and intellectual enigmas, leaves spotty juveniles groping for direction. For this audience, the horror film is mythic Clearasil®: It helps the young find their way free of dizzy uncertainty, it delivers workable home-truths in answer to life's great riddles, and it quells their fiercest fears—especially, the dread of death. (And what, at bottom, is adolescence but the painful demise of the child's soft larval skin prior to the emergence of the nascent adult?)

Myths work "by demonstrating order"; consequently, they are appropriate vehicles for tempering the immensely troubling complex of confusions that accompanies sexual maturation (Ausband, 1983, p. 5). If this is the case, and as Cassirer argues, "mythic thought is especially concerned to deny and negate the fact of death and to affirm the unbroken unity of life" (quoted in Vickery, 1966, p. 10), then we should expect to find the horror film irrevocably linked with the ageless trauma of becoming a sexually mature adult.

Myth steadies an audience that has lost its bearings by giving it an "experience both of accord with the social order, and of harmony with the universe" (Ausband, 1983, p. 21). When the monster, nothing more than a thinly veiled symbol of pubescent chaos, is finally brought to heel in the last exciting reel, we tell our children that they too shall emerge triumphant from the beastly trial of maturation.

In this case, Hollywood really is a mythmaking machine. The constant stream of horror films, now reaching 90 uninterrupted years of production, points not to a vacuous, wholly unimaginative industry that steadfastly refuses to innovate for fear of missing the bottom line but to the continued need for confrontation with the primal.

Horror films are primers for the primitive. Just as it would make no sense to disparage an elementary school textbook for printing the alphabet in the exact order it has assumed for hundreds of years, it makes no sense to criticize the horror film for spelling out, to the apprehensive youngsters in the audience, the common ancestral urges they have been bequeathed. For those older members of the audience who still enjoy horror films, and who also have some understanding of what it means to be sexually active, horror films work as a refresher course in the instinctual: "Yes, that is what we are all about, isn't it"? Returning to the horrible allows us to keep sight of the fundamental desires that rule the species.

Through any particular work, as horror films are nearly all identically constructed, an individual audience member can come to know not only the entire history of horror but also his or her biological/psychic destiny.[17] An understanding of horror, a familiarity with all its timebound rules, is an introduction to two genealogies: the story of one particular type of film production and the development of the sexually mature individual.

Horror is our vision/version of a primitive's dream. Never bemoan seeing the same thing on the screen time and again, as what is important here is not artistic innovation but the revelation of our fundamental condition. Through the dark glass of the horror film we can learn who we are. Look elsewhere for cinematic innovation.[18] A trip to the cinema is a valuable retreat to Plato's cave, and there many critics have enshrined the horror film.

Around this primeval site, where we usher our anxious children into the mysterious vagaries of maturity, our screen fears are sanctified by horror genre criticism. Maniacs, killers, goblins and ghouls, vampires, mummies, big reptiles, giant ants, power tools, holy water, crypts, and summer camps are legitimate icons of inborn terror because they allow us to pass through the trial of puberty relatively unscathed. We can be reassured that these monsters and weapons of destruction, along with the scary sites, are nothing less than our oldest extant memories rekindled on the screen with the help of an altruistic movie industry that recognizes that quality gets in the way of race memory. In irrevocably linking horror to the unconscious we dismiss, all too hastily, the possibility that horror films have something to say about popular epistemology, about the status of contemporary community, or about the fearsome power of modern technology.[19]

There is, however, another pole in psychoanalytically informed criticism that still clings to an unchanging human psyche while maintaining a provisionally progressive impulse for at least some of the cultural artifacts defined as horrible. The whole subject who occasionally plays out repressed desires within the safe confines of the instructive horror film is replaced, in the revisionist perspective, with a fractured subject. This new subject, who is theoretically unstable, provides the ground for making the argument that as there is no fixed subject it then follows that there is no solid footing from which to produce, and view, images of the social world and the monsters who dwell there.

The addition of a mutable psyche would seem to suggest the possibility for social change, as a shifting subject is capable of living in multiple worlds; however, this change from solid to rocky ground, vis-à-vis the stability of the subject and the representation of antisocial desire, is still moored to a universal and ahistorical deep structure. Even though the model of the psyche has been reconfigured, and its relationship to bloody imagery redrawn, all horrible texts continue to exert a uniform effect across individual audience members. That is, while the effect that horror films have on subjects has changed, as we now have a different subject seated before the screen, this new effect is still one that is universally experienced by nearly all viewers of the horror film.

Following this recension, instead of offering imagery that reins in inappropriate desire, horror films actually work to provoke the expression of aggression. Spectacularly excessive productions, according to Kristeva (1980/1982), let loose an aggressive drive in unstable subjects through an insidious attack: "There looms, within abjection, one of those violent, dark revolts of being . . . opposed to *I*. . . . A massive and sudden emergence of uncanniness, which . . . now harries me as radically separate, loathsome" (pp. 1-2).[20] Somehow, our fantasies turn back against us, and once secure subjects find themselves beset from within.

Kristeva, like many other psychoanalytic critics, argues that as a regular part of the maturation process we have all adopted ideal representations of ourselves as whole egos ensconced in relatively healthy bodies.[21] Occasionally, our all too perfect images of self are exposed to attack. The source of distress, that which lies behind the revolt against self, is the abject. The abject are those objects, oftentimes bodily detritus, that desecrate our narcissistic mirage of self by effacing the boundary between myself and that which is not "I." The abject provides proof that our idealized portraits of pristine flesh and whole egos are, unfortunately, nothing more than brittle fantasies.

If we are to maintain the integrity of our illusions of self, we must work to expel from conscious consideration those objects or abjects that reveal the true constitution of the subject. Abjection, the attempt we make to cast the abject out of mind, is, as Creed (1989) reads Kristeva, "a means of separating the human from the non-human and the fully constituted subject from the partially formed subject" (p. 64). We are not, however, always successful in this endeavor. The abject can return to consciousness, as in the horror film, and we are forced to restyle the unsullied self-images we manufacture for ourselves. The screams we let loose in the theater as the horror film plays on do not signify the release of tension or the expulsion of pent-up libidinal energy: They are the shrieks uttered whenever cherished fancies about self are shattered.

It is altogether unlikely that the lovely images I conjure up whenever I think about my appearance will include any tangible signs of my ever advancing decrepitude. My images will almost always be good, reassuring images that work to preserve the ideal pictures of self I find so very pleasing. In contrast, the abject marks us as always already fallen and decayed—always moving toward nothing. It is not death that the abject signifies; rather, the abject represents just how close my body is to death. Flesh that fails us,

> a wound with blood and pus, or the sickly, acrid smell of sweat, of decay, does not *signify* death. . . . These body fluids, this defilement, this shit are what life withstands, hardly and with difficulty, on the part of death. There, I am at the border of my condition as a living being. My body extricates itself, as being alive, from that border . . . until, from loss to loss, nothing remains in me and my entire body falls beyond the limit—*cadere*, cadaver. (Kristeva, 1980/1982, p. 3)

We would like to live farther away from death than is possible. Those signs that give us the real measure of distance between ourselves and death, like the nasty fluids detailed above, are inevitably going to be treated as abject: They place life and death at too close a remove.

The most menacing piece of waste, far more threatening than any mere bodily excretion, is the corpse. A dead body has nothing to do with what is really human; yet once animation escapes, it is the most tangible reminder of the life that has just slipped away. Unfortunately, even as the corpse is the most powerful reminder of an entire life now ceased, it is also the least permanent reminder of earthly existence. The corpse decomposes quickly and, as it putrefies, it offers up more than just an affront to the delicate senses. In death, the rotten flesh of even our dearest relations becomes an excessive burden that should be hastily interred or incinerated, as "a decaying body, lifeless, completely turned into dejection, blurred between the inanimate and the inorganic . . . the corpse represents fundamental pollution. A body without a soul" (Kristeva, 1980/1982, p. 109).

The corpse must be packed away if we are to survive the psychic damage inflicted by the dead; however, even if the abject must be removed, we simply cannot treat the flesh of our loved ones like just any disposable bit of waste. We must reconcile our desire to stow the dead with the equally powerful need not to forget the beloved soul that once animated the cold meat. Only by manufacturing pleasant memories of the dead, a nonthreatening simulation of the lived body, can we successfully negotiate the difficult contradiction between the abject status of the dead and our love for the person whose body was not always a noxious corpse.

Once the body is taken from the human world and boxed up or burned up, it is the recollection of a fantastic lived body (the ostensible referent of these memories is ashes and dusky shards of brittle bone or something even worse) that takes the place of the forgotten corpse. Our memories of the deceased, a highly romanticized collection of insubstantial reveries, replace the now stinking flesh, and in a grand delusion, we keep the body pristine with spurious fantasies. Only ignorant children, too young to yet catch a glimpse of their own bodies breaking down, sing of the worms crawling in and through the odious meat of the corpse. In turn, only adults think of the dear departed, so they fatuously believe, as they imagine the corpse would like to be remembered.

When we take account of our chary connection to the dead, we must also consider our relationship to the monster. What is a monster other than a reanimated corpse? We may turn our back on the dear departed and hurry home once the coffin lid is strewn with dirt, but the horror film returns us back to the dead and forces us to confront that which we had hoped to confine to the quiet grave. Whatever abjection we strive to avoid, the corpse being the most potent of all abjects, we can be assured that the contemporary horror film will most certainly accommodate its grotesque return.

The spectacle of gore is then a messy moment of truth and confrontation. As Creed (1989) notes,

> The horror film abounds in images of abjection, foremost of which is the corpse, whole and mutilated, followed by an array of bodily wastes such as blood, vomit saliva, sweat, tears and putrefying flesh. . . . When we say such-and-such a horror film "made me sick" or "scared the shit out of me" we are actually fore-grounding that specific horror film as a "work of abjection." (p. 67)

Creed's list could go on and on if she wanted to make a fetish of comprehensive detail; watch any gore film and be prepared to see an incredible, near infinite number of nauseating bodily discharges stream from broken flesh as the living body is transformed into a corpse. Whatever distance we seek to put between ourselves and the dead, we can be sure the horror film is more than up to the task of bringing it all back home.

Unlike the positive critics who see horror as a generally beneficial enterprise, Kristeva (1980/1982) underlines the negation at work in disturbing texts. She argues that the abject signifies the terrible lack that marks us as empty or, even worse, filled with decay. The violence of the horror film is then the attempt to return to a zero state. Get rid of the bodies, the civilizations, the knowledge systems, and any other worthless fraud that masks the true emptiness that characterizes the most basic human state. We are literally filled with shit. The rotting corpse, the fetid stool, and the worrisome symptoms of disintegration that accompany any illness are the clearest signs of what and who we really are.

Critics who see a stable superego in confrontation with the mercurial id as the source of horror and fantasy must look aghast at Kristeva's revolutionary revision, especially in light of the fact that they see the horror film as a salutary representation of civilization's success at restraining or surmounting the nasty bits that are part and parcel of us all.[22] As Jackson (1981) notes, for those who do not take the extreme position represented by Kristeva, "fantasies make up for society's prohibitions by allowing vicarious fulfillment. Fantasies express libidinal drives towards satisfaction, the libido being that part of the self (according to Freud) which struggles against submitting to the reality principle" (p. 70).

Where other critics are reassured that these unpredictable and unsettling tendencies are kept to the screen and reality is kept intact, Kristeva (1980/1982) sees the ego struggling for its destruction: "a drive overload of hatred or death, which prevents images from crystalizing as images of desire and/or nightmare and causes them to break out into sensation (suffering) and denial (horror), into a blasting of sight and sound (fire, uproar)" (pp. 154-155).

According to the negative position, horror is a great deal more than just a safety valve engineered from nightmare images. It is categorically not a prophylactic representation portraying humanity acting inhumanely; rather, it is the positing of real desires for real destruction. Here, there is no dissimilarity between war and film. It makes not a whit of difference that real humans die agonizing deaths on the battlefield and in horror films gore is a special effect. War and the desire to see the flesh riven are both fueled by a destructive drive that erupts from deep within the psyche. Whatever drives the war machine also drives the production of horror.

Horror wakes us to the fact that, beyond all the good objects with which a subject seeks to identify, there is a vacuum. This vacuum is expressed in the unwavering commitment the masses have made to the production of horror. As horror films are so alike, there must be a basic need to confront the same story time and again.[23] The recurrent return of the always identical must speak of some fundamental absence that cannot be filled. It is a junkie's habit, an addiction that can only lead to further degradation. This need is not based on the desire to see wayward sexual impulses restrained. It is a need to tear away the veil and see the truth of human existence emerge as living death.

What we see on the screen is something far more terrible than the monster's visage and the temporary damage it can do to humanity. The fascination with the abject, with whirring chainsaws biting into tender flesh and the terminal destruction of community, is a metaphorical assaying of the primary human condition. Behind the monster lies our insatiable appetite for destruction: "The more or less beautiful image in which I behold or recognize myself rests upon an abjection that sunders it as soon as repression, the constant watchmen, is relaxed" (Kristeva, 1980/1982, p. 13).

The darkened auditorium, or cozy den, is one of the spaces where the censor lets down its guard and the devouring absence, which is our center, can erupt.[24] We try, as our century-long hunger for the horror film testifies, to again and again find an adequate representation of our internal chaos.[25] When the body is blasted apart on the screen, all the cherished illusions we hold about the subject are momentarily vanquished as horror lays siege to the narcissistic shields that protect our pretty pictures of humanity.

A blasted corpse looks just like any other. It has no individual identity, it has no animating personality, it screams of nothing as the menace reduces humanity to a suppurating heap of viscera. The marks of difference that we mistakenly take for defining characteristics of what it means to be human are revealed as minor irrelevancies once the flesh is torn asunder:

> These abjects disturb identity, system and order. They respect no definite positions, rules or limits. They are forms of the body's acknowledgment that such boundaries are arbitrary, that they are fantasies or projections rather than pre-ordained norms or biological rules. They signal the precarious grasp the subject has over its identity and bodily boundaries, the possibility of sliding back into the chaos out of which it emerged. (Grosz, 1986, p. 111)

For Kristeva (1980/1982) and other like-minded analysts, there is **nothing** to learn from terrible tales. We already know what horror films depict; we need the courage not to forget it as we leave our seats and file out from the theater. Horror tales give you the same directive, no matter when they were written, no matter for whom they were originally told:

> Their only sustenance lies in the beauty of a gesture that, here, on the page, compels language to come nearest to the human enigma, to the place where it kills, thinks, and experiences jouissance all at the same time. A language of abjection . . . where any ideology, thesis, interpretation, mania, collectivity, threat, or hope become drowned. (p. 206)

We can go even further. Horror stories and

> all literature is probably a version of the apocalypse that seems to me rooted, no matter what its socio-historical conditions might be, on the fragile border (borderline cases) where identities (subject/object, etc.) do not exist or only barely so—double, fuzzy, heterogeneous, animal, metamorphosed, altered, abject. (Kristeva, 1980/1982, p. 207)

Obviously, this is the strongest possible case one could make for the transcendental meaning which lies behind every ferocious monster. Kristeva's final nominatives capture all the famous beasts: The double is Hyde; fuzzy is the Blob; heterogeneous are Cronenberg's sickly mutations; the animal is the great white shark and rat; the metamorphosed is the Wolfman; and so on. Whatever blurs the human frame, whatever disturbs the line between human and nonhuman, every unclear delineation between the not-us and the subject with constitutional integrity is horrific.

To characterize Kristeva's summation as reductionistic is to miss the point of structural/psychoanalytic criticism. Yet what alternative is left when this mode of analysis "confines every desire and statement to a genetic axis or over-coding structure, and makes infinite, monotonous tracings of the stage on that axis or the constituents of that structure" (Deleuze & Guattari, 1980/1987, p. 13)? Must every taboo shattered on the screen refer solely to an unconscious tape loop spinning endlessly through every mind and body in the audience? Without exception, the answer is an unconditional yes. It is all a matter of unconscious drives.

This position refuses to admit the unconscious is no longer that. We live in an age in which everyone is at least nominally aware of a great deal of Freudian vocabulary. Taboos need no longer be broken for the sole purpose of satisfying some unnameable desire. We know the names of all these things; isn't it boring (boredom being the only state that pop culture refuses to inhabit) to demonstrate the same savoir faire when it comes to the no longer forbidden? This is not to say that it is time to entirely dismiss the idea of the unconscious, but might terror work on planes other than the extraordinarily vast territory claimed for the unconscious?

At the very least, we would expect the imagery produced and consumed by the unconscious to vary when the existence of the forbidden is no longer a secret.[26] A useful example of the surplus of Freudian imagery in the popular film, and what happens to Freud when everyone knows a surplus exists, comes from Meltzer's (1987) description of the first Beatles film:

A scene in *A Hard Day's Night* [is] full of explicit Freudian overtones (if you want them that way). The Beatles are in a compartment of a real/symbolic train, symbolically encased with a middle-aged gentleman who refuses to allow them to reduce their symbolic intimacy by opening a window. John

Lennon introduces "homosexuality" by asking the man, "Give us a kiss?" and "pervertedly" placing a soda bottle to each of his nostrils. Later Ringo turns away from the advances of a beautiful woman with the explanation, "She'll just reject me and I'll be frustrated," adding that he therefore must "compensate with me drums." Such intentional and obvious psychological references are so blatant as to *be* the surface appearance itself, supplying an explanation itself with no further need to reach below: yet this type of self explanatory surface is such an overstatement that it baffles the analytical critic far more than ordinarily. (pp. 13-14)[27]

Or at least it should. When John introduces (with a suitably jaundiced eye) perverse themes, he also subverts earlier presentations of the youthful violator. He knows he is mocking youthful excess just as he continues to break cultural taboos. Rebellion in the Beatles' films is not only the anarchic shattering of rules, it is also a put-on; however, when earlier teen rebels, like the anguished James Dean and surly Marlon Brando, confronted authority there was nothing funny about the situation.

The social standing of the teenager changed markedly during the years between *The Wild One* (1953) and *A Hard Day's Night* (1964). By the time the Beatles had become film stars, teenagers were empowered with far greater freedoms than had been granted the teens who cheered as Marlon rolled into a soon-to-be-terrorized town; consequently, early youth flicks were rather somber affairs. Marlon and the other "villains" in the early teen pictures were never secure enough to laugh freely at authority. *Cry Baby Killer* (1958), Jack Nicholson's first film, *Hot Car Girl* (1958), and *Stakeout on Dope Street* (1958) along with many other troubled adolescent pictures usually ended in pitched violence as misguided and terribly unhappy youths were led away in handcuffs.

When the Beatles made their screen debut, youths had acquired a certain amount of cultural capital and real money. Teens could afford, both symbolically and with actual spending power, to blithely reject almost anyone or anything smacking of authority. Violence had been superseded by secure fun with the arrival of *A Hard Day's Night*. A new film-going community had been established, a community that now possessed a certain measure of power. The changes in teen films had everything to do with changes in the social world and nothing to do with biological destiny.

Contemporary horror films have broken just as dramatically with their predecessors. One shift may be seen in the altered connections today's films, as contrasted with earlier films, make between violence and humor.

Earlier films made obvious which moments on screen were to be laughed at and which were supposed to be frightening. Today's films do not draw clear distinctions between moments of levity and horror.

Currently, the most successful films make the fan laugh and squirm with terror in his or her seat. Freddy, the Elm Street molester and murderer of countless children, is also a quotable raconteur, stand-up comic, and pitiless slasher. Contemporary films, as in *Dawn of the Dead* (1979), will show an unwitting victim having his guts ripped out as he checks his blood pressure on a self-service diagnostic machine in a shopping mall. After the slippery intestines have puddled to the floor and been sampled by ravenous zombies, the camera glides to a meter blinking SEE YOUR DOCTOR Blood Pressure: 0/0. Perhaps not the most hilarious film sequence, but what kind of humor is possible once you have seen awkward zombies clumsily disembowel an unlucky mark concerned with his cardiovascular fitness?

The contemporary horror film moves from laughter to terror with unsettling ease. Punch lines and gory destruction appear randomly throughout the erratic narrative. These films make a virtue of putting climactic jokes where violent set pieces should appear and vice versa. Yet they do not simply alternate laughter and escapism with blinding terror. Gags and violence are distributed randomly. The viewer must take the film seriously as some scenes are incredibly threatening, but it simultaneously demands detachment as what could have been an exceedingly graphic scene turns out to be a joke.[28]

The audience must willingly engage these disturbing effects. When watching a contemporary shocker, they must not only suspend disbelief, an action all films require, they must also cooperate by laying their bodies on the line. Laughter and fright both require gut reactions. The body must react to a "successful" death or humorous interlude; however, each reaction involves the body in diametrically opposed physical states. The audience must willingly allow the film to put blood pressures up a notch and tickle macabre funny bones. Films will not work if we refuse to involve the body in the spectacle; however, when we give ourselves over to the film we put our own flesh at risk.

What happens when the joke looming ahead turns into an endlessly protracted and extraordinarily realistic death scene? Or instead of letting loose an anticipated shiver, you have to laugh? This is more than the simple frustration of expectations; in your flesh you experience not only one of the extremes of contemporary horror—laughter or fright—but you are always in a state of unrelieved tension as to which direction you will be thrown. The film audience continually surveys the screen wondering what to do. That experience creates viewers who expect uncertainty and narrative collapse as a matter of course.[29]

The nonfan cannot make sense of these films without the knowledge of, and willingness to accept, radical discontinuity. These films are deeply dissatisfying if you are not prepared for this sort of didactic tension. Horror films entertain only when audience members refuse to predict the film's direction as narratives careen about like wicked drunks assaulting more temperate guests at a genteel soiree. Filmgoers who like predictable movies cannot take brutalization as part of the entertainment package. Since new horror is not told with rational narratives, these films are stupid, incomprehensible, offensive, and just plain ridiculous to the uninitiated. Forced like a captive ball bouncing between death and glee, the experienced viewer knowingly takes a very cynical ride over the bodies of assorted victims.

Where Kristeva and the other critics have gone wrong is in arguing that terror, in whatever form it manifests itself, is always a matter of the unconscious "I." Their readings make all forays into the forbidden a private escapade, a lonely search for solitary satisfaction, a simple matter of individual psychological economy. They have neglected the fact that film viewing is primarily a social experience. Even in the age of the private home entertainment center, we watch and make sense of film culture in units larger than one. The most popular film rentals are always films everybody is talking about. When they are seen at home, far from the numerous irritations of public life, they are still viewed with the knowledge that lots of people responded positively to this particular selection.

Dracula, Frankenstein's monster, the Martians and the Big Beasts of the 1950s, Norman Bates, Rosemary's little tyke, Regan (of 1973's *The Exorcist*), Romero's zombies, and now Freddy, Jason, Chucky, Michael, and Hannibal are understood by millions. They do not belong to a private world where each represents a particular solution to some singular process of psychic maturation/disintegration. Horror films are not integrated into each viewer's consciousness (or unconscious) without regard for how others see the menace. It is only as a group that we make sense of our heroes or antiheroes. The significance of a celebrated killer is a public phenomenon and, for reasons as yet unexplained, fans like killers who star in movies that do not make conventional sense.[30]

Whatever the new terrors mean, they can only be understood in conjunction with a much larger world than that of the solitary misfit coming to grips with his or her own discomfiting sexuality. By consistently reading the audience as an individual psyche, horror films have been turned into tokens of universal, unchanging, and, ultimately, undifferentiable archetypes or psychic black holes with no historical relation to the times of the people who made and understood them. In reading a culture and its attendant texts, Freud and his varied followers

> move rather too quickly from the individual to the social, attempting explanations of such collective phenomena as group dynamics, art or religion in relation to the operations of the psyche, writ large. By collapsing the social into the psychic life of the individual, Freud risked losing the social, and a similar problem exists with regard to our theoretical understanding of horror films. (Prince, 1988, p. 20)

There are other places to look, places where horror does not always come back to "I."

Finding the new horror film a pleasurable experience means joining millions of others on a roller coaster. This ride does more than rub you raw in a painful cinematic trek through the horrors of adolescence. Our horror films offer something more than the reassuring platitude that society is not such a bad place to live once we are freed from the pains of galloping hormones. Our horrible visions also do more than take you to the site where the fundamental monstrosity of the human is confirmed. New horror films refuse to entertain the unconscious as they, instead, offer meaningless death in response to the terrors of everyday life. Contemporary horror will dispense with the conventions of the past and terrorize the body in ways unthinkable to all but contemporary audiences. It will, however, take a little time before Jason is as beloved as any other Hollywood movie star.

Notes

1. See Todorov's (1975) influential reading of the fantastic, Wood (1984) on the horror film, or Wright (1975) on the western.

2. It should be clear that Cawelti (1985) is not endorsing this method unreservedly but is only serving notice that it is a common practice among genre analysts.

3. Waller (1986), in his significant account of noteworthy shifts in the vampire tale, underscores and furthers Neale's complaint when he observes that "the all-too-common

tendency to underestimate individual generic texts and to oversimplify the history of a genre is matched only by the tendency to disregard the complex relationship between a genre and the social, political, and cultural values and institutions that make up our world" (p. 12).

4. Not all critics are committed to policing change in genre studies. In particular, Schatz (1981) has demonstrated how change is inevitable in even the most obviously stable film genres.

5. It is crucially important to note that Altman (1986) does not use "discontinuous" to imply any sense of historical development within a genre over a period of time. Discontinuous succession simply means that each film is a "different basic version" that reformulates the defining characteristics or codes of the genre within a discrete performance.

6. The failure to appreciate the tremendous changes worked in the horror film leaves us with a rather too narrow analysis of the genre's long-standing appeal. For example, Dickstein (1984) reduces all horror films to thrill rides in which "getting caught up emotionally, walking out drained and satisfied, waking up relieved to deal with more workaday problems—this is the secret of all horror films" (p. 77). Not only does Dickstein's conclusion conflate disparate texts within the genre, it also conflates the genre with all leisure activity used for cathartic stress reduction.

7. See Shaviro (1993, chap. 1) for a more extensive critique of psychoanalysis and film criticism.

8. Certainly, paradigmatic elements may be substituted by adept filmmakers, who, when they create a "well done" generic work, demonstrate the sophistication an expert linguist can take to the most intransigent lexicon. The accomplished genre film showcases a kind of grammatical mastery. It has been done countless times before but never with this particular analytic elegance.

Praising films in this manner allows critics to preserve a film's semantic purity while accounting for its syntactic fluidity. For example, the Balkans and other gothic locales have been overused, and in their place the ingenious director will substitute suburbia as a locale, as in *Fright Night* (1985). The genre analyst may then argue that community is still the primary locus around which eternal evil swirls. That earlier manifestations of menace erupted in Eastern Europe instead of suburbia is epiphenomenal.

9. In somewhat greater detail, uncanny experiences stem, as Freud sees it, from two very different acts of repression. The first source is those discredited beliefs we have inherited from our distant ancestors. While we no longer believe in animism, magic, and so forth, we are not completely confident in our rational powers of explanation and sometimes fall back on dated superstitions to make sense of the world.

The uncanny may also arise when infantile complexes, once banished from consciousness, are revitalized. When fears of castration, "womb phantasies," or "animistic beliefs" are rekindled we are frightened. In both cases, the uncanny involves a return to an earlier, more naive state of comprehension. To experience the uncanny, says Freud (1971), is to experience the world like a newborn babe or Pleistocene primitive. On a practical level, it is quite difficult to decide, when a subject is struck by the uncanny, which source is responsible for generating the experience of fear (pp. 248-249).

10. Given Twitchell's (1985) assumption that old forms are continually being reconditioned, producing the latest incarnation of the horrible is only a matter of updating the images dealt to the audience without changing their essential value. Bela has aged a wee bit, so take him out of the pack and put in a seductive lamia. When a card has been nearly worn through from being continuously in play, one need only insert an updated replacement.

This process is analogous to the periodic updates to which tarot cards are subject. Now, tarot cards are available in renewed formats emblazoned with endangered animals, Native American totems, and African Americans; however, just because a griot, cougar, or Navajo *hataalii* appears where the Queen of Cups used to hold court does not mean the symbolic valence has changed. The values supposedly always remain constant, but as the original pictures no longer speak to some of their users as well as they once had, the cards have been reillustrated. Still, a death card is a death card is a death card.

11. In his reconfiguration of the uncanny, Twitchell (1985) finds that horror films have four important functions: Scary tales define socially correct sexual behavior; these same tales are animated by adolescents' need to know the truth about sexual desire and society's concomitant obligation to tell its young what it is they need to understand about sex; horror is important to the young only until they successfully graduate from adolescence; and horror tales are collections or "memory banks" of wisdom proffering socially appropriate direction and prohibition to the young (p. 104).

What matters most about these conclusions is how completely Twitchell isolates the meaning of horror films within the world of the unconscious. He leaves no room for horror to deviate from the wellspring originally detected by Freud, no space where horror films could respond to something other than an inbred psychological imperative. If Twitchell is correct, then horror films are nothing more than thinly veiled bits of instructive solace meant to mollify anxious and horny teens.

12. The adolescent is the perfect biological figure for a psychological construct of taboo desiring. Who would deny that adolescent angst and sexual confusion are not driven by innate biological and psychological imperatives? Yet, can we really trace all figures of horror to a sexual base? The Wolfman may have spent too much time abusing himself, hence all the unwanted hair, but are Jason and others of his ilk nothing more than misguided seekers of sexual release? Furthermore, are the giant bugs that supplanted the spooks of the 1930s and 1940s sprung from the same pit of sexual apprehension that purportedly created their antecedents?

It is also worth noting that adolescence is a relatively new chronological-psychological construct; yet horror criticism often assumes that the psychic/sexual drives of the pimpled teen are as old as the mythic figures that have ostensibly circulated through all horrible stories.

Philippe Aries (1962), who specializes in the history of private life, would argue otherwise. In his work on the development of child-rearing practices and the constitution of the modern family, Aries dates the appearance of the adolescent to sometime in the late 19th century (p. 30).

13. Twitchell (1985), who obviously concurs with Evans on this point, argues that the ageless monsters who haunt adolescence may live for eternity. Just as they survived the childhood of our parents and grandparents,

> the dominant monsters of the modern imagination—the vampire, the
> hulk-with-no-name, and the transformation monster—will endure for some time to
> come. They will endure, while other beasts come and go, because we will continue to
> search them out in the dark, continue to listen to what they have to say and watch
> what they do, and continue to be terrified by them out of ignorance. We may not
> appreciate them, let alone want to have them around, but they have been with us for a
> long time, and for good reasons. Unless these reasons change, we had best be
> prepared to see them again and again, illumined by the full moon of adolescent
> curiosity. (p. 301)

14. In Les Daniels's (1975) survey of horror, *Living in Fear: A History of Horror in the Mass Media,* the author argues that Franken Berry and Count Chocula "are simply safety valves that make our grim world, if anything, a little less monstrous" (p. 242). They may

allow little children to experience some measure of cathartic release, but they also show how terribly feeble some monsters have grown with age.

15. This is in the face of numerous changes in the adolescent body and in teenagers' behavior. For example, the average American girl began to menstruate at 14.3 years in 1900; now she begins at 12.9 years ("*Harpers* Index," 1985, p. 13).

In addition, see "Blackboard Jungle" in *Harper's Magazine,* March 1985, for a comprehensive list of the radically different discipline problems facing American schoolteachers from about the time of Frankenstein's last appearance in Universal pictures and Jason's debut in *Friday the 13th* (1980).

For a more in-depth and incredibly depressing look at how the lives of American teenagers have changed for the worse, see Gaines (1991). Her field observations make teen suicide appear an eminently rational act of self-improvement.

16. The information we need must not be confused with news of everyday life. If it were, you could read the *New York Times* or *USA Today* for guidance instead of seeing a fantastic horror film. Scary films based on events taken from today's headlines would generate something like trivia, not useful information, under the model many critics use to explain the meaning of horror.

17. Genre criticism in this case is cultural genetics. Somewhere deep in the brain or collective unconscious there lies a subterranean structure that orders the production of horror. This structure also maintains a permanent process of decoding, which ensures that monsters will mean the same thing across audiences and across time.

One important problem with this hypothetical construct, assuming it does in fact exist, is that it is fashioned from such an indeterminate mix of sexuality, biology, and hard-wired mythology that it is impossible to figure out where sexuality leaves off from biology, where cultural artifacts cease being genetic bequests, and when contemporary horror films do more than simply retell oft told tales.

18. When works are overtly intertextual, when they make obvious their association with other texts, it is often the case that the critic who enjoys them must apologize for such overt quotation and, in place of originality, offer a vision of group storytelling. If stories are patently derivative, then perhaps they have some measure of value as communal glue.

Any artwork, even that which satisfies the cultured tastes of the most well-educated audience, has its progenitors; however, no one would dare to picture the well groomed sitting around the campfire/artwork telling and retelling common tales of hardy sustenance. So, not only is the ritual function patronizing, it has a class bias as well. The masses have generic reruns, the rich possess uniquely original masterpieces.

All cultural works have a generic makeup, but some textual assemblies are a bit squeamish about freely revealing their lineage. The apparent lack of originality in genre work is only more craftily disguised in "difficult" work. It is a part of high art practice to disguise debts, to fragment overt quotations, and to use only strategic portions of earlier works in such a way as to make any quotation ambiguous. Nonetheless, plagiarism is rife in any cultural endeavor. High art is just more particular about revealing crib notes.

19. Film criticism informed by psychoanalysis need not always refuse the influence of factors outside the purview of the unconscious. For example, the readings of Williams (1983, 1989), Penley (1989), and Clover (1992), while firmly grounded in psychoanalytic film theory, do engage, in a constructive dialogue, other modes of criticism.

20. It should be noted that when Kristeva (1979) develops her concept of abjection she does not do so in reference to horror films (p. 46). Kristeva draws her "horrible imagery" from religious texts and transgressive literature. That said, just because Kristeva does not traffic in low art is no reason to suppose that horrible visions produced for a less well read audience may not be abject as well.

21. This process, theorized by Jacques Lacan, begins in the mirror phase. In the mirror phase, the baby learns that she is not all the world. Prior to this stage, the baby experiences all that goes on about her as nothing more than an extension of her own body. Now, the baby learns to differentiate between me and not me. Following Laplanche and Pontalis (1967/1973),

> the mirror phase is said to represent a genetic moment: the setting up of the first roughcast of the ego. What happens is that the infant perceives in the image of its counterpart—or in its own mirror image—a form (*Gestalt*) in which it anticipates a bodily unity which it still objectively lacks (whence its "jubilation"): in other words, it identifies with this image. (p. 251)

The mirror phase marks the beginning of socialization because when the baby recognizes herself, at one and the same time she also recognizes that others are not she. When we identify with the image, that which shows that we and the world are two different entities, we are then ready to signify. We may then adopt systems of meaning that are shared throughout the social system.

The mirror phase also marks the first time we adopt what we see as a picture of who we either are or want to be. We will continue to identify with images, especially in the movies, because images "[deliver] my identity which reassures me" (Kristeva, 1979, p. 42). Unfortunately, all our choices are ultimately dissatisfying because, no matter what images we choose to identify with, these images are never of our own making. They are productions or reflections produced outside ourselves. When we adopt an image, regardless of how flattering it may be, we are adopting an ideal imposed from without. And no matter how much effort we put into the process, we cannot realize, cannot become, the mirror to the image.

Kristeva proposes abjection as counterbalance to the immense dissatisfaction that arises from identifying with images that can never truly be our own. In abjection we reject all images "in order to compensate for the painful process of becoming a social self" (Stone, 1983, p. 43). We recognize that all images are lies, that they never capture who and what we are; consequently, in abjection we work to destroy all the pretty pictures placed before us.

22. Twitchell (1985), for instance, finds Kristeva "almost impossible to read" (p. 10). We may well wonder, does Twitchell consider her impossible to read because she writes like most erudite poststructuralist critics or because of what she has to say about the human condition?

23. The minor adaptations whereby horror is more explicitly and more powerfully splashed across the screen do not reflect an alteration in the fundamental meaning of the terrible. Audiences are very well versed in how films are produced and will not be frightened if they catch a glimpse of the wires that allow a hungry vampire to glide across a victim's bedroom. They cannot suspend disbelief should the camera cut away as Dracula has an oak stake driven through his sternum. We must now see the gore as monsters attack. The new horror, which is increasingly bloody, has not re-created monsters with a different symbolic value. It is only that we have too much technical knowledge to be satisfied with a glimpse of the Phantom's grisly face. The turn toward the graphic is only a condition of increasing literacy.

24. Early horror films ended with the death of the monster. Contemporary horror films end with the certain death of the living; this shift, if Kristeva (1979) is correct, signals nothing more than the censor's relaxation. Familiarity with the genre has led to acquiescence on the part of the superego. Any move toward a more nihilistic brand of horror does not mean the central message of the spectacle has changed.

25. We try to know the beast in the mirror, to give it a title or face, but no image can capture the form of the nameless thing. Even if we assembled all the horrific images ever produced, we would have a terrible dictionary that gave us numberless portraits of the monstrous, but nowhere could we find the real face of the beast.

The beast exists in the subject prior to the acquisition of language, prior to the mirror phase, but it can be evoked by telling endless stories about destruction. Only the endless procession of horrible imagery tells us it exists; however, no remotely accurate portrait of the void inside us can be produced. Our vacuous center is impervious to precise definition. Any effort at description is sucked into a black hole that engulfs all light thrown near. Horror films are, in the end, just failed approximations fascinated with the empty fury inside us all.

26. Many films, including *Psycho*, a touchstone for the contemporary shocker, are not shy about demonstrating a contemptuous familiarity with Freud. When *Psycho* concludes, "the film debunks Freud," as Kendrick (1991) observes, "by squeezing him into the prosings of a smug callous psychiatrist who comes on near the end to dispel shadows" (p. 232). This is not an uncommon trope. Windy, opining psychiatrists and other boring authority figures are often the subject of sport in the contemporary horror film.

27. The most obviously post-Freudian horror film is *The Rocky Horror Picture Show* (1975). This film and the stage production from which it is adapted make a virtue of mocking all the sexual secrets that purportedly fuel the production of horror.

In *Rocky*, Dr. Frank 'N' Furter, the film's mad scientist, is perfectly frank about why he is making a man from scratch. He wants someone who will meet all his many desires and what better lover than one built from the ground up; unfortunately, even with his own custom-made sweetheart, Dr. Frank 'N' Furter is still insatiable. He continues to want more.

Dr. Frank 'N' Furter is not an exception. Everyone in *The Rocky Horror Picture Show*, as in a psychoanalytic critique, is driven by perverse wishes. Brad and Janet, the two straight visitors to the Doctor's swinging castle, find their long-repressed desires mysteriously stirred by the strange goings-on in the inaccessible mansion. Soon enough, Brad and Janet have gleefully sampled the forbidden pleasures of the opposite and same sex. There are also a host of lascivious secondary characters who obviously represent both a panoply of monsters and an impressive range of paraphilias.

In addition, Andy Warhol's *Dracula* (1974) and Andy Warhol's *Frankenstein* (1974) are particularly notable Freudian send-ups. In this *Dracula,* the poor vampire is continually betrayed by wanton women who welcome his advances; sadly, none of the bloodsucker's willing victims are virgins. Dracula spends half the film throwing up bad blood as he complains about being unable to find a sexual neophyte.

Warhol's *Frankenstein* is best remembered for its literal reading of a bit of dialogue swiped from *Last Tango in Paris* (1972). The stolen, and slightly amended, line "You can't say that you know life until you've fucked death in the gall bladder" is taken quite literally in the film.

28. As the genre has aged, more often than not ultraviolent horror is played for laughs. In *Army of Darkness* (1993), *Dr. Giggles* (1992), *The Return of the Living Dead* (1985) and its sequel (1988), and the later *Elm Street* films, the jokes outweigh the dismemberment. Yet, even as the genre turns toward parody, these films feature a great deal of violent play that is anything but funny.

29. Carroll (1990) argues the opposite: "The locus of our gratification is not the monster as such but the whole narrative structure in which the presentation is staged. . . . These stories . . . revolve around proving, disclosing, discovering and confirming the existence of something that is impossible" (p. 181). If Carroll's description of narrative pleasure is limited to films made prior to our epoch he has a point. The sequence noted above does cover a great many old horror films.

New horror films are, however, not governed by such a tidy narrative structure. Although new films are conventional—they do follow relatively fixed formulas—the dominant convention running through the genre is that common sense is at an uncommon premium. In these films, pleasure comes from the destruction of reason, irrational plot lines, and the extinction of all those who try to think rationally in the face of death.

30. In the case of the contemporary shocker, this group includes more than just those fans who regularly watch horror films at the movies. Most studies on the horror film assume that this group is, in the main, composed of adolescent males. This is an accurate description of the audience who buys tickets at the cinema. Young males are among the most active movie-goers and are likely to be in attendance for the latest horror film and just about any other film down at the show.

It is also likely that through video and cable distribution the original audience has been greatly expanded. Even if they have never met at the cinema, everyone knows the slasher. In addition, the violent tableaus and nihilistic passion for spectacular suffering have infected a wide range of productions ensuring that nearly all of us are familiar, to one degree or another, with the pageantry of gore.

3. NOSFERATU

Beauty provokoth thieves sooner than gold.
—William Shakespeare,
"As You Like It,"
Act I, scene 3, line 108
(in Bevington, 1988)

For transcendental critics, there must be a wellspring, an original source, out of which all horror flows. Novel images of the horrible, constructed from what appear to be new elements, are interpreted as a gloss on old fears. In arguing that the history of horror films should be read as a broken series of disjunct moments, responsive to more than the prerogatives of the static unconscious, it will be necessary to mark out a number of different shifts in the genre.[1] If there are notable differences across the genre we cannot rely on the immutable unconscious as the solitary source of horror's effects.

Many films, once the source of sure-fire thrills, have been forgotten and deleted from memory as new, more capable visions of the monstrous replace impotent chillers. Radical breaks now separate what is considered scary from what was once thought to be frightening and is now, at best, lively entertainment for impressionable children. That films do not work, that they scare no one, should alert the reader to transcendentalism's excesses; especially when, under the transcendental model, it only seems logical to presume that all films in the genre should, for any given audience, strike some universal primeval chord.

Does *Nosferatu: A Symphony of Horror* (1921) make your blood run cold?[2] Does *The Golem: How He Came Into the World* (1920) force you to screw your eyes shut? These are not isolated examples designed to brace up a wavering straw man; no matter how long we obsessively pore over obsolete celluloid, it is an exceptionally difficult task to find many moments from any horror film made before 1960 that can raise the least shudder from any audience. Not only do these films fail to scare, they are positively boring—the chill is gone.

Whatever might have caused the audience's skin to crawl has vanished. Perhaps these films were successful because the audience for them willingly manufactured the effects that once sent crowds screaming. For a horror film to work, the audience must not only suspend disbelief, they have to manufacture particular kinds of belief. Watch *The Rocky Horror Picture Show* (1975) once without its regular group of active participants and again with its usual audience of dedicated fans. The film would lose most, if not all, of its loony charm without the merry audiences who create an extraordinarily successful duet. Horror works in the same fashion. For a film to scare, the crowd must respond—eagerly.

Like decayed filmstock, the passage of time makes horror ineffective. Old horror films, like many aged pop artifacts, have only sociological worth. They tell you what once enthralled audiences just as they now fail to satisfy contemporary tastes. In most cases, the experience of watching a film once known as truly terrifying is an utterly mystifying experience. People were scared by this? If not a soul is scared by it, there is little sense in valuing an old horror film as a masterful bit of movie magic. That strategy may work for other film antiques as a way of celebrating early breakthroughs in film craft and directorial panache, but horror films that provide no thrills are worthless, except for what they say about older screen-audience relationships. Yet, in this regard, dated horror films are priceless relics. Surveying old films is, without question, the most reliable way to establish just how far the latest genre entry has drifted from its putative roots.

Today, *Nosferatu* is welcomed only by audiences who enjoy doing time in the art house; Godzilla hawks Dr. Pepper®; buxom lamiae and gregarious werewolves sell Bud Light® and Coors®; and cardboard stand-ups of Universal monsters push new, cheesier Doritos® and Pepsi® at the end of aisle 7 in the Piggly Wiggly.[3] When old-time spooks turn up on the revival circuit or on glossy supermarket packaging intended to fuel impulse purchases, we ought to recognize that these beings no longer carry the same arresting charge they once did.[4] When an image can be licensed and splashed across all sorts of delicious merchandise or marketed as a welcome return to the cinema's glorious past, it is something other than scary; it has a share of public memory certainly, but as a useful source of terror it is empty and weak—well-known but not even remotely threatening.

To map out some of the consequential transmutations undergone by the genre, highlighting the chain of succession as new visions of the dreadful replaced spent depictions of the horrible, we need to turn to the films themselves. To chart a portion of the meandering course that horror has traced over the past 80 years, I survey a series of films, from the silent movie era to the time of Jason, that offer markedly different visions of the horrible. For each of these readings, I, first and foremost, establish the character of the menace. Once its nature has been determined, the question is how, if it is vulnerable, can it be defeated? What does it take to slay a beast, and are we up to the task? In addition, what are the social relations the menace disrupts? When monsters are being monstrous, how do their black behaviors affect the lives of the film's protagonists? Finally, I consider the relationship that each film constructs between knowledge and our ability to make the world a safer place. When we are under attack from a menace, will these films allow us to imagine a better day, an untroubled tomorrow, when we shall live mercifully free from monstrous violence?

Like any nascent medium, early films were produced by scavenging preexisting formats for lucrative plots and styles of presentation that could be feasibly adopted for the moving camera. All new communication technologies, especially those designed to entertain, plagiarize previous modes of transmission and content. Silent films were no exception; certainly, they reshaped plagiarized material and integrated some new elements with stolen ideas, but for the most part, silent horror films were a messy combination of recast gothics, folktales, staged melodrama, and potboilers.[5] When it came to producing horrible visions on the screen, new ideas came at a premium.

According to Hardy (1986), author of *The Encyclopedia of Horror Movies*,

> Horror had little role to play in the earliest days of the cinema. In the flickerings that resulted from the combination of the trickeries of science and magic, the emotion engendered by horror had little place. . . . It was only as films grew longer and audiences more sophisticated that the horror film took its rightful place in the cinematic spectrum. In retrospect, the

speed with which the subsequently identified "traditional" themes and sources of the horror films then emerged is quite surprising. (p. 16)

Hardy goes on to describe the ancient debuts of all the earliest embodiments of cinematic terror. In just the first years of the medium's existence, the Wolfman, Frankenstein's monster, the Vampire, and the Maniacal Scientist, among others, all made it to the screen; however, none of these stock prototypes are remembered in their initial public appearances by anyone other than film scholars and devoted film buffs with an affection for archival research.[6]

Chief among the pioneering early screen demons is the broken-down vampire featured in F. W. Murnau's *Nosferatu*. The plot for Murnau's film was borrowed from Bram Stoker's *Dracula*. In a fruitless effort to evade copyright law and the wrath of Stoker's litigious widow, screenwriter Henrik Galeen renamed the principal characters and shifted the scene of Dracula/Nosferatu's eventual destruction from London to Bremen. Unfortunately, at least for Murnau and his production company, *Nosferatu* was so obviously lifted from Stoker's work that all copies were ordered destroyed for copyright infringement.[7] Despite the burning permit, not all copies of the unauthorized film were put to the match. Some prints escaped the law, and the film eventually made it to American screens in 1929. The survival of *Nosferatu,* thanks to mechanical reproduction and multiple copies, allows us to directly measure the distance between our frightful entertainment and early horror.

Nosferatu begins, after a brief establishing shot of Bremen, in the tidy home of the Harkers as the couple prepare themselves for the coming day. Jonathan and Ellen Harker are comfortably middle class and, from all appearances, relatively happy with their shared station. Beautiful tokens of domestic calm—gilded sunlight, a cozy and nicely decorated parlor, a playful kitten, and a bountiful flower garden—underscore the altogether pleasant nature of family life in the Harker domicile. Clearly, for the time being at least, this is an enviable family situation. As Waller (1986) puts it, we are witness to a

fanciful image of the bourgeois home as a comfortable, private domain contiguous with domesticated, ornamental nature—a modern Garden of Eden, in which the man goes and does, while the woman entertains herself with idle childish diversions or passes the time with needlepoint before her husband returns from his sojourn in the public world of commerce. (p. 179)[8]

This serene world is about to be severely tested. Here, against the backdrop of domestic space, is where we learn to take the full measure of Dracula's abominable powers.[9] The Harkers are going to have their charming home torn apart as Jonathan precipitously leaves kith and kin to serve Dracula. The moral of this film is obvious given Murnau's glorious depiction of the home. Even before we catch sight of the vampire we know that it is a sin to misjudge the boundless importance of domesticity.

Jonathan will seriously underestimate the value of his family and, as a terrible consequence of his poor judgment, expose himself and his wonderful wife to the pernicious desires of the undead. He errs in the appreciation of home and hearth and find himself condemned to suffer endless torment. By the end of the film, the Harker home will house only a shattered widower. The life of his wife and the blissful union the Harkers could have shared long into the future will have been painfully lost through spiritual mismanagement.

As the Harker home is brought to ruin, the audience is going to learn that one should never devalue the bond between spouses; they will also learn that all spouses have the power, if only they choose to use it, to save their uniquely precious alliance. Initially, it seems that Ellen is the weaker vessel in the Harker home. How many heroines, women of iron will and many talents, seem reasonably happy to occupy **all** their time with the delicate intricacies of embroidery and matters of home economy? No matter how much we appreciate the fact that women can make their own way in the world, the repertoire of images that come to mind when we think of distaff strength is unlikely to include a woman meticulously embroidering home decorations for hours and hours on end.

We are even less likely to consider Ellen a possible saviour when we notice that, despite her generally happy air, she appears rather nervous as Jonathan gets ready to leave the house. How can we expect a contented, albeit high-strung, hausfrau to emerge as a monster slayer? In comparison to his edgy wife, Jonathan is a level-headed man of action whose fiscal concerns establish him as a force to be reckoned with in the wider world. These are not, however, the roles they will live to the end of the narrative; by the film's conclusion, Ellen will become an extraordinarily powerful figure and Jonathan a weak, disbelieving child.

The Harkers' avoidable troubles ensue when Jonathan's superior, Renfield (the vampire's mad confederate), presents the unworthy husband with the promising opportunity to sell Dracula some choice Bremen real estate. Jonathan mistakenly assumes Dracula is just one more firm handshake in the creation of a brilliant career as the lure of wealth seduces the grasping mate away from home. To consummate the deal, Jonathan must visit the Count in his far-off castle lair and personally collect the vampire's signature on the offer to purchase and contract. He readily abandons his anxious wife to the care of friends, a poor substitute for a husband's full attention, and sets off on an ill-fated trip that will lead to the fall of the House of Harker. In the end, when Jonathan eagerly offers the Count the chance to reside in Bremen, he barters his life and wife for a better overstuffed sofa, more bric-a-brac, and a more suitable neighborhood.

Along the journey to Dracula's den, Harker's coach stops over at a rustic country inn. Jonathan exits the carriage and is immediately marked as out of place by his smart city clothes. His elaborate traveling coat, ruffled shirt, and dandy hat all clash sharply with the traditional peasant garb of the stage driver, innkeeper, and various townsfolk. Harker enters the way station and titles announce his urgent need for refreshment as he is late for an appointment at Dracula's castle.

Upon being served, Harker consumes his drink with extreme disdain for the innkeeper and barmaid. He swigs his lager with the messy gusto of a bratty child knowingly creating a scene in a restaurant. Jonathan behaves as if his genial hosts and the other patrons either did not exist or were only there to watch him enjoy slaking a gargantuan thirst. Jonathan's appalling table manners demonstrate the depth of feeling he has for those of a lower station. It is a shameless, narcissistic display. Obviously, common courtesy need not be employed if the only people who can observe your miserable comportment are ignorant peasants. The man may have money and a good tailor, but he has no respect for those whom fate has relegated to the working class.

With this display of callous immaturity the audience cannot have all that much concern for Harker's eventual fate. Perhaps Dracula will teach him something about raging egoism and the precarious nature of existence. Should he survive his encounter with the living dead, Jonathan might learn just how ignorant he is of the many secrets that make up this difficult world. He might also acquire a deeper respect for the little people who must, if they are to feed and clothe their own needy families, serve him.

When Harker self-importantly mentions the castle, with the expectation that he will be treated with even greater deference, the peasants react with obvious concern and a little fright. They are not, however, wildly terrified. The mention of the vampire's home does not send them into paroxysms of quaking terror. Their reaction is closer to the face one would make on hearing that a rabid dog or ravenous bear is loose in the woods. Apparently, they have a healthy respect for Dracula, but they are not driven witless by the mere mention of the beast's name.

And why, after all, is Dracula soliciting the aid of a real estate agent? Why should the vampire have to leave Transylvania and travel all the way to Bremen if he is so powerful? The peasants must know how to control the beast and come very close to defeating the vampire if he must pack his bags, call Century 21, and, after three centuries, remove himself to Bremen. Surely, the peasants have succeeded in drying up the blood source as Dracula is now compelled to forage far afield for the nectar of the dead. To Jonathan's regret, the rough peasants do know the ways of the vampire and are willing, caring stewards if given the chance to educate the unschooled. They will try to aid the boy but are stupidly rebuffed whenever they offer Jonathan a much needed measure of assistance.

As Harker has his refreshment, all the while reveling in his patent superiority, the film cuts to the wilds surrounding the village. Instantly, the peasants are given additional credibility and the audience knows Harker is in desperate trouble as we witness a foul-looking hyena descend to the town pasture. If we doubted the peasants previously, the camera forces us to accept their world. The alien animal is an envoy, Dracula transformed, or the kind of miserable pet only a nightstalker would keep. If feral animals like this roam the woods, then vampires are probably here too. We can now be certain that Jonathan's narcissistic bubble will not survive this business trip. We do not yet know what will happen to Harker—we only know that something must as the ominous animal stalks the earth. The quick cut from Jonathan to the wild creature unites them for the audience; as they have been so closely paired, it is only logical they will eventually meet in the same frame—instead of on opposite sides of a splice.

While the hyena prowls the countryside, the townpeople's horses flee the area, having picked up the scent of the beast. Like the peasants, the horses have learned how to elude the vampire. They have the sense to vacate their territory whenever they apprehend the presence of the enemy. Watching the horses run to safety reveals something important about the vampire: Dracula cannot be an entirely supernatural creation if the galloping horses have the sense(s) to detect him or his familiar. Obviously, vampires are an oddity, but if animals, and the peasants as well, are endowed with the ability to detect the presence of a vampire, then such vile beasts are not entirely otherworldly. If the vampire did not have to obey some natural law, then the horses and their owners would not be able to detect his presence and protect themselves from the unearthly predator.

Vampire detection for the work animals is just plain horse sense. For the peasants, knowing how to best a vampire is like husbandry, cooking, the preparation of medicinal teas, and the brewing of beer. It is a skill that can be acquired by attending to the ancient lore and practices of one's elders.[10] It is also a skill that requires a close relation with the things of the earth. We see then how the peasants have defeated Dracula: They live near to the land and have maintained tight-knit communities that make it easy to pass on the accumulated learning of the clan.

Jonathan has a chance, if only he will listen to the peasants. To survive outside the busy metropolis, one needs either a native guide or a lifetime of schooling. Not surprising, a city boy risks his life if he too readily depreciates the talents and wisdom of the peasants. As Jonathan is a self-important fop, he is in serious jeopardy. Not all city folks are doomed, but to survive they must pay heed to those who know more than they. Ellen will defeat Dracula as the film concludes because she, lacking Jonathan's obnoxious vanity and dreadful ego, trusts the lore of the peasants.

Jonathan retires to bed and is greeted, as Waller (1986) humorously notes, by the peasant version of Gideon's Bible conspicuously placed near the bed in a last attempt to enlighten the vapid guest (p. 180). He glances through *The Book of Vampires* and hurls it to the floor with a derisive laugh. When Jonathan blasphemously slams the truthful text to the ground, laughing hysterically at the nightstand reading of his backward country cousins, we are reminded, once again, that Harker's ruin is certain.

Jonathan's vulgar exhibitionism and contemptuous treatment of invaluable informants makes it difficult, if not impossible, to pity his end. He is so exceptionally self-satisfied that wanting to see him taken down a peg or two is not unnatural or inhumane. He needs some seasoning. The audience may not want him killed, but a lesson in humility would certainly be a useful exercise. Jonathan too often erupts in childish displeasure whenever he is faced with someone who attempts to awake him to the fact that others know better than he. He never listens, pauses over what he has been told, or in any way tries to engage in dialogue with a willing mentor or able confidante.[11] How many times can aid be freely dispersed and just as freely spurned before the audience abandons him to his sad fate?

Once Jonathan leaves the inn and boards the coach that will take him to the Count (and we are ready to leave him for dead), the film takes a startling departure from the narrative. For just a moment, the technology of film assumes the foreground, and plot advancement is displaced for thrills. Jonathan's coach travels perilously fast as the camera is under-cranked. To the modern viewer, the speeding coach has the herky-jerky look of a discombobulated paddy wagon trailing Buster Keaton. Murnau then switches to a negative print and the entire world of the film is reversed. This blazing ride, which trades day for night, is meant to entertain us. The crazy pace of the drive, not to mention the magical conversion of black to white, is not designed to take Jonathan to his wit's end, as his bland reaction to the uncanny trip merely consists of asking the driver to lessen the blistering speed of the coach.

Later, when Dracula hurriedly departs for his sea voyage to Bremen, we are treated to further cinematic spectacle, or more appropriately, what once passed for theatrical magic. Dracula loads a number of earth-laden coffins atop a wagon. He climbs into the last bier and we see the casket lid float unaided to close the vampire's resting place. The scene is shot from Jonathan's astonished point of view; however, it is really shot from the point of view of an audience eager to be mesmerized. In a strict narrative sense, there is nothing to be gained by breaking the story line and enjoying some film legerdemain. Any information gleaned from this scene will only aid in understanding the nature of cinematic spectacle, not in further illuminating the meaning of Jonathan's futile struggle with darkness. Jonathan already knows Dracula has uncanny powers and so does the audience. This scene, like the undercranked and negatively imaged journey to the castle, serves one simple purpose: It allows the audience to revel in technological sleight of hand.[12]

The film returns to Jonathan's travails, and the technology of film recedes to the background, when the boy from Bremen is unceremoniously dropped before an ancient and decayed fortress. The forlorn castle initially appears uninhabited. It is a crumbling relic only faintly suggestive of another time when the inaccessible keep represented black power and infamous glory. It is likely that the once forbidding abode represents an ignoble retreat from the dangerous plains controlled by the able peasants below. Dracula has been driven up and away like a frightened rodent whose lower warren has been flooded. He must remove himself to the remote high ground. The castle is no longer an impregnable aerie, hanging over the hamlet like Damocles' sword, as much as it is the last limb of refuge in reach of a hunted/haunted creature.

Dracula himself greets Jonathan, remarking that the servants have already been dismissed for the evening. No matter what the hour, regal presences do not greet unannounced callers at the front door unless they have fallen on difficult times. As the missing servants never appear the following day, it is likely Dracula has been abandoned. The lack of allies and the depressing condition of his castle-hovel reveal the dire straits to which the bloodsucker has been exiled.

His worn clothing and wizened appearance complement the state of the decrepit castle. He is clad, like a very poor undertaker, in a dusty, threadbare black suit that tightly cloaks his gaunt frame. The vampire is frightfully lank, bald, moves arthritically, and has fragile-looking rat cuspids, not impressive razor-sharp fangs. There is nothing hair-raising or seductive in his look. Nosferatu is no father to the suave brood soon to follow him to the screen.

Upon Jonathan's arrival, the favored guest and worn host adjourn to the dining room as Dracula, ever the caring familiar, wants to treat Harker to supper. Jonathan, still oblivious to the fact that he is in peril, is more than happy to sup with his host. In vivid contrast to the rest of the barren castle, the dining room is well furnished and the dining room table itself is overcrowded with delicious foods.

Dinner with the Count mimics, in reverse, Jonathan's savage drink at the way station in the valley. In the castle, Jonathan goes out of his way to make a good impression. If down below, among the working poor, he was a moneyed boor, then here Jonathan is a very well mannered executive in conference with an important prospective client. At the table of the mighty, he civilly cuts his food (and later himself as well) in small manageable bites while paying avid attention to his affluent host. He does not fling his glass about like a loathsome lout lucky to have a couple of bucks in his pocket. Because the noisome peons below had no money or social standing, they were not worth the bother of simple courtesy.

The Count, however, is another matter entirely. With him Jonathan acts politely, as he deems men on their way up in the world should when dining with those of similar or better station. All the appropriate niceties that accompany deals and meals are rigorously observed. This last supper becomes even more ironic when Jonathan accidently cuts himself while paying too much heed to his hungry dinner partner. He inadvertently slices his thumb when startled by the ringing of a clock. It is not coincidental that he happens to be carving a loaf of bread when he injures himself. We know he will become for Dracula what bread is for humans—the staff of life.

Although it was extremely doubtful that he would wake up when the alarm rings, as we have seen so many stupid behaviors on Jonathan's part, the self-inflicted incision seals his fate. He should have recognized his danger as the clock rang with a skeleton beating out a tocsin; instead, he ignores yet another clear warning and digs his grave a bit deeper. Jonathan, deafened by material lust, fails to note the warning call and spills his own blood for the vampire.

Aside from the dining hall, the only other well-furnished location in the bleak keep is Jonathan's bedroom. The bedroom and dining room are the two most significant rooms for the care and maintenance of domestic relations. Here, all the necessary rituals that preserve a close community or inseparable dyad occur.[13] In these small, private spaces, a variety of essential acts take place as we strengthen old ties and forge new bonds. Here, we make love, break bread, talk of the day, and share common interests and rare insight with friends and lovers. And only indoors with family, friends, ignored aides, and the beast itself are clues offered to rid the world and the Harkers' lives of the night menace. Of course, such clues may not be apprehended no matter how patently obvious. Witness Jonathan's shallow understanding of what it means to be human and have meaningful relations with those who live nearest to hand and heart. If one cannot recognize love, if one confuses comfortable furnishings with the household, or if one negligently refuses genuine offers of care and refuge, then one cannot apprehend evil.

Jonathan's last important scene, and also the moment when the focus of the film shifts permanently to Ellen, occurs shortly after the evening's first meal when Dracula feeds on Jonathan. Finally, aware that his worthless life is in peril, Jonathan flees his avaricious host in a supremely cowardly manner: He withdraws to bed and pulls the blankets over his head. In this yellow retreat, Jonathan becomes a frightened and egocentric tyke who assumes that what cannot be seen must not exist. Dracula's prey, with the exception of Jonathan, do not play peek-a-boo when about to be bitten. Other victims make, at the very least, token attempts to save their skin when confronted with the killer. One only feels disgust with Jonathan's utter lack of spine as the scene fails to evoke a hint of fear. No one else duplicates Jonathan's insipid posture, and Murnau does not film another assault with the camera dispassionately perched above the killing tableau. This is a special scene that prepares us for Ellen's assumption of the film's narrative and spiritual center just as it comments on the ability of others to die honorably.

As Dracula is poised to tear the coverlet off Jonathan, we see a medium close-up of Dracula's threatening shadow imposed over Jonathan's blanketed form. Emblazoned against the bedroom wall are Dracula's shadow arms, his elongated fingers form dark, greedy claws, and we know the vampire is ready to dig his teeth into Jonathan's quivering neck. The film then cuts to Ellen's bedchamber, where her arms are outstretched in a similar attitude. While Dracula is made manifest in shadow, we see the corporeal form of Ellen opening herself to Jonathan. The metaphorical difference between these contradictory figures is immense. Dracula, the phantom of the dark, is an incomplete and parasitic simulation of the living; Ellen is represented as a whole and complete being. Ellen's loving embrace gives care and refuge, whereas Dracula's rapacious hold painfully drains life from animated tissue.

Ellen cannot actually release Jonathan from his cruel torment—he must make his own way back to Bremen—but she is able to keep him alive. There is an undeniably affirmative power in her inviting embrace, just as there is an almost equally negative power in Dracula's venomous clutch. Ellen is hundreds of miles away and still her profound love offers protection. As Jonathan shrinks into a feeble ball unable to defend even himself, Ellen extends her transcendent love over sea and land to penetrate the heart of Dracula's ravaged castle, and her husband is saved.

Although the contrast between Dracula and Ellen is striking, the difference between the postures of Ellen and Jonathan is equally notable. Ellen, vulnerably clad in only the thin film of a sheer nightgown, exposes her flesh and soul to save another. Faced with danger, Jonathan implodes. Not only does he fail to fight for his own life, he cannot even bear to look at his assailant. He flees to the imaginary security of the bedcovers and tucks himself in deep. No image better captures the enormous spiritual difference between the couple. For the rest of the film the resistant life force belongs to Jonathan's selfless wife.

Dracula departs by water for Bremen, having felt Ellen's spiritual presence, and the exhausted Jonathan trails along by land. At each port,

Dracula replenishes himself. These unnatural events are reported in newspaper clippings that cite an unknown plague crossing Europe. The attacks, noted only by printed report, are impersonal and of no real interest to the audience. Like the shots of prop planes circling a spinning globe in 1930s travelogues, these inserts do nothing more than chart Dracula's inexorable progress as the vampire makes his way to the Harker home.

Also interwoven with the documentation of Jonathan's and Dracula's travels are scenes of Doctor Van Helsing, Harker family confidant, lecturing his students on the Venus flytrap and other vampiric specimens of nature. These lectures have traditionally been interpreted as symbolic of contemporary man's inability to understand the real meaning of evil. According to Waller (1986), only the detached, soulless humanist, isolated in his antiseptic laboratory, would use the vampire as the source of a monstrously inappropriate, anthropomorphic explanation for nature's mysteries. Van Helsing and the other scholars have lost sight of evil's existence in the world and can only catch a glimpse of good's enemy in a wholly discrepant metaphor (pp. 183-184).[14] When real vampires take to the black night, only the blind discuss them metaphorically.

This is an unfair insult, as Van Helsing and the other studious naturalists are never given a chance to confront the beast. We cannot be sure what Van Helsing and his compatriots would do in the presence of the undead, as Ellen refuses to discuss the real explanation for her complaint with anyone other than Jonathan. Furthermore, during Jonathan's trip, Ellen's anxiety over her husband's lengthy absence is not treated as a wild aberration of feminine hysteria by the Doctor. He does want to know why she is so unsettled, but again, Ellen refuses to tell Van Helsing or anyone else about the terrible beast that is the source of her agonizing misery. Van Helsing is not out of touch with spiritual Truth and the real meaning of evil; he is simply, in contemporary parlance, out of the loop. Until she takes matters into her own able hands, Ellen relies solely on the love of her husband to save her from the vampire. It is not abstract knowledge and the scientific community that fails Ellen—it is Jonathan who must shoulder the blame. Jonathan betrays Ellen when he fails to live up to the sacred contract between husband and wife.

As the two members of Ellen's domestic triangle make their way to Bremen, we see the loyal wife seated forlorn on the otherwise deserted Bremen beach. Because she sits at the water's edge on a dreary beach scattered with white crosses, it is likely she is waiting for Dracula and not Jonathan. Her powers of compassion and love for Jonathan are so strong she can sense the site where Jonathan's nemesis will appear and prepare herself for the coming confrontation. While sitting watch on the lonely sands, Ellen is given a letter that announces Jonathan's imminent return by land and his battles with horrible nightmares. If she took the note to heart and believed Jonathan's feeble attempt to calm a prescient soul, she would appear vastly more relieved; instead, she looks even more plaintive as she registers Jonathan's pathetic white lies. Ellen knows that whatever troubles her husband's sleep is not a figment of imagination brought on by ingesting a bit of bad meat. She retreats to her home, leaving friends bearing bad news behind, to resume her vigil in the sanctuary of domestic space.

By this time, Jonathan's face has begun to resemble his wife's worried countenance. He has stopped grinning and the audience wish for comeuppance has been granted. No longer will we be repelled by the smug expression Jonathan wears to alert all about him that the world could not be a better place. This look is not, however, a sign of hasty maturity. It only represents his baleful encounter with the vampire: No growth has occurred.

The departure of Jonathan's smile allows us to make an important discrimination between the films of today and those of the past. If later horror films destroy the body with a combination of inventive hysteria (the latest special effects) and fanatical detail, then the early horror film is extraordinarily subtle and, by today's standards, dull when it comes to marking the toll that terror has taken on the body of a sorry victim.

Horror has, however subtly, impressed itself on Jonathan's body. He has been visibly disfigured—the maddening smile is gone. Jonathan is now compelled to bear the knowledge of evil on his mournful visage. Jonathan is lucky—the damage to his body is only cosmetic. Later films will banish subtlety and simply mark horror on the bodily surface with indiscriminate gore. In our time, Jonathan's glad smirk would have been ripped apart and replaced with a vulgar red-rimmed hole.

Jonathan's little mark, a delicately inscribed frown, also carries an instructive moral that further differentiates the violence of yesterday from the gore of the present. We can watch Jonathan's unhappy face and recognize the obvious teaching: Marriage is an awesomely weighty responsibility that cannot be entered into lightly. Marriage demands sacrifice. Do not fail to discharge your marital duties when trouble pays a call, or you too will find yourself unable to muster even a glimmer of a smile.

One of the prime reasons why most critics loathe contemporary horror films is the notable absence of such tutoring. We simply do not encounter characters like Jonathan who are pupils as well as victims. Our violence is meaningless. What lessons are we to glean from the shattered dead of today? Future victims are bloodily erased and not given a moral send-off when they die. They simply perish. Whatever happens to the body in the contemporary horror film just happens. There is only nothing to learn. We are not allowed to exit the theater with an instructive adage echoing in our heads. We leave our spectacles with bloody and blank images resonant of nothing.

The distance between now and then, even at the level of how monstrous violence impinges on the body, is already great. It becomes even greater when we consider the character of the protagonists in *Nosferatu*.[15] Ellen's role as tortured martyr and Jonathan's role as a domestic Peter, always denying what he should defend, leads us to ask if Jonathan is worthy of Ellen's self-abnegation. For the modern audience, especially one familiar with the selfish acts that pervade contemporary horror, the answer is an unequivocal no. We are supremely unprepared to accept the psychology of masochistic suffering motivating Ellen's death. There is no contemporary equivalent for this amazing sacrifice. Nothing—not the dated special effects, not the film's slow pace, not the histrionic acting— makes the film more difficult to read and enjoy than Ellen's self-willed destruction.

We are currently incapable of either believing or presenting such actions on the screen. Ellen's incredible behavior seems as remote as the holy acts of spiritual grace which lead the Church to find the occasional true believer fit for beatification. Given the religious tenor of self-denial that characterizes Ellen's gift, it would only be fitting that her image be glazed in stained glass with the Virgin and other divine heroines.

Contemporary films do not attempt scenes of evil's destruction occasioned by valorous acts. Should horribly misplaced acts of altruism, like Ellen's offering, arise in contemporary horror films, they will almost certainly become the impetus for deeply cynical jokes. Nobility is a signal for vicious teasing to commence. If Ellen found herself transported to today's horror film, she would be endlessly tortured for presuming that noble victims are a narrative possibility.

Today, monsters like Freddy only become stronger in the face of probity. The good is no longer a barometer of the monstrous. In *Nosferatu,* we know the vampire is very evil because Ellen is so very good.

The reverse is now a cinematic convention: The moral vacuity of mere mortals is indexed by the omnipotence of evil.

As the film draws near its end and we await Ellen's inevitable transport to heaven after she finishes with Dracula, a strange comic interlude interrupts the denouement. Pitted against the moral depth of Ellen's angelic efforts is an abbreviated comedic romp. In this little detour, Renfield escapes from the local asylum and capers through Bremen with a horde of angry citizens in tow. Like the vignettes with Van Helsing, the crazed Renfield's dizzy chase is only of local interest. He and the others prevent the film from being too uncomfortably claustrophobic. Marginal characters merely add some depth to the Harkers' lives; they do not play a central role in Jonathan's moral failure and Ellen's consecration. To imagine they do would be similar to finding the grave diggers in *Hamlet* of paramount importance in defining the despondent Dane's troubles.

Renfield's wild run through and out of Bremen begins when he is found perched on a steep-roofed house, chucking rocks and pieces of slate at the understandably overwrought Bremen folk gathered below. The townspeople are consumed with worry over the devastating disease sweeping through their fine town and now they have an escaped madman pelting them with stones. It is all too much. The idiot's attack is met with a return barrage of their own, and soon the game is on. Renfield seems to find undeniable pleasure in annoying the assembled Bremenites. He performs acrobatic feats, capers about with remarkable ease, and swings from cast iron lamp brackets like a lithe gymnast 30 or more years younger. As Renfield is none too svelte, the idiosyncratic picture of a chubby burgher gamboling with exceptional grace is amusing. In contrast, the mob moves awkwardly, aimlessly seething to and fro, losing its way, and herding down meandering blind alleys. This is to Renfield's benefit as he is an obvious scapegoat for all the bad luck that has befallen the plagued city of late.

In one particularly memorable shot, Renfield's grinning head bobs up behind a close-up of a gnarled stump. His bald pate, framed with upraised wisps of thin white hair accenting the ears, apes Dracula's far graver image. Renfield's oafish caricature of Dracula's fiendish head leads us to wonder, "How can anyone believe that ludicrous face is dangerous?" The intensity of the pursuit is totally out of proportion to the menace that Renfield presents. This narrative dead end, like the displays of technological whimsy that precede it, stops the movement of the film toward the final confrontation and allows us to relax and revel in the town's hasty folly.

Murnau does a wonderful job of composing activity for seated patrons as he invites us to play in the streets and forget, for a brief moment, the oppressive despair of Ellen Harker. In keeping with the frenetic nature of the search, the editing for this scene is more animated than in any other sequence in the film. The snappy pace of the cutting doubles the hectic commotion of Renfield's wild tail. Multiple camera positions complement the cutting, giving us the liberty of a playful viewer who can alight anywhere in Bremen. At different times the lens places us before, behind, and above the crowd. At one moment, we are temporarily stationed at the end of an alley, as if both we and Renfield were ahead of the pack, casting a furtive glance backward to make sure the angry throng is still following. We see the mob negotiate the corner and hasten on—a quick cut—we are taking a long view of frenetic silhouettes running against the distant horizon—another swift cut—we are staring Renfield in the face and sharing his malicious enthusiasm as he continues to elude the harried mob.

Our spurious physical pleasure easily distracts us from the weighty concerns the narrative has so far thrust on us. Slapstick legitimately excuses the audience from worrying about Ellen and her uncertain future. Once the match is concluded, we are sufficiently refreshed to resume our burden. Humor functions like a sorbet between rich courses that can overwhelm the palate if they follow too closely after one another. The extraordinary compassion that Ellen's plight demands could not be met without a pause from the negative exposition.

The interchange between horror and lighter moments represents a restorative balance. In the midst of pain and anguish the heart can still grow light and take leave from a world of trouble. The scene of Renfield's chase is successful because we are totally immersed in a child's game that masquerades as adult enterprise. Such reassuring moments will be quite common until our jaundiced era. In time, humor will cease to occupy its optimistic role as relief and counterbalance to evil.

Early horror films had an ecclesiastical optimism (there is a time for every emotion under heaven) that is absent in the shockers of today. In Nosferatu, there are no problems in identifying whether or not something is funny or sick. Black humor, the humor of overworked and near deadened outrage, is nonexistent in the silents. In the future, knowing what is fit for a belly laugh and what is a scene requiring disgust will be radically unclear. Humor, when only some of the audience laughs together, will veer hysterically from glee to terror in an instant. The line of demarcation between tears and chuckles will grow dim. Laughter will become a question of relative perversity and self-doubt.

After Renfield's refreshing escapades, we are turned back to the Harker household where Ellen again sits, delicate embroidery in hand. In a domestic tragedy, the bedroom is the perfect site for ultimate failure and transcendent victory within a sacred union. It is here where Ellen is beatified and Jonathan is transformed into a lonely widower. In this room, lovers caress, lie, dream, quibble, and hammer out the innumerable pacts any couple must of necessity forge if they are to create a workable life together. It is not a space where strangers are long welcome.

Against this backdrop, Ellen must reluctantly invite Dracula to enter and for a short time take Jonathan's rightful place in the bed. Although one of the marriage partners is undeserving of the other, their bond is still holy. Ellen honors her sworn commitment to such a degree that she will engage in a monstrous version of the wedding night to save her husband. She is forced to surrender her body in the very place where it should be revered. Where she had been tenderly caressed and kissed by Jonathan, she must be torn by the claws and fangs of Dracula.

Contrary to her husband's feckless wishes, Ellen has read *The Book of Vampires* provided to Jonathan by the scorned peasants. If Jonathan had only heeded the wisdom of the learned folk, then he and Ellen could have escaped the curse of the vampire. Of course, Jonathan's business trip would have been for nought and he would have to return home with empty pockets; yet, even without a new account, he would have the largesse of his wife's undying love. Public space, an occasional source of deep disappointment, still remains brimming with opportunity when the hearth provides healing solace to lovers momentarily disenchanted with the outside world.

Jonathan's impatience with Ellen's justifiable curiosity is fueled by wounded pride and an insurmountable fear of dealing with the unknown. Ellen's interest grants Jonathan one last opportunity to attempt a solution with his wife's aid. He fails to respond to Ellen's plea, for what can a woman possibly do?—she lives out her life within stifling walls, her limited experience ends where a man's just begins, and she could not possibly understand the overwhelming complexity of the situation. Such are the realizations of an irresponsible husband who has not discovered the real worth of marriage. Why else his petulant rage when Ellen suggests she knows of Jonathan's unhappy misadventures with Dracula?

In response to being castigated by Jonathan, Ellen exhibits some unangelic behavior of her own when she scolds Jonathan for having to

encounter Dracula's ominous form night after night through the bedroom window. As if to lessen our intense revulsion for Jonathan, Ellen
must descend from her pedestal, if only for a brief period, and demonstrate she carries a human flaw—a temper. All Jonathan can do when
scolded is run to the window, ball his fists, and stamp his feet. The
posture hardly signifies the fiery wrath most spouses would feel if their
home were held siege by a nightmarish killer.

Dracula has been content until now to browse among the other
Bremenites; he has not yet made any final advance toward the Harker
domicile. His attack is, however, inevitable. If Ellen could feel Dracula's
demonic intentions across Europe and the Balkans, what she feels now
must be infinitely more painful. When the Harkers should be allowed to
retreat to one another's arms in relative safety, the vampire looks on,
invading the couple's dearest refuge. With Ellen's acknowledgment of
Dracula's presence in the Harker bedroom, the horror of *Nosferatu* is
realized. What evil can do attains its full measure when it reaches between
two lovers in their inner sanctum.[16]

To rid herself of Jonathan's presence, for he is now an obstruction, Ellen
feigns a swoon and sends her husband out of the bedroom to find Van
Helsing. It is ironic that Ellen must pretend to suffer from a stereotypical
female complaint to save her husband. Two sets of presumptuous assumptions are exploded by Ellen's counterfeit faint. Men are not the sole gender
capable of ridding the world of evil, and passive resistance can expel the
undead from the land of the living. There is unimaginable strength in this
feeble and quintessentially clichéd performance.

This act is also striking because Jonathan has been permanently exiled
from the innermost domestic circle. The woman who has stood steadfast
beside him now wants him gone. Ellen is, of course, too selfless to
consciously send Jonathan on a lifelong guilt trip, but he will have earned
many sleepless nights with Ellen's passing. To Jonathan's eternal regret,
he will always have the memory of being driven from Ellen, by Ellen,
when the aid of a powerful lover would have been most desired. The
audience may have rejected Jonathan, but the loss of his wife's faith is
unprecedented. She will still die expressly for him, but she will do so on
her own terms.

The Book of Vampires explicitly details how a vampire may be vanquished. Ellen has read its directions and knows a vampire will perish if
kept by a pure woman of virtuous heart until the sun has risen. The
sacrifice, which cannot be coerced, ends in death. Any woman who elects

to follow the ancient instruction must do so freely and completely. There are no half-measures allowed. If Ellen resolves to take Dracula away from the Harker home, then she will be gone as well.

Upon Jonathan's misguided exit, Ellen approaches the window overlooking Dracula's nest. She attempts to open the window but cannot bring herself to undo the clasp. Like the time she berated Jonathan, this short lapse of will underscores Ellen's humanity. She is not quite perfect. With each tiny misstep we can come closer to identifying with Ellen. Her sacrifice is not altogether beyond human comprehension when she loses her temper and has momentary doubts about letting the abominable vampire feed on her. She is still probably too good for our planet, but we can detect the faintest hint of clay upon her feet.

Recovering from her brief failure of nerve, Ellen flings the window wide and waits. With Ellen's signal of apparent submission, Dracula steals into the Harker home. He has long been waiting for the divine moment when Ellen capitulates and allows him entrance. As Dracula creeps up the stairs and into the bedroom, Ellen retreats to the bed. Unlike Jonathan, when Ellen is beset she does not bury her head beneath the covers. She is woman enough to accept her chosen lot. The shadow of Dracula's taloned hand crosses her unprotected breast and brutally mimes crushing a capacious heart. Ellen writhes in real pain as Dracula's phantom image lances human flesh. Ellen lets her heart be broken for love as Dracula consumes the animating core of the Harker home. The bedroom has worth only while Ellen's heart still beats. When she is gone, Jonathan will sleep alone and find the room a cold vacuum.

Many of the vampire epics that follow *Nosferatu* depict the women who fall under a vampire's spell being willingly seduced. There is absolutely no indication of perverted romance in Ellen's bedding of Dracula. Ellen has no dirty need to lie with the beast; there is no hidden danger lying within her breast. Jonathan has been so severely structured as an illegitimate husband that to make Ellen contemptible as well is a cynical transposition that blatantly refuses the obvious terms the film sets forth. Jonathan would make almost anyone else's eye wander, but such is not the case with Ellen. The film is not an unconscious rape fantasy; it is a paean to the home and the possible glories that await a couple in which each partner is worthy of the other.[17]

Dracula is a malignant curse, bringing sickness and danger to Ellen's family. Her marriage to Jonathan gave Ellen lifelong vows to honor and she does. She takes Dracula to heart only to ensure his destruction. It is blasphemous to suggest that Ellen is aroused by Dracula's embrace (Fieschi, 1980, p. 710). The idea that she may enjoy her enemy's foul touch taints her sacrifice and is a projection of perverse criticism. Reading the film in such a manner is akin to the resentment certain critics feel toward Freud's judgment that memories of childhood seduction were really unconscious fantasies.[18]

We are free, however, to refuse the message of the film as speciously optimistic without denying the film's structural integrity. Who can help wondering what kind of destructive socialization led a worthy woman to sacrifice her life for a man with Jonathan's less than endearing qualities? A contemporary audience is likely to find this idealistic conception of marriage more horrible than anything Dracula can do. How could anyone owe so much to a man worth so little?

The scene of Dracula's last feast is shot from across the soiled bedroom with Ellen's back to the camera. The camera's remove from the assault and the shielding of Ellen's face preserves her privacy. The attack takes place without excessive violence as Dracula kneels, almost tenderly, over Ellen's prostrate form, quietly sucking. Although Dracula's assault on Ellen is shot without any sign of gruesome struggle, the horrible depravity of the violation is registered by the position of heroine and beast. As Dracula cradles his all too lovely prey, the posture of demon and damsel blasphemously recalls the manner in which Mary attends to her dying son in any of Michelangelo's *Pietàs*.

Nosferatu does not explore a victim's death agony in obscene detail. We are not allowed the voyeuristic thrill of complete access to the death struggle. It is not necessary to show gore in detailing early horror. We do not see barbed teeth sink into a delicate throat. We see no spurts of blood spray from gaping entry wounds. There are no close-ups of horrified eyes trembling in terror. Ellen's dignity is maintained with discreet camera work that would rather not show that kind of thing. The idea of Ellen's end, her holy offering, and the appreciation for her gift are all that is necessary to establish the grave harm that has come to a good woman.

Although *Nosferatu* scrupulously avoids gore, there are scenes that do work to underline the terrible pain that comes with the vampire's fatal bite. No images suggest the agony of Ellen's excruciating ordeal better than the intercut scenes of Van Helsing and Jonathan strolling through a lovely garden discussing Ellen's vague symptoms as Dracula kills. They calmly amble to the Harker house along a pleasant garden path, chatting of many things while Jonathan's wife is being quietly tortured. What must it mean to suffer such terrible degradation and know that one's lover is promenading amidst the greenery?

The draining of Ellen continues without tension or terror. It is as if the attack were over once Dracula had trespassed in the bedroom. With that violation accomplished, nothing more terrifying can occur. The sucking continues unabated until a cock crows announcing the dawn. Dracula leaves off his meal and realizes he is doomed. He moves to the window as sunlight courses down the buildings outside, grasps his throat, and vanishes in a puff of smoke.[19]

Ellen returns to life, apparently still worried about Jonathan, and calls out her husband's name. He and Van Helsing enter the bedroom to hear her call his name again. As she lay under Dracula's fetid mouth all she could think of was Jonathan. The errant spouse rushes to Ellen's side and cradles her broken body as she, in her final act of Christian selflessness, makes sure he is still alive. She dies with Jonathan's name on her lips. Until the end, Ellen's only concern is her worthless husband. Knowing he is safe, Ellen collapses and dies. The film ends with a brief epilogue affirming Bremen's survival as it tells of life returning to normal. Those who were weak recovered. There is no further mention of Jonathan.

Our final memory of *Nosferatu* is of a couple bound together on the marital bed. Unfortunately, one of the partners is dead. This pose could have been preserved until a natural end had some important lessons not been neglected. The moral of *Nosferatu* is clear: Good defeats evil—at a price. Remember those things you swore to hold dear. Let nothing take you away from domestic bliss.

Men of worldly action, too involved with the secular arena beyond the home, either do not know what it takes to preserve the hearth or, much worse, cannot bring themselves to make the necessary sacrifices to maintain the stability of the family unit. Doctors and businessmen, in fact any sort of spouse, will be derelict in their duties if they do not keep an eye on the home as they make their way in the world. All civic accolades, fiscal perks, and bourgeois accoutrements that mark worldly success mean nothing when the precious hearth is left unattended.

Evil comes from outside the domestic circle. If both partners are not equally cognizant of the dangers that lie across the threshold, then evil will steal into the home. Love needs ever alert sentinels to survive the assaults of this world. Peasants, grounded in tradition, have remembered this lesson, but so has Ellen. All Ellen needed was a workable mode of sacrifice. Both peasants and urban dwellers can drive the beast away if they recognize the towering importance of family and care. Horror arises in the absence of regard for love. Where love flowers, horror has no place.

Notes

1. See Andrew Tudor (1989) for a more inclusive look at the varieties of breaks in the history of the horror film. Tudor's wide-ranging survey provides an admirable taxonomy of the horror film's impressive number of subgenres.

2. Hereinafter *Nosferatu: A Symphony of Horror* is referred to as *Nosferatu*.

3. Only a high-art European director (Werner Herzog), would bother to remake *Nosferatu* as *Nosferatu the Vampyre* (1979) when it is clear that other sorts of menace have long been the focus of audience attention. To commemorate the original film's restoration, *Nosferatu* has also been recently rereleased to the art house circuit. These are clear signs that *Nosferatu*, in whatever incarnation, no longer has any significant relation to contemporary horror. Imagine the confusion that art house patrons would experience if a *Nightmare on Elm Street* production was co-billed with the latest Zhang Yimou or Yvonne Rainer picture.

4. Madison Avenue cannot, at present, appropriate today's slasher for sales promotions. There have been no ad campaigns featuring contemporary monsters selling anything other than the films in which they themselves star and the ancillary merchandise (printed T-shirts, baseball caps, Halloween costumes, etc.) that comes with any successful Hollywood release.

5. Kendrick (1991) does a good job mapping out all the various materials filmmakers drew on to produce the earliest films in the genre.

6. Willis (1972-1984) provides the most complete catalogue of horror films.

7. Even though important thematic elements were dropped from Murnau's film, the work is an overt theft of the Stoker novel. Stoker's story was itself based on vampire tales that had already been told many times and in many ways prior to the publication of *Dracula* in 1897. As Hogan (1986) notes,

> Poems, stories, and novels that date back to "Hecuba" by Euripedes helped shape the course of the literary vampire. Homer, Aristophanes, and Philostratus explored vampirism—from a chiefly moralistic point of view—while Goethe's 1791 poem "The Bride of Corinth" is about a repressed girl who is free to marry her lover only after she has died and been resurrected as a vampire. The poet Coleridge gave us "Christabel." . . . Lord Bryon's outline "The Vampyre" . . . inspired Bryon's companion John Polidori to fashion a finished story of the same title in 1819. . . . Finally, J. Sheridan Le Fanu's 1871 novella *Carmilla* . . . and Theophile Gautier's story "The Dreamland Bride" (1836) revolve around female vampirism. . . . Dracula is a character whose fictional lineage is impressive and clear. (p. 139)

8. Waller (1986) also argues that, to appreciate Dracula's power and the melancholy chaos he creates, it is necessary to find the misery borne by Bremen equal to the pain suffered in the domestic arena. Although many Bremenites do perish after the arrival of Dracula, their deaths are a footnote to real distress.

In contrast to the beset Harker home, the Bremen sequences are abstract portrayals of general strife. The trials and tribulations that Bremen suffers are shown in only a few long shots of funerals and the boarding up of plague-stricken houses. We are like gods watching the death of Bremen. The citizens are imperiled, but there is nothing horrifying about their suffering. Their problems could just as easily be the result of starvation, influenza, or a "real" plague, and no one feels the same frisson watching a monster kill as they do charting the course of an anonymous microbe.

Waller overrates the Bremen sequences, even though he calls them "brief," because he wants to read the suffering of the Harkers, a domestic struggle, against the mass confusion affecting the other citizens. Waller's allegorical interpretation finds that the battle of the Harkers, especially Ellen's blood sacrifice, is not justified by the survival of sterile bourgeois Bremen. He wants to extend the battle of good versus evil beyond the domestic sphere, when the film is essentially a bloody mystery. The extraneous Bremen deaths are mere addenda to the intense domestic chaos Dracula brings to the home of a happy couple. What happens to Bremen does not really matter; something has gone dreadfully wrong with Ellen's family and it is up to her to solve the puzzle, even if she has to die in the process (pp. 178-196).

9. In the late 1960s and 1970s, there is a return to the domestic scene. This time, in a paranoid turn, evil makes itself known from within domestic space. *Alice, Sweet Alice* (1976), *Rosemary's Baby* (1968), *The Omen* (1976), and *The Exorcist* (1973) all feature an eruption of evil from inside the home. *Rosemary's Baby* is particularly noteworthy as evil appears in perhaps the most domestic space of all: the womb.

10. Rarely do we see these sorts of skills employed in contemporary horror films. They usually appear only in parody films like *Buffy the Vampire Slayer* (1992), *Fright Night* (1985), and *Fright Night, Part 2* (1988). When a latter-day film appeals to the lore of the ancients you can almost always be sure the genre is being sent up.

11. Contemporary victims are similarly incapable of learning anything of real worth; however, this inability to learn stems not from choosing to remain ignorant but simply from the fact that no matter what someone learns, learning can, in no way, be said to have any ameliorating effect on bad situations. Jonathan is a callow idiot; if he was a little more mature he would stand a much better chance with the vampire. In contrast, today's victims, whether they be smart or dumb, are equally without power when evil strikes.

12. Contemporary horror films have been castigated again and again for ceasing to tell stories to satisfy brute pleasure in film excess. This is one item that has not been transcended historically. Even the earliest silents found time to revel in film's technological possibility. Of course, what film can do changes over time, but in nearly every horror film one can find moments of technological whimsy. *Nosferatu* is no different. Even this stale, academically revered chiller leaves off storytelling for a bit of spectacular exhibitionism.

In comparison to contemporary horror, earlier films had less spectacular spectacle, but that is only because film technology advances so very rapidly. At some point, almost every memorable horror film engages technology with excessive fervor. This is especially true of contemporary films. A horror film without visible hyperbole does not generally work. It collapses under the weight of good taste and will not satisfy the fan, as any vestige of good taste has been relegated to other venues of cultural play by the horror audience.

13. Many silent horror films had monsters who would kill to enter domestic space. When the Phantom falls in love with his talented operatic pupil in the 1925 version, it is the aborted love of the disfigured monster that fuels the film's depiction of the horrible. The Phantom is banned from the domestic scene. The same is true of Lon Chaney's other well-known role from the 1920s. As Quasimodo in *The Hunchback of Notre Dame* (1923) he is involved in a hopeless romantic engagement that ends in death. The 1921 version of *The Golem* also

features a central love story that is not found in any authoritative version of the ancient Jewish legend.

14. In this story, science plays no role as exemplar of modern man's unholy distance from the past. The scientists are just a little slow to catch on. In fact, as Fieschi (1980) argues, the "lecture at the very heart of the film . . . extend[s] the principle of vampirism to the heart of the universe" (p. 707).

15. This vast remove from the horror of the early years of cinema is not so obviously apparent when viewing other silent genres. For example, the films of Mack Sennett, Buster Keaton, Harold Lloyd, and, of course, the Little Tramp, are all within easy reach. Only silent horror is so inimical to contemporary viewing practices.

16. The domestic scene has also been a source of fascination for many recent thrillers. Latter-day thrillers seem to prefer going after victims on the private stage. *Pacific Heights* (1990), *The Hand That Rocks the Cradle* (1992), *Deceived* (1991), *Fatal Attraction* (1987), and *Unlawful Entry* (1992) all feature the happy home under assault. These films, like *Nosferatu*, all contain errant protagonists who unwittingly allow trouble entry into the home. If the family is to survive, then individual family members must wake up to the danger outsiders present and, as the group bonds together, the family must attack evil as one dynamic unit.

Another notable parallel between these films and *Nosferatu* is the fact that all the above movies feature protagonists who are comfortably or very well off. Today, when evil calls, it seems that only the tastefully decorated yuppie split-level, Soho loft, or Painted Lady is of interest to the malefactor.

Unlike Jonathan Harker, the victims in contemporary thrillers are not chastised for living the good life. It is true that they have failed in keeping the wolf from the door; however, their error lay not in material lust but simply from failing to remember that the worst evil is oftentimes disguised as the most innocuous good.

In contrast to *Nosferatu*, the message these films deliver has no religious component or ethical reminder. Indeed, contemporary thrillers offer only the simple argument that raging paranoia is the best and only defense against evil.

17. See Bram Stoker's *Dracula* (1992) for a movie that argues that women are dying to sleep with a monster. In this version of the vampire tale, whenever women think about Dracula they seem compelled to don décolletage and writhe against any available male substitute should the Count be otherwise detained. No film is more obvious in demonstrating the vampire's appeal to the fairer sex.

18. See Masson's (1985) controversial book for a "real life" analog to the idea that Ellen truly desires Dracula.

19. Deleuze (1986) makes explicit the spiritual nature of Ellen's gift as he describes the immolation of Dracula in the Light. When Ellen brings Dracula to bed she unleashes

> the dynamic sublime: *the non-organic life of things* culminates in a fire, which burns us and which burns all of Nature, acting as the spirit of evil or of darkness. But this latter, by the ultimate sacrifice which it demands of us, unleashes in our soul *a non-psychological life of the spirit*, which no longer belongs either to nature or to our organic individuality, which is the divine part in us, the spiritual relationship in which we are alone with God as light. (p. 54)

4. THE MONSTER

That there is a we and a they will have to be mended before long.
—Julian Beck (1987, p. 115)

In *Nosferatu,* horror made itself known as a source of family strife. Pledged to protect each other against the bad things of this and other worlds, Ellen and Jonathan Harker found themselves the object of monstrous attention as Dracula took to the night. If we were to learn what it meant to be horribly threatened, to understand the eruption of exceptional evil, it was necessary for us to intrude upon private space. We must peer behind closed doors, as the most horrible assaults one could suffer occurred within the province of domestic life.[1]

With the passing of the silents the most memorable horror films were consistently produced by Universal Studios.[2] Between 1930 and 1950, Universal Studios produced the most indelible and long-celebrated incarnations of Frankenstein's monster, Dracula, the Wolfman, and the Mummy.[3] In the Universal Age, these monsters secured a lasting place in the Hollywood pantheon of screen greats that most of us carry around in our heads.[4] When Dracula's name is uttered, the image that first springs to mind is not likely to be that of a fragile Max Schreck, a glowering Christopher Lee, a tottering Al Lewis, or an urbane Frank Langella but, rather, the immortal Bela Lugosi. Similarly, if the results of Dr. Frankenstein's wayward experiment are recalled, we generally think of Boris Karloff's portrayal of the Creature as the foremost representation of the handmade Monster. Unfortunately, although these efforts are, collectively, the source of some of the most durable images of the monstrous, they no longer afford much of a thrill.

Like *Nosferatu* or *The Phantom of the Opera,* films from the Universal Age are not extraordinarily scary experiences for contemporary audiences. Only sly, small children who have skirted precipitously early bedtimes appear fascinated by Frankenstein's hulking creation. For a more experienced audience, a sense of winsome nostalgia, not rekindled fear, accompanies the experience of re-viewing Universal classics.[5] The old days of horror films seem so much sweeter and so extraordinarily distant when we think of the rapacious killers who splatter their shrieking victims across the screen today. After all, Universal's first talking horror films were released only a scant 60 years ago. That is a relatively short period of time in comparison to the truly staggering span between what was once deemed fit horror and what is now considered worthy horrific entertainment.

Although it is terribly unlikely that we are going to be even slightly frightened by Bela the Balkan vampire or anyone else in the infernal coterie of Universal stars, it should still be obvious, even to now jaded viewers, that Universal's creations demand a different reaction than do earlier incarnations of the monstrous. Universal reconfigured the strict moral balance between human protagonists and eerie antagonists by radically redrawing the boundaries between good and evil and mortal and monster. These creatures do sometimes behave just as appallingly as their mum predecessors, but Universal monsters are also many times more appealing than the creatures of the silents. Even if we sometimes wish they were dead, we oftentimes end up sympathizing with these abnormal beasts and their miserable plight.

Universal films made it much harder to fully loathe the monster. At some level, all the members of the studio's cast were beguiling. Each empathetic curiosity demanded a measured evaluation of the meaning of the monstrous.[6] They had formidable personalities as complex as those of their human counterparts, and audiences were often compelled to root for them against their human foils—for it was the humans who would send the monsters to perdition.[7]

This important break with the silents, the creation of monsters for whom one feels pity, forces us to rethink the meaning of horror. Anytime there is a permutation in the nature of the monstrous, any change that forces us to reconsider what we are fighting against, it also becomes necessary to ask ourselves what it is we are fighting for. When monsters are accorded a new ontological status, what it means to be human changes as well. Monsters, because they are our enemies, work to define who we are by offering us an inverted portrait of ourselves. The ideal image we have of ourselves, based on what we struggle to extinguish, is altered when who and what we hate is changed. Anytime that monsters are created anew, humans are also remade. Universal gave us a host of monsters who all seemed to have their reasons for acting awful; consequently, we end up having to rework our conception of what it means to be human.[8]

Frankenstein's monster was a misguided brute—good but dim and easily unnerved (a bit like Lennie in *Of Mice and Men*); Dracula was a seductive and suave Lothario whose charms were amplified by his ability to engage his victims in charming, dangerously attractive repartee; the Wolfman was a kind of hairy, low-brow Hamlet, always in anguish over his unshakeable curse; the Mummy, while the least charismatic monster, being little more than a terrifically irate rag doll, was too often called to consciousness by irreligious archaeologists and power-crazed priests who trespassed on sacred ground.

In addition to complicated personalities, the monsters of the 1930s and 1940s were consumed with profound misery. They found the world as difficult a place to reside as many humans commonly do. What kind of monster says, as Bela Lugosi did in the 1931 version of *Dracula,* "To die. To really be dead. That must be glorious"? Karloff echoed Dracula in *The Bride of Frankenstein* (1935) when he cried, "We belong dead." Yet they must continue to live. They are compelled to go on no matter what the cost. A group of disenfranchised killers, the Universal ensemble nobly adopted a will to persevere. At times they sound like world-weary characters from more erudite fiction, outcasts who feel "life is visually too hideous for one to make the attempt to preserve it. Let it go. . . . At the same time, I am still part of life, and I am bound by this to protect myself to whatever extent I can" (Bowles, 1979, p. 83).

A monster who loathes his own life and contemplates existence with a downcast eye exhibits troubling parallels with depressed humans. Monsters with existential burdens? Beings who dread the future and find carrying on with life a terrible weight are truly eerie creatures. How can Universal monsters be considered a negation of the human when they agree with the revulsion humans feel for their species? They even make each other sick; consider the Bride's anguished exclamation when she finds out to whom she has been betrothed. Such unanimous agreement in regard to what is good and beautiful cancels the strict line that distinguishes the human from the nonhuman. Opposites, beings who share no common ontological ground, would never find themselves in harmony over what constitutes physical beauty and a worthwhile existence. We might wage war together, but we are not categorical opposites.

All these creatures were at some time us.[9] The Universal monster is nothing more than a converted human: one who has been cursed with damnable abilities and frightening characteristics that make him an oppressive and oppressed minority. The only real difference between them and us is that we just missed out on certain formative experiences. Their present situation is nothing more than a horrible twist of fate that could have happened to anyone. Their tragic struggles to find a viable place in the world, ill-starred quests that cannot possibly succeed, offer visions of the misbegotten whose path we are lucky not to share.

Dracula was himself a victim, nipped and forced to continue an ancient trade. He was unwillingly apprenticed into eternal damnation; consequently, he is driven by two strong and definitely human traits: the urge to survive and a distaste for cannibalism. In the tenuous balance of these two urges, with the "life force" being slightly stronger, he is exquisitely miserable. Every moment he stalks the night is a dark hour for his own soul.

Frankenstein's creation might be in a worse situation. He was any number of dead men who had found glorious peace in endless irenic sleep. He is assembled from a hodgepodge of stolen corpses and one abnormal criminal brain and electrovivified back to life. The monster's real creator, makeup wizard Jack Pierce, worked hard to create a monster who embodied discomfort. Frankenstein's creation was really a hack job:

> I did some research in anatomy, surgery, criminology, ancient and modern burial customs, and electrodynamics, I discovered six ways a surgeon can cut the skull, and I figured Dr. Frankenstein, who was not a practicing surgeon, would know the easiest. That is, he would cut the top of the skull off, straight across like a pot lid, hinge it, pop the brain in, and clamp it tight. That's the reason I decided to make the Monster's head square and flat like a box, and dig that big scar across his forehead, and have metal clamps hold it together. The two metal studs that stick out the sides of his neck are inlets for electricity-plugs. The Monster is an electrical gadget and lightning is his life-force. (Pierce, quoted in Gifford, 1983, p. 86)

Awkwardly sutured from a melange of graveyard inhabitants, a butcher-block caricature of humanity, he is selfishly returned to life, and people are surprised when he runs amok. Laden with residual memories of having lived before, he awakes from death with the horrible apprehension that he is a mix-and-match human, not only again dreadfully alive but self-conscious of being jury-rigged from foul bits of partially decayed flesh. What Hell could be worse than to be returned to life in a counterfeit jumble of a body with the expectation that you will behave peaceably, happy to have been returned to the living?

The Mummy was in suspended animation for thousands of years and brought back to a world without a shred of respect for his religious heritage. He was interred as an eternal guardian for his ancient religion, and when the new world threatens his beloved temple he must react violently against the blasphemous defilers. Our existence is a constant threat to the sere altar boy's sacred values. To the Mummy, we are a pack of bloody infidels as we threaten to destroy not only his world but his gods as well.

The film that best exemplifies the new relation between the human and the monstrous is *Frankenstein.* The movie's portrayal of a monster who had his reasons was duplicated in all other Universal efforts until the corpus collapsed from overexposure. By the time all the Universal monsters had been paired together in variable combinations (costarring with Abbott and Costello), there was nothing left to say in the Universal language. The model was no longer current. The audience was bored, and new horrors, like the Atom Bomb, were revolutionizing the meaning of terror. One formerly dead man roaming the countryside means nothing when entire cities vanish under man-made explosions set off with the express consent of a nation's rulers. Genocidal acts by allies and enemies also did little to make Universal films scary. Until that time, however, Universal monsters were popular horror.

Frankenstein opens with an explicit recognition of its status as show. A tuxedo-clad gent with boutonniere, obviously an emcee, steps from behind a worn stage curtain, bids us welcome, and delivers an important announcement from Universal Studio head and film impresario Carl Laemmle.[10] Mr. Laemmle is concerned for our safety. He wants us to know the show might be too frightening for the faint of heart in the auditorium. The prologue is obviously a bit of corny hokum; whoever sees it has already paid the entrance fee and found a choice seat.

Moving a barker from outside the tent, where a crowd must be baited to enter, to the inside of the venue changes the meaning of the pitch. It signals that the pact between audience and filmmaker in producing workable horror films has been understood by the studio. The only reason why a shill is put in a film is to wink at the audience and say "Here comes the show!" The emcee speaks to us, and teases all the patrons beyond the footlights, in an attempt to further whet our appetite for the film. It is a moment of attempted seduction: We are being wooed. Like a prayer before a football game, the filmmakers want the audience on their side. *Frankenstein,* and all horror films, cannot work without the intercession of an audience—and Mr. Laemmle knows it. Whether or not the film does work—the audience might dismiss *Frankenstein* as a failure—all horror films come with similar, if not so dramatically stated, invitations to participate. The audience must join Dr. Frankenstein in his laboratory and operate beside him.

Invitations distributed, the story proper begins. Like countless earlier horror films, the tale commences in a forbidding graveyard. The heavily atmospheric lighting suggests that whoever died is being buried at night. Funerals as the moon rises are somewhat uncommon. The burying of the coffin in the middle of the night has all the loving warmth of a morose satanic ritual. There is something perverse in sending a loved one on an eternal voyage after the sun's rays are extinguished. The scene is perfectly dismal. If this is good morality in operation, how much bleaker can wayward ethics seem?

The depressing graveyard scene is made even stranger when the supposed hero, Dr. Frankenstein, is spotted waiting in the bushes. The good doctor, hidden behind the shrubbery, waits for the corpse's survivors and grave digger to exit—so he may avail himself of the corpse's parts. Grave robbing is an old and necessary partner of medical inquiry in the horror film. Many well-intentioned scientists, and many more bad ones, have had their important research hampered by ignorant God-fearing folk who want their kin left undisturbed in hallowed ground. Grieving, limited thinkers, constrained by improbable moral fantasies, find the thought of their relatives being coolly eviscerated in operating theaters outrageous. Facing such determined resistance, grave robbers are an unavoidable evil.

Usually this activity is reserved for seedy low-lifes, workers who are relegated to the least appealing jobs society can offer. These scabby ne'er-do-wells are the scavengers of wage labor. Their wretched status in the social pecking order is probably lower than the positions held by almost all members of the criminal element. If you are going to steal, take something with respected exchange value, like money, jewels, or furs. Stealing dead bodies is disgusting and not all that profitable. As criminals, only pedophiles might be held in greater contempt by the general public and felons themselves.

The ambitious scientist is usually distanced from such nefarious activity by having it done for him. Purloined corpses are delivered late at night to the loading dock or servants' entry in illicit transactions that leave the doctor clearly troubled. Men of learning are distinctly uncomfortable having to deal with the lesser men for whom grave robbing is a necessary calling. If left unfettered vexed researchers, like Dr. Frankenstein, believe such experimentation could quickly come to fruition for the greater good. Grave robbing, then, is simply part of the high cost of being a visionary as legitimate society stupidly thwarts exploration at unsavory medical frontiers.

In *Frankenstein,* the doctor is an equal party to the theft. He and his diminutive hunchbacked aide work side by side in stealing the newly buried corpse. The body has not had even a moment's quiet in the ground before the body snatchers are feverishly after it. Dr. Frankenstein is so driven that each shovel of dirt he removes from the gravesite ends up showering a grim cemetery statue that presides over the holy land of the dead. The rain of filth cascading over the stern specter demonstrates the depth of feeling the good doctor has for traditional morality. He is utterly unmoved by normative Christian precepts, although he does care for the body in his own irregular manner. As the fresh coffin is levered from the dark pit, he embraces it and says, "He's just resting, waiting for a new life to come." The tender clutch carries with it the distinct odor of perversion. There might be some nasty portion of necrophiliac desire mixed with the Doctor's dream to restore life to the dear departed.

The Doctor and friend have one more stop on their apparently regular collection route. Having collected the consecrated dead, they now move on to more unsavory specimens. They are delighted to find a criminal still swinging from a roadside gibbet. The highway gallows are erected for the evildoer. He is left to openly putrefy, exiled forever, as a festering example that community mores must be obeyed. The convicted criminal lived as an outsider with no care for the law; henceforth, he will spend eternity banished from common ground. Even worse, his body will be destroyed as part of a spectacular production designed to keep the rest of society in line. The Doctor is not impressed.

When Frankenstein comes to collect the corpses of criminals he transgresses not against religious law but against the civil order. It is the

law of man that bars the criminal from a decent burial. When Frankenstein snatches the dead from consecrated ground he defies the Law of
God. As the Doctor makes his way through the night, he trespasses all
conventional boundaries, refusing to distinguish between the good who
should be left respectfully undisturbed in their sacred graves and those
who should be shunned as they dangle and rot in the open air.

The question of duty to civil commandment and religious stricture
matters not a whit to the Doctor. Bandit or good soul, there is no
difference to Dr. Frankenstein. The Doctor does not care how the dead
came to their sorry end. Frankenstein will gather up whoever is interred
in the family plot, even if the sacred ground of the cemetery is meant for
those who felt they had earned the right to spend eternity in the peace
of blessed soil. He is also just as happy to garner the broken bodies of
outlaws, being the one professional in town beyond mundane notions of
good and evil.

The Doctor had wanted the brain of the dead outlaw for his pressing
work. At this time, Frankenstein makes the same mistake his bumbling
research assistant will later make when he is forced to steal an abnormal
brain from the local medical school. A good brain makes for a good man;
therefore, one should always make sure to get the best possible specimen
when it comes time to reanimate the dead. Criminals should be excluded
from the search for viable brain tissue because crime is an organic
problem. Trouble with the law stems from misshapen crania and mal-
formed gray matter, and only a medical dilettante would fail to know
this obvious neurological verity.

The failure of Frankenstein's operation, the creation of a dangerous
freak, is usually blamed on the hunchbacked dolt who drops a perfectly
good brain and must, if he is to please the master, replace the ruined
brain with an intact criminal organ. Here, Frankenstein is about to make
the same blunder. He too would have put a criminal brain in his prodigy;
even though, when it comes to brains, science is confidently prescriptive
on this point: Criminals have abnormal brains that will not perform
reliably should they be reused in a new skull. Fortunately, the felon's
neck was broken (a real surprise considering he was hanged) and his brain
is useless. How could a physician capable of creating a new man from
dead bodies not realize a hanged man probably died from an insult to
the neck? The Doctor may not be as bright as we commonly believe if
he does not think hanging until dead has precipitous effects on the
brainstem.[11]

As soon as a disappointed Frankenstein finds the dead man's neck is snapped, the film cuts to a medical school where an anatomy lecture is in progress. The juxtaposition between the Doctor's midnight foray and the brilliantly lit, antiseptic research hall works to establish some telling commonalities between Frankenstein and his erstwhile peers. While cutting from the midnight raid on a lonely road to the teaching lab does locate some common ground among the physicians, the transition also works to demonstrate exactly where the Doctor's research concerns diverge from the professional interests of his ostensible equals.

Frankenstein's ambitious search for extraordinary knowledge takes place on lonely roads deep in the night. His only colleague, a moronic near dwarf, would not be one's first choice for an evening of stimulating conversation. The school, in contrast to Frankenstein's world, gleams as if cleanliness were really next to Godliness. It has the hygienic sheen of fastidious respectability. Beyond the utilitarian purpose of killing disease-bearing germs, all surfaces glow to demonstrate that nothing untoward could happen here.

The institute bustles with teachers and students who clearly delight in the presence of one another. No one from this elite circle could ever run afoul of the law in the impassioned effort to understand the sparks of creation. They are too happy to be physicians, too happy to have the fine titles and untarnished reputations that gravitate to the cautious professional. They may never do the deeds for which Frankenstein will be responsible, but neither will they do very much to further scientific knowledge. They and their sterile scientific sanctuary are resplendently haute bourgeois. There will never be any sort of trouble with moral guardians here—and no fiery controversies leading to the advancement of medical knowledge either.

Frankenstein has left the fold and is far, far outside the normal limits of scientific enterprise; yet this respectable place has its dark side as well. The students and teachers are callous and enjoy lording their superiority over the dead. They are unconscionably smug in the fact that they continue to breathe and can do whatsoever they please with the dead flesh at their disposal. Jokes about the stiffs are common fare during the school day as everyone has a good laugh at the expense of the dead. Frankenstein may experiment beyond conventional boundaries, but these doctors are less saintly than they care to believe. They will react in professional horror over what their one-time colleague has done without ever suspecting their own indiscretions. They too are arrogant, self-righteous egoists who should be thankful their own sins are muted by the frightened deference paid them by an awed public.

The first set of *Frankenstein*'s conflicts is now established. What are man's intellectual limits? This is a social question and not a question that is answerable within the domestic sphere. The outside world, the community, must be consulted before a satisfactory reply can be fashioned. Many of the operations that go on in the well-kept medical school were once taboo. The lab employs corpses; is Dr. Frankenstein so different just because he is forced to collect his own subjects? Are we being overly squeamish simply because he has been denied rubber-stamp approval by the bureaucratic machinery that regulates trade in dead flesh? Is Frankenstein's problem just one of funding? Would he be considered a degenerate renegade if he performed his work while ensconced in a clean, orderly lab instead of mucking about in moonlit graveyards with a contemptible homunculus? Should an ambitious intellectual ever stray so far from the present-day borders of sanctioned scientific inquiry? The Doctor could simply be ahead of his time. His transgressions may only be a matter of running before the calendar; he may not be violating permanent standards.

Years ago, the fiends who practiced anatomy on a cadaver could be put to death; now, anyone who is licensed to soil his or her manicured hands in the guts of a corpse gets a ceremonious tip of the hat from the average man on the street. What lies beyond the pale is sometimes located just the other side of an always evanescent boundary. Most of what goes on in the estimable medical school today was black magic, nonsense, or scientifically implausible a few years earlier. In his improbable effort to bring a man back from the dead, Frankenstein may only be establishing the right to claim as his rightful heirs Dr. Christian Barnard and the pioneering xenocardiologist who implanted a beating baboon heart in little Baby Faye.

Finding the medical establishment unyielding in the face of genius, Frankenstein abandons the suffocating university and squirrels himself away in a remote watchtower. There, free from the irritating limits imposed by dogmatic and reactionary colleagues, the Doctor continues his research. Without any peers to keep him from his pressing work, Frankenstein devotes all his time and energy to answering the question of existence. In so doing, in giving his all to returning the dead to life, the Doctor leaves off performing his other duties; consequently, his friends are in an uproar. While his compatriots do think his work is worthy of encouragement, as Frankenstein has established himself as a superior and original thinker, they are sure he is working beyond the limit of physical endurance. They are also concerned that his current aim to rekindle life in inanimate tissue is simply too far removed from legitimate scientific inquiry.

Perhaps even more unsettling to the members of his immediate circle, Frankenstein has rejected his beautiful and trusting fiancée, Elizabeth. Their impending nuptials have been put off indefinitely. The traditional marriage and safe job have been abandoned. To the hidebound mediocre eye, Frankenstein has forsaken the good life for a foolish dip into necromancy.

In the face of such abnormal behavior, a scheming troika of best friend, fiancée, and former mentor conspires to return Dr. Frankenstein to his rightful place. He simply must return to his fiancée's side and the scientific mainstream; not unexpectedly, considering the pact between coconspirators, Frankenstein is paranoid. These fools, wrong about the possibility of his visionary research succeeding, want him to abandon his grand dream, a dream that will put the Doctor on equal footing with the Creator. As Frankenstein notes, in a snippet of dialogue edited from the original American release, "In the name of God, now I know what it feels like to be God!"

The scenes of fretting among Frankenstein's extended family might be considered so much narrative boilerplate. They quickly sketch out all the wonderful facets of bourgeois camaraderie the Doctor is relinquishing: a pretty lover, who earnestly believes in her man; a teacher, who is convinced of his wayward pupil's genius; and a worried male comrade, who sees honor, love, and a tested friendship being cast aside for toxic distillates and test tubes. Like the melodramatic household episodes in *Nosferatu*, *Frankenstein*'s portrayal of familiar networks in disrepair and career opportunities in decay conveys how close others are inexorably pulled into painful chaos. Unlike *Nosferatu*, which only directly involved two people with the monster, *Frankenstein*'s actions will affect not only loved ones and friends but the entire community as well.

The rosy depictions of the conventional good life create an unfair opposition to Frankenstein's outrageous plans. The healthy well-rounded life, composed of abiding love, rewarding work, and hearty friendship in equal measure, is, on the face of it, a more pleasant use of time than are long days and nights spent toiling away in deserted graveyards and a desolate laboratory. The team of companions and townspeople who intervene when the Monster escapes the laboratory are also immeasurably more agreeable associates than the mentally and physically stunted imbecile who slinks annoyingly about the test tubes and electronic gadgetry.

Until he does create a man, Frankenstein's aberrant behavior fits the evaluations his friends have offered to the audience. These comparisons are ultimately rendered illegitimate because they precede Frankenstein's staggering success. When the Doctor raises the odds and ends of basted graveyard pickings to the boiling storm clouds and returns with a living being, we are forced to reconsider both Frankenstein's raving and the condescending reactions of his conservative clique. As the Monster's fingers tremble with new life, the Doctor's hysterical pronouncements regarding the imminent success of far-fetched investigations into "chemical galvanism and electrobiology" are proven correct. The man may have deserved to act strangely when he was so close to revolutionizing science and becoming Prometheus's first cousin.

With the creation of a being who, for the first time, is animated by the grace of Man, we are given an additional conflict: what price victory? What is worth surrendering if the elemental mysteries of life can be understood? Should the love of a decent, if unadventurous spouse, be sacrificed for lonely, if fruitful, work outside the home? If unimaginable success means social exile, are such achievements equal to the status of leper? These questions are the humanist version of Dr. Faustus's problem. In this case, however, there are no steep bargains struck with the Devil. A man must decide if he wants the powers of creation by the sweat of his own brow. Is it worth it to make yourself God when no one will recognize you are a deity? Dr. Frankenstein puts it eloquently when he asks,

> Have you never wanted to do anything dangerous? Where should we be if nobody tried to find out what lies beyond? You never wanted to look beyond the clouds and stars, or to know what causes the trees to bud, or to change the darkness into light? But if you talk like that people will call you crazy. Well, if I could discover just one of these things: what eternity is, for example, I wouldn't care if they did think I'm crazy.

Eventually, the Doctor will abandon his grand work, acquiesce to the desires of friends and fiancée, and return to the fold. The person most responsible for Dr. Frankenstein's eventual compliance is his father, Baron Frankenstein. The Baron is enormously wealthy and lives surrounded by inherited opulence and loyal servants who adore being awash in the reflected glory of the Frankenstein empire. Among his varied possessions is the utter allegiance of an entire village. The town, populated by servile citizens, functions as an extension of the family's domestic staff who more directly cater to the Frankensteins' boundless wishes.

The serfs in town are content to live under their lord's boot as they never dispute his right to rule. The Baron may be a relatively benign tyrant demanding no more than happy faces at a long awaited wedding carnival, but he is a dictator nonetheless. The clear-cut hierarchy between father and town doubles the paternal hold the son has attempted to elude. The son is different from the villagers; he wants to escape his heritage in a palace revolt. His experiments might go wrong, but there is a healthy distrust in the son for the wishes of the father.

To the Baron, the son's scientific fervor has blinded him to more important duties. Incredibly, Dr. Frankenstein seems not to care that he was to the manor born. This lapse in assuming one's responsibilities to the family is Frankenstein's real madness. The family enterprise is in need of another scion. Like a determined foreman who will not stand for a slowdown in output during his shift, the Baron wants a grandson manufactured in his lifetime: Babies need to be made and they need to be issued forthwith.

The Baron would make a good transcendentalist critic as he is certain that his son's cavalier dismissal of the good life and good wife stems from sexual intrigue. According to the Baron, another woman has his son in thrall and now, under the spell of another, he no longer desires the lovely Elizabeth. The elite mind cannot encompass the idea that normal passion can be redirected by an overwhelming interest in something other than procreation. If the Baron lived with a rudimentary knowledge of Freud, then he might deem his son's unworthy evasion of responsibility a clear case of sublimation. The son, so the Baron might surmise, is afraid of adult sexuality and cannot bear the thought of using his penis to extend the family line. He escapes through endless tinkering in the laboratory; even worse, all his work seems to take place mostly at night when most other men the Doctor's age couple with their wives and create real flesh. The Baron's diagnosis would be supported by Twitchell (1985), who writes in *Dreadful Pleasures* that, for Dr. Frankenstein, "the sexual, or rather asexual, nature of his character has been changeless. He is a neuter, sublimating his erotic energies into the mechanical creation of life" (p. 180).

There are a couple of caveats to be taken with this analysis. First, the Doctor has clearly already won the deep love and admiration of his fiancée. No one, but especially not a flaccid anhedonic neuter, could engender the intensity of feeling that Elizabeth has for Frankenstein. How could his beloved come to love him so, if the Doctor were always and forever working off blocked sexual tensions in a cloistered laboratory? Sometime before his experiments began to achieve promising results, the Doctor had successfully courted Elizabeth. Geldings, with or without advanced degrees, do not go on dates, and should they somehow venture into public with the object of their affection, it is highly unlikely that they will have the good fortune to win their lover's hand in marriage. Is it really likely that Elizabeth would respond so strongly to a man with zero interest in consummating a relationship with her? The film may have a Victorian cast, but we need to remember that the absence of public displays of heated affection does not mean that nothing is expressed in private as well.

Second, if the possibility of creating new life would not keep a researcher in his lab for long hours, nothing else would. This is, after all, a question of solving the great puzzle of the universe. The Doctor is authoring his own book of Genesis. Just because a fatigued God rested on the seventh day does not mean man must follow suit. Married life, with the additional expectations that the Doctor will take over the Frankenstein holdings, would be an invasive waste of precious time. And all visionary intellectuals know that " 'the intolerable burden of thought' is a burden when the conditions make it burdensome. . . . Every man whose business it is to think knows that he must for part of the day create about himself a pool of silence" (Lippman, 1946, p. 54). Some epochal discoveries are worthy of single-minded pursuit; becoming a world-renowned scientist, even if one's social life deteriorates badly, could merit the misery of putting all else aside.

Escaping, for the moment, the wishes of father, friends, and family, Frankenstein perseveres and finishes his creation. Our first introduction to the Monster is a revelation.[12] The Creature shuffles backward into the laboratory as the camera slowly zooms in on the back of his head. The supposedly ferocious beast, who looks like a set of large rectangular blocks packaged in human form, walks like a drugged toddler. He moves with hesitant plodding steps and seems always on the brink of tumbling over. His gait and bulky form evoke not fear but some odd mixture of pity and a desire to shield the poor stumbling lug from harm.

These movements communicate unsettling ideas about what the thing really is. He does not move like a killer. Death incarnate is usually depicted as swift, agile, and unmercifully cunning. The ponderous thing before us has none of these deadly attributes. Seeing Frankenstein's creature is like greeting a good friend's severely traumatized infant for the first time and comprehending the life of unending despair to which it is almost certainly doomed. The Monster's initial steps in the world are so terribly vulnerable. He appears as a forlorn bastard foundling who needs tender care, a dedicated physical therapist, and hours of patient instruction.

Finally, he turns, slowly and awkwardly, and we are confronted with a face that is ugly but not evil. The big head appears impossibly delicate. The close-up softens the crude brow and extravagant cheekbones as it blurs the crisp right angles of the Creature's fractured scalp. The eyes are moist as if the beast has been weeping. They are not angry slits or clouded holes bespeaking dangerous fury. The shot approximates a formal portrait of a depressed and moony-eyed cow. He does have a cumbersome head, but there is something gentle and innocent behind those awkward ridges and plaintive eyes.

Frankenstein urges the beast to sit. The Monster is confused and leery. He must be told to rest several times before he settles himself into a wooden chair that, ironically, resembles a throne. His inability to easily follow the Doctor's commands is not a manifestation of combative will. He is a scared and dyslexic newborn who desperately wants to perform well but is not quite sure if the actions he is taking are what he is supposed to do. The Monster is not being intransigent. He does not know what to do because the neurons are rusty and send out confusing directions; eventually, he understands what he is told and does it.

As a reward for correctly obeying his orders, Frankenstein chooses to let the Monster bathe in sunshine. The Doctor opens a skylight and showers the beast in brilliant light. The Monster's attitude is one of awestruck reverence. He tilts his head back, casts his eyes to the sky, raises his hands, palms up as if in prayer, and lets the beams play about him. No creature of the shadows would so relish the act of sunbathing. He takes a deep and simple joy in being in the light. When the Doctor closes the skylight the Monster reaches imploringly for more. The camera cuts to the roughly sutured hands that beg to remain illuminated. This shot echoes the earlier close-up of the Monster's damp eyes. Clearly, the Creature has a good soul. He may be misshapen, a terrible mistake, but he responds to the light like a anemic flower left for too long in the cold shade. What are we to make of a monster who esteems open air and sparkling sunbeams, who seems deeply content when left unmolested in the cool, healing light?

Immediately after his meditation, the accommodating Monster is exposed to another sort of light, one that casts a poor reflection on the Doctor and his aide. The hunchback has burst into the lab fearing the Monster has escaped. His hysterical cry announcing the loss of the Monster is motivated by more than concern over the beast's possible absence. His tormented screams are animated by hate for the Monster. He spots the Creature and assaults him with a blazing torch. The Monster goes wild with fear. He lashes out blindly and must be pummeled unconscious.

This terrible scene presages the Monster's eventual fate. As long as the Creature is not needlessly provoked he is a calm giant. How else is a 7-foot-tall babe with the undomesticated strength of several men supposed to react when he is menaced with fire? Tellingly, it is an imbecile who first besets the Creature. Idiots attack unthinkingly, destroying what they cannot understand. If the hunchback had taken the time to study the beast as we have, then he would see that the Creature represents no immediate danger when handled with reasonable care.

After he is subdued and chained, the Monster is again assailed by the Doctor's miserable helper. The little monster whips the shackled beast with malevolent glee. There is a definite element of sadism in the extended punishment allotted the imprisoned Creature. There are no positive disciplinary returns from whipping a chained being:

> "If you whip, you are cruel." . . . The pain of the whip is that which is
> applied to slaves, prisoners, and inferiors. For the one that orders it, or the
> one that carries it out, it is a sign of absolute, essential power; and for the
> victim, the harrowing proof of his actual inferiority, and his eventual
> submission. (de Coulteray, 1965, p. 104)

De Coulteray, a strange film critic who attempted to catalogue all the scenes of particularly gratifying sadism in the movies, knows whereof he speaks. The Monster is being gratuitously punished for the sheer joy afforded by flaying a weak creature. Unfortunately, the Doctor knows all about these brutal episodes and lets them continue unabated. In *Frankenstein,* punishment flows downhill. Eventually, the weakest, or the least protected, receives the brunt of all the unfair blows rained down through the food chain. Only the Monster is lower than the hunchback; consequently, like the dog in the tired witticism, he gets kicked last.

Why does the Doctor allow the beatings to go on? Why is his most cherished experiment allowed to be ruthlessly tormented? The Doctor treats the beast humanely, so why does he silently endorse sadism on the hunchback's behalf? The answer can only lie in Frankenstein's unconscious regard for the hierarchical caste system that orders social position. He may rebel against his place in the system, but he still harbors deep respect for the structure as a whole. Like many a megalomaniac, Frankenstein must feel his special abilities leave him free to ignore the rules that legitimately constrain everyone else: Some are meant to obey, and a few elect others are destined to lead. Even his own creation is not entitled to any special privileges; it too must accept its inferior lot and attendant dearth of natural rights.

The hunchback's disciplinary regimen is left undisturbed because even the most pathetic natural-born human specimen is innately superior to the handcrafted version of the human. A superior's role, of necessity, must be made clear. Superiority means nothing when not continually on parade. If it takes physical abuse to demonstrate power, then such abuse is mandated. Restraint has no place in the celebration of hierarchical prerogative.

Frankenstein is exempt from directly carrying out corporal punishment. His lackey will eagerly do it for him. The Doctor does not have to sully his surgeon's hands with the whip, a crude cutting instrument, when he has servants to indoctrinate the Creature in common wisdom. Frankenstein will go only so far with his favored minions. He will grave rob alongside them, hunting select portions of the anatomy like a warped truffle fancier, but he will not whip the Creature himself. He realizes that to spare the rod is to spoil the lower classes, but such distastefully menial work can be hired out.

The townspeople will also share in the aide's enthusiasm for inflicting pain on the Monster. When they learn the beast is loose and has killed, albeit accidentally, a little peasant girl, the mob is demonstrably bloodthirsty. The judicial imperatives inherited from the Old Testament are fairly benign compared to what the townspeople desire in retribution for the girl's demise. They do not want to simply capture or kill the reputed predator. They want him drawn and quartered. They want to hear him writhe in pain as his bones crack and splinter.

Sadistic impulses, dedicated to crushing those who are damnably different, run through the entire society. The laboratory should have offered an enlightened example for the unwashed below; alas, science can create a new man but not a new world for man to live in. The surface antisepsis of Dr. Frankenstein's laboratory only serves to cloak, like the scrubbed halls of the medical school, the same dirty drives that lie unmasked in the filthiest peasant hovel. Polite obeisance is paid to those above one in social stature, but for those unlucky many scrambling lower down the ladder, only a stiletto heel is offered.

The practice of raising welts on another's hide in *Frankenstein* does not lead to orgasm, as these spiteful impulses carry little, if any, erotic charge. Beating another merely serves to release the tension that arises when living underfoot. If one happens to reside more comfortably within the social register, then sadistic practices are the most expedient method to maintain one's exalted space. In the end, both peasants and elites want the Creature in pain, finding equal, if structurally different, levels of pleasure in treating the wretched monstrosity badly.[13]

That the Monster is obviously being tortured raises some interesting questions. Defining any action as torturous implies that some moral commandment has been trespassed. When the Monster is felt to be unnecessarily harmed, we are condemning the moral code by which all the so-called protagonists live. The act of inflicting gratuitous pain carries with it the abominable distinction of moral vacuity—a lack of consideration so low that whoever is responsible for such actions resides outside our system of moral reference. The Creature's enemies, given their treatment of him, are reprobates. In denouncing the savage humans of *Frankenstein,* we again find ourselves in a different relation with the Monster. Would we treat him like an ominous Thalidomide baby and, an even more difficult question, would we punish those who trespass against the beast?[14]

In reply to the torture, the Monster kills the hunchback. Thus the first death for which the beast is responsible occurs in self-defense. Traditionally, self-defense has been understood as the permissible use of deadly force when all other avenues of escape from perilous insult have been foreclosed. Threat may be justification enough to use self-defense, but the possibility of imminent extinction assures its acceptability as a defense of one's own violent actions. The notion also carries with it the premise that whatever is being self-preserved is worth preserving. Anything that acts in self-defense must have, if only to the selfsame being, a valuable self.

Discovering that the vicious hunchback has been exterminated, Frankenstein and his onetime mentor agree that the Monster must be put to sleep for his crime. The act is to be performed by the good Doctor's former professor as Frankenstein no longer has the heart to continue his research. He quits the laboratory and seeks a coward's comfort in the welcoming arms of his relieved family. Tellingly, before he abandons his creation to the good hands of his former mentor, Frankenstein calls their decision "murder."

The Creature is not to be killed outright—he must first be dissected. This fraudulent scientific exercise helps Frankenstein's teacher assuage his conscience. Murder is the act of a cold-blooded criminal, but dissection is a scientific procedure performed by admirable professionals. While preparing to eviscerate the Creature the attending physician notes that the difficult patient has required stronger and stronger doses of sedatives to keep him unconscious. The doctor then jots down "dissection at once"—underlined with a flourish—and the Creature's eyelids roll back. Once again, an eminent practitioner of the medical arts makes a stupid miscalculation. Sedating a normal patient or ordinary murder victim is a fairly mundane task. The doctor errs in assuming that the larger dosages of sedatives injected into the new Creature are sufficient to keep him under. Since this is a medical miracle, caution might be advisable when drawing up a workable intravenous barbituate schedule.

No matter whom the Monster comes into contact with, doctor or idiot, everyone wants him dead. The relation between the professor and beast is the same association maintained by the hunchback in his interactions with the Creature. The major difference between foes lies in the relative refinement with which they would dispatch the beast. Undoubtedly, had the silver-haired sage succeeded in killing the Creature, he would have sewn the twice-dead corpse closed with small, tidy sutures, leaving behind a razor-thin scar as testament to his wonderful training. The surgeon's sharp blade would have provided an altogether cleaner death than the bloody end desired by the furious hunchback. The little killer would have covered the rough plait of his stinging whip with bruised tissue before the beast expired.

The Monster liberates himself by strangling the physician poised to slit his torso wide. Again, Frankenstein's invention kills intentionally for only one reason: self-preservation. The shot sequence during the second attack makes this abundantly clear when the film cuts from the word "dissection" in the research record to a shot of the Creature stirring to consciousness. The segue dramatically implies an awareness of impending danger. Strapped to the operating table, with belly naked, barely awake, he is aware as the doctor wheels a frightening array of surgical instruments to the Creature's exposed side. Before the surgeon can neatly gut him, the Creature kills another of his many oppressors.

The Monster has done nothing for which unimpaired humans would be found culpable. He has merely defended himself against an active sadist and a scalpel-wielding assassin. The killings are identical except for the fact that one of the deceased criminals held an advanced degree and was well respected by the community. This minor distinction fails to mitigate the more learned corpse's responsibility for his own demise. The two deaths, wherein both the highest and the lowest of society are destroyed, serve to bracket the entire community and show how moral turpitude runs through all classes in *Frankenstein*.

The death of the malpracticing surgeon leaves the Creature free to roam the countryside and experience, for the first and only time, the exhilarating feel of fresh air on his cross-stitched skin. Knowing how the Creature reacted when he was last washed by sunlight, he must find his brief lark delicious. Unhappily, the Creature's exodus also means the entire population is free to attack him.

The confused beast fumbles his way out of the laboratory and is gone. He eventually finds his way to a beautiful alpine lake and there, by the sun-dappled water, the Creature makes the acquaintance of a charming little girl. This is the last time we will see the Monster in a lovely natural setting. The Creature later reappears in Dr. Frankenstein's cluttered mansion and on a midnight moonscape, where, hunted by a raging mob, he is treed in the laboratory and burned alive.

The episode with the peasant girl offers further reassurance that the Creature is good as he responds in the appropriate fashion to an offer of friendship from the young child. Even the moment when he adores the feel of sunlight playing across his cracked brow is less powerful than the time he spends returning the good wishes of a loving human. His reaction to the light could have been nothing more than a phototropic response denoting bodily comfort in the presence of a pleasant stimulus, as even deadly rattlesnakes seem to enjoy lazing on sun-baked rocks. It takes the interlude with the girl to make us completely accept the idea that the Monster is intrinsically good.

Initially, the little girl frightens the Monster when he chances upon her. The Monster is scared, torn between fight and flight, because he knows from experience how humans feel about him. She, with no sense of fear based on adult stereotypes, takes the Monster as a godsend.[15]

Lonely and forlorn, she has been granted an unexpected playmate. The girl offers a beckoning hand and strolls to the lakeside, Monster at her side, for an afternoon of joyous play. She takes no notice of the Monster's readily apparent physical abnormalities and inability to communicate beyond Neanderthal grunts and a broken smile. She shows the Monster how to make boats from wildflowers, and together they happily toss pretty toys onto the water's placid surface.

During their game, the Monster beams and enters into a short-lived epiphany. He is extraordinarily joyful with his unexpected reception. This is the only time he has ever been treated in such a kind manner, and his body language bespeaks utter happiness. That we can easily read the plain signs emanating from the Monster's body is proof enough that the beast is human. He speaks our language, without training, revealing his ability to be as fully expressive as any other pleased human being.

The satisfying interchange ends when the Monster makes a terrible mistake. He accidentally drowns his new friend when he treats her like the beautiful flowers they have been tossing on the water. Like many other young learners, he does not know how to construct error-free extended syllogisms. Reasoning from sign, the Creature constructs the following conclusion: Pretty things float. By analogy, he moves to his second and fatal syllogism: Girls (like flowers) are pretty things. Pretty things float; therefore, girls float. Of course, the minor term is undistributed and the Creature inadvertently assumes all pretty things do not sink in the water. The Creature, with limited experience in the wide world, moves too hastily to the dire conclusion that all girls, like all flowers and other pretty things, will ride the calm skin of the water. He follows his deductive line to its logical end and drops the girl in the lake to join the flowery armada.

The Creature was not acting with evil intent. He errs in logic but not in feeling. His actions are the natural consequence of trying to figure out how he should play with the girl. He meant to treat her as delicately as she treated the lovely mountain wildflowers. She perishes, and the Creature is doomed for the crimes of being both a monstrosity and a child murderer.

What is important in this scene is the variety of judgments and behaviors the Creature is capable of performing. First, he can befriend others and engage in gentle play. He reciprocates compassionate gestures when given the slightest opportunity. In so doing, he shows definite evidence of recognizing alterity and having mastered complicated cognitive processes. These higher-level mental machinations enable him to comprehend the selfhood of other beings and the complex mixture of emotions and motives that drive the behaviors of those he encounters. He is not some slapped-together juggernaut who mindlessly demolishes all things, human or otherwise, with the bad luck to lie in his path. That sort of monster arrives later, when unnaturally high levels of radiation or some other equally perfidious invention escape from government research centers, transforming the most benign things of the world into giant killers.

Second, the beast can make aesthetic choices. Monsters of the Creature's type are not known for their judicious eye in matters of beauty. I am, of course, not referring to any of the oft-told versions of beauty and the wolf, which always involve a hairy, fanged misanthrope searching out the loveliest, most succulent virgin in the community for a delectable feast. The stories of beautiful and vulnerable innocents beset in the gloomy forest by lascivious predators are patently designed to warn prepubescent girls away from unloosed male sexual energy. Frankenstein's creation is not some thinly disguised portrait of an illicit erection. He has an eye for beauty, but that eye is not dependent on dangerous levels of testosterone for visual acuity. The beast in *Frankenstein* is not monstrous because of wanton erotic desire.

The Creature can appreciate the flowers swaying along the shore just as any weekend naturalist spending his precious free time in the country would. He can also see, in an entirely nonsexual sense, that little girls are attractive as well. The recognition of beauty is not an apperception made by lower animals. Only the most developed animals are capable of seeing what the Monster sees and calling it good.

Finally, even though his judgment is flawed, the Creature can construct elaborate chains of reasoned association based on natural observation. He can imagine the future, with some degree of accuracy, based on past experience. He is a thinker; perhaps he does not think as ably as we would like, but there is no denying that his cognitive abilities are the same as ours.

Following the death of his one and only friend, the Creature reappears in the House of Frankenstein. The mansion is awash in expensive tchotchkes, wedding decorations, and tipsy revelers. Here, scuttering peasants, servile help, and good citizens are happy to share in the sundry wines and foodstuffs the Baron has had prepared for the enthralled town. The wedding festivities not only serve to unite the errant Doctor and his beloved, they also renew the townspeople's debt as indentured servants.

It is a corrupt carnival; the participants are unleashed to dance and drink and play—as long as they understand that tomorrow they must be back on the job tending to the Baron's desires.[16]

In the midst of the gala, the Monster searches for his duplicitous maker. He fails to locate his chief nemesis, although he does manage to frighten the lovely Elizabeth into a dead faint. Even with the perfect opportunity to mightily distress his opponent, the Monster does not harm the fearful bride. He only wants the guilty Doctor. Once more, no harm comes to those who have not directly abused the creation.

The mansion reeks of privilege and the Creature's horrible visage clashes severely with all that is terribly dear in the household. The juxtaposition between the Monster and personal effects of the Franken-steins' is a surrealist exercise. Everything becomes something else when paired with the Monster. At this moment of transgression, things that are normally totally inimical to one another are brought into unnatural proximity and, in a strange couplet, produce something original and heretofore unspoken.

What do we see when the fine house becomes a monster's latest haunt? What connotations does a monster have when shot against baroque umbrella stands, silver crystal, and massive morris chairs? What are these objects that should never be seen in tandem? When they conjoin we finally see the complete scope of Frankenstein's desire. It takes a most grotesque and avaricious imagination to encompass the fusion taking place in the Frankenstein mansion. With his base desires satisfied by the peasants' labor, Frankenstein has turned to science to create new things to own. The man wants all things alive and dead arrayed about him.

Unlike *Nosferatu,* where the vampire is always a complete outsider, the Monster in *Frankenstein* has some claim on the household adorn-ments and the house itself. In comparison, Dracula was an unwanted guest, an invasive plague guilty of trespass. When Dracula comes for Ellen's pure blood the moral balance between the two is not altered. Ellen is eternally good and Dracula irredeemably evil, no matter where the two meet. Dracula, the murderous burglar, only desires to have what is not legitimately his; he enters quietly and, if successful, spirits away his loot before being discovered. The thief who does not belong cannot lessen the value of the things in the home. In fact, the opposite is true: He emphasizes the value of the bourgeois cache.

The Monster's case is very different. When he is loose in the Franken-stein home we must reappraise the value of the stuffed domicile and its wealthy owner just as we must reconsider the Creature's worth. In entering Frankenstein's manor and fomenting a slave's revolt, he demonstrates his own utility. When the Creature comes, his entrance proves that the only thing in the house of any intrinsic merit is himself.

The corrupt system that spawned the Creature, finding the idea of him intriguing, sends him packing simply because he does not fit preconceived notions of the good and beautiful. This system is based on a grotesquely greedy aesthetic that violently rejects any object that thinks first of its own utility. The beast is just not a fit possession. Nothing demonstrates the Monster's unsuitability for ownership as clearly as his abject contrast with the rest of the Frankensteins' property. He is an unfortunate acquisition, a stupid purchase, which must be removed posthaste from the premises.

The Doctor's experience as a Frankenstein has not well prepared him for an object that does not cater to his every whim. The Monster declines to reside in the space for which he was created. Frankenstein has literally sown/sewn his own destruction by fusing pieces of rebellious property that fight being forced to serve an illegitimate patriarchy. The Monster is, however gross in form, a human being with a intractable will of his own. He will not be treated like a disposable bauble that, alas, clashes with the rest of the estate.

The monstrous is nearly always identified as that which disturbs normality. Implicit in this observation is the idea that what is accepted as standard operating procedure is good. As Robin Wood (1984) has noted when making a similar observation, "One must firmly resist the common tendency to treat the word [normality] as if it were more or less synonymous with 'health' " (p. 175). Is the system that allowed the Frankensteins to put together an awesome collection of household goods, and the servile staff to maintain it, worth preserving?

No one in the film, with the exception of the Monster, would think the Frankenstein empire should fall. Although a muted undercurrent of resentment toward the family runs through the film, no one disputes their right to rule; it is only the Monster who wants to destroy Frankenstein and cripple the House.[17] What is a monster who, however inchoately, acts as an insurgent Marxist? Admittedly, his political struggle is as rough-hewn as his body, but he is committed to overthrowing if not the government at least his wealthy governor. When the repressed returns, it is not in the form of sublimated sexual outrage; it reappears as the most hideous prole imaginable.

From the well-appointed mansion it is only a short hike to the barren lunar region where the Creature is hunted down and killed. It is not coincidental that his last stand takes place in this harsh area. The ground is dry and broken, a plane of rough scarp and multifaceted rock, denuded of almost all vegetation. The landscape, in its extreme brutality, is identical to the Monster's own physiognomy. Had the Creature lived and escaped his enraged pursuers, this ravaged land, a rough aerie fit only for superhuman exiles, would be his home.

The Monster is flushed from the glorious mansion, where "normal" humans dwell, and forced back onto the rocks where the laboratory is located. During the hunt, one of the mob is wounded by the hapless Creature. Once again, the Monster kills no one. He only wings a solitary pursuer in self-defense, avoids the mad crowd, and patiently waits for an opportunity to honor his final appointment with the Doctor. He brings no lasting harm to the innocent. Even when he is pursued by bloodhounds and fanatical agrarians, all of whom are dying to sink tooth and blade into the beast, eager to have their pound of reanimated flesh, he commits no vengeful acts.

Eventually, the two meet and Frankenstein is toted, over the Monster's burly shoulder, back to the laboratory. It is fitting that this time the Doctor is a reluctant captive, taken against his wishes, and returned to the scene of his epochal triumph. The owner/scientist has been found wanting by his principal subject. The Creature, reaching the acme of self-realization, acquires the Doctor's body and intends to use it as he pleases. The beast will perish—but only after carrying out his own desires and sending the Doctor to the black soil from which the Creature was unwillingly sprung. They fight, and the Doctor is defenestrated, landing unpleasantly on a windmill blade as he plummets to the earth. The laboratory is set ablaze and the Monster immolated.

The film was to have ended here—with Doctor and patient dead. However, the producers felt that Frankenstein's death sentence was too negative, that audiences would not fully appreciate the double end of Doctor and Creature. In a subsequent cut, *Frankenstein* was released with a revised ending that allowed the Doctor to live long and prosper. He married and had his necessary heirs, although the Doctor is never seen or even heard after being pitched out the window. He is only referred to, in effusive terms, by the ebullient Baron who, at long last, now has his privileged progeny to carry on the family name.

The extension of the Doctor's life in the contrived denouement leaves *Frankenstein* with an inappropriate finale, an end that is not helped by the on-screen absence of the supposed hero.[18] It feels as if the producers were embarrassed at letting the wayward physician continue to exist. We are supposed to rejoice in the cessation of Frankenstein's woes and the birth of new family members, but there is little vicarious pleasure in the restoration of equilibrium. The film fraudulently guarantees a solid footing for the Frankenstein family when the filmmakers have previously shown the institution to be bankrupt.

Frankenstein concludes with the audience and cast split over the meaning of the monstrous. We despise the craven Doctor and pity the innocent Monster. The status of pariah has been shifted to the most celebrated in the community; it is now the hunted outcast who is worthy of our tender concern. The townspeople would find these sentiments obscene, but they are pawns and cannot possibly think such thoughts. It would be blasphemy for any vassal to suggest their lords were of the Devil. We are a bit freer and capable of deviating from previously established norms. Anyone who has seen *Frankenstein* can never again automatically assume that the monster is everything we are not. Some monsters may be wholly dangerous or evil incarnate, but after *Frankenstein* we must reserve judgment and once again pose the question of whether or not the worlds visited by beasts deserve to exist unchanged.

Notes

1. Many of the most horrible assaults one can suffer continue to occur within the province of domestic life. According to Costello and Thurber (1993), women are more likely to be killed, raped, or injured by their male partner than by an unknown assailant. In fact, each year the number of women attacked by their partners exceeds the number of women injured by automobiles.

Although contemporary horror films do not place the same value on the domestic scene as silent horror did, new films do recognize that the worst killers are many times those we believe we know best. See, for example, any of *The Stepfather* films (1987, 1989, 1991).

2. The production of a new kind of monster was made possible by technological improvements in moviemaking machinery, in particular the introduction of sound, implementation of new acting techniques, and the refinement of the studio production system.

First, many of the early horror films were either expressionist or strongly influenced by expressionism. Actors in expressionist films played their roles using a form of acting technique called pantomime. Pantomime involves adopting a set of broad stereotypical gestures to communicate meaning to the audience (Naremore, 1988, p. 61). When actors brought a monster to life or portrayed an unhappy heroine they employed "conventionalized poses . . . [to] indicate 'fear,' 'sorrow,' 'hope,' 'confusion,' and so forth" (Naremore, 1988, p. 51). With the introduction of sound and the move away from expressionist styles of filmmaking, this form of acting was replaced by a more "natural" and less obviously formulaic acting style.

When actors are liberated from reproducing rigidly conventional signs, signs meant to exactly indicate the particular emotion the actor is experiencing, they are freed to produce more complex emotional states. In this way, heroes and heroines cease to be as patently good and monsters cease to be as entirely bad when pantomime is no longer employed. This dual liberation from a style of storytelling (expressionism) and character presentation (pantomime) led to radical changes in the way horrific stories were told.

In addition, we also need to consider how the major studios produced motion pictures in the 1930s and 1940s. The most efficient way to run a profitable studio was, and still is, to hit upon a remunerative formula and repeat it until the fans stop buying tickets. According to Gifford (1983),

> Only when Universal found their mid-budget picture building into their biggest money maker of 1931 did they declare their intention of making "*another* horror film." . . . It was Hollywood law that every success must have its successor: the standard contact was a two picture deal. For Lugosi's follow up Laemmle [Universal studio head Carl Laemmle] found *Frankenstein*. (pp. 82-83)

With the huge success of *Dracula*, Universal now had a template for producing profitable horrible tales.

3. This is not to say that the other Hollywood studios produced no decent horror films. Some critics have argued that many of the films listed below are, on an individual basis, better than most of the Universal films. Still, while other studios may have made better films, only Universal can lay claim to defining the genre after the introduction of sound. Among the films produced by other studios, RKO brought *King Kong* (1933) to the screen and released Val Lewton's subtle productions, which included *I Walked With a Zombie* (1943), the original *Cat People* (1942), the sequel *The Curse of the Cat People* (1944) and *Isle of the Dead* (1945); Metro-Goldwyn-Mayer released Tod Browning's *Freaks* (1932) and *Mark of the Vampire* (1935); Paramount produced *Island of Lost Souls* (1932) and remade *Dr. Jekyll and Mr. Hyde* (1931). The independent studios released a slew of low-budget horror films, although only *White Zombie* (1933) is today remembered by anyone other than hard-core film buffs. See Turner and Price (1986) for more on the mostly forgotten work of the independent studios.

4. See any copy of *Famous Monsters of Filmland*, the precursor to today's *Filmfax*, to get a sense of just how adored the Universal monsters were by fans of these old films. When the Universal films were broadcast for the first time on television in 1957, a new crop of young fans was introduced to the double pleasure of rooting for and against its favorite fiends. *FMF*, targeted at these doting fans, debuted in 1958 one year after Universal horror came to television (Daniels, 1975, p. 202).

5. Universal monsters are closer in feeling to the Cookie Monster on "Sesame Street" than they are to the hordes of slashers in contemporary horror films. It would seem the creators of children's television programming realize this as a fanged puppet called the Count (Dracula's title) teaches tots simple mathematical operations on "Sesame Street."

The Universal Monster also teaches adults useful lessons. In print advertisements, underwritten by the Miller Brewing Company, a portrait of Frankenstein's Creature is accompanied by copy that admonishes irresponsible drinkers, "Don't be a monster. Don't drink and drive."

6. We rarely experience this sort of affection for cinematic monsters today. One of the few places where we do meet monsters we can love is in the novels of Anne Rice. In particular, her series of vampire sagas has garnered a large audience that is clearly enamored of her bloodsuckers.

Witness the PR fiasco that accompanied the announcement that Tom Cruise would play Rice's most beloved vampire, Lestat, in the movie version of *Interview With a Vampire*. Fans of the book, including the author, were altogether dismayed that a simple "all-American boy" would be allowed to play the very complicated character of Lestat. Given Cruise's previous performances, most Rice fans felt he lacked the depth of character to make an audience fall in love with a killer.

7. The vast difference between Universal monsters and more current monsters is successfully explored in *Nightbreed* (1990). In this film, honorable creatures of the night, who elicit a response from the audience close to that evinced by Universal monsters, do battle with a psychopathic psychiatrist who frames innocent mental patients for his terrible deeds. Now, as *Nightbreed* demonstrates, Universal monsters, or their close contemporary kin, are more human than our multimurderers.

8. The most famous line from Jean Renoir's *The Rules of the Game* (1939), "The terrible thing about this world is that everybody has his reasons," could also have been used as an epigram for any monster tale from Universal. Even monsters had their many reasons.

9. King Kong, the other famous beast of the era, while not a Universal creation, shared the same mix of good and bad attributes common to the other Creatures in the Universal menagerie, although, in a reverse of the Universal formula, we were all, at one time, him.

The great ape was given a substantial range of anthropomorphic traits that covered the psychological spectrum. He was alternately a feral antagonist and a guardian angel. In being both dangerous and loving, King Kong could be neither wholeheartedly detested nor completely adored.

Kong should never have been disturbed by the star-making machinery thirsty for a truly profitable sideshow attraction. He was God on his island, revered by natives who venerated his miraculous strength and awesome physique. In an act of incredible profanity, he is drugged, shackled, and toted off to New York for the lead role in a Radio City dog-and-pony show.

The ruin that Kong brought to New York was a direct consequence of inexperienced handlers imprisoning a 50-foot-high gorilla in poorly designed constraints. The exploiters, who desired a profitable P.T. Barnum spectacle for all of America, misjudged the mighty Kong's power. He could not be held culpable for lashing out against his irresponsible captors.

Unfortunately, once loose in New York City, Kong's demise was a tragic necessity. He died a brutal death that was ultimately touching. When Kong dies, after a plunge of 1,250 feet, his magnificent chest pumped full of machine-gun bullets, we are saddened that such a great beast has come to such a terrible end.

10. The emcee is Edward Van Sloan. Sloan played the learned vampire killer Van Helsing in Universal's *Dracula*. Here he steps out of character and through the fourth wall when he becomes a barker.

11. Frankenstein's tunnel vision will become a recurring character flaw in the overachieving scientists who follow him in later horror films. At some point, nearly all theoretical madmen become painfully stupid in Universal films. In their zeal to perform experimental breakthroughs, they forget basic scientific principles and make simple errors. These dangerously absent-minded professors, who eventually always screw up, share an inability to work safely.

In 1950s science fiction and horror films, this hallmark of scientific hubris becomes even more apparent. Countless radioactive experiments go awry because of easily avoided error. Visionary lab technicians are always human—all too human. They may destroy the world, reagent in hand, with the laboratory equivalent of slipping on a banana peel.

These errors help humanize cool and collected eggheads and demonstrate that even powerful intellects fall far short of perfection. They also point to the necessity to work very conservatively with new technology as destroying the world is only a tipped beaker away. The world is a fragile thing and no matter how high our IQ scores soar, we are innately clumsy.

12. The interlude before we confront the beast's face is obviously a director's stunt; it forces us to explore less overtly important aspects of the Creature's body while wondering what he really looks like. Were audiences granted an immediate close-up of the Creature's misshapen features, before having the time to evaluate less obviously telling body parts, we might rush to judgment.

13. There is no contemporary equivalent for these scenes. Slashers are never tortured or treated inhumanely. Humans, even if they so desired, do not have the power to mistreat the monster of today. Slashers reside at the top of the food chain, and as a consequence of their splendid position, no real harm can be brought to them.

14. *It's Alive* (1974) and its multiple sequels use this question to ground their respective stories. In these films, ferocious babies pit loving parents against agents of the state who want to destroy the newborn menace. The proto-punk band The New York Dolls directed a similar, albeit more decadent, question to their fans when they sang "Do you think that you could make it with Frankenstein?" in "Frankenstein (Orig.)."

15. See Colin McNaughton's (1994) children's book, *Making Friends With Frankenstein: A Book of Monstrous Poems and Pictures* for a more complete description of the joy kids feel when in the company of a really good monster.

16. I am using the idea of carnival as Bakhtin (1965/1984) does in *Rabelais and His World*. For Bakhtin, the true carnival of the people is characterized by "the suspension of all hierarchical rank, privileges, norms, and prohibitions." In contrast, "rank was especially evident during official feasts; everyone was expected to appear in the full regalia of his calling, rank, and merits and to take the place corresponding to his position. It was a consecration of inequality" (p. 10)

17. When the little girl's corpse is discovered, her lifeless body is carried by the bereaved father to the House of Frankenstein. The body is borne to the right address; it is the Doctor who bears full responsibility for the death of the child. Unfortunately, even though the distraught father has come to the correct house, blame is shifted to the Monster. The Doctor's mighty position works to shield him this time, but for how long can the villagers bring their troubles to the overseer's residence without realizing that their rulers might be responsible for the grief they suffer?

18. Filmmakers do not usually end triumphant narratives celebrating the conquering hero without a laudatory appearance by said champion. It is likely that the actor playing Dr. Frankenstein, Colin Clive, could not return to the set for the additional footage. Whatever the reason for the Doctor's untimely absence, the ending is totally inept and out of flavor with the rest of the film.

5. THEM

Do you fear this man's invention that they call atomic power?
There is no way to escape it. Be prepared to meet the Lord.
                                        —Louvin Brothers (1989)

The Louvin Brothers, one of the great country music duos of the 1950s, might be in error as to the clear possibility of heavenly intercession when the Bomb drops, but they are absolutely correct in attaching eschatological significance to the most destructive invention of all time. The great atomic power made the utter waste of the Earth imminently plausible and, in making the planet disposable, produced a superior, less opaque, vernacular counterpart to the elliptical threats contained in the final book of the Bible.

We could now unleash an explosive terror that would go well beyond the plodding (40 days of inclement weather) or local plagues (amphibians, locusts) of the Good Book. This time, however, our world would not be threatened by an outraged Deity unwilling to further tolerate humanity's infinite capacity to err; instead, having had the perverse wisdom to aggressively pursue the systematic development of doomsday armaments, we would kill ourselves. We drew the atomic blade to our own throats and seemed ready to pull the exploding knife across.

Even more incredible, our end would be complete. Omnipotent gods, even in their most extreme moments of righteous fury, have always left scattered samples of the beasts and humanity to repopulate a cleansed globe. No vengeful deities **ever** went so far as to eradicate all their subjects, failing to make some pointed discrimination between the innocent and the sinful. We would, however, take more drastic measures and exceed the wrath of any angry god.[1] All humanity, every man, woman, and child, and the bulk of the natural world could conceivably be extinguished when the missiles left their pods.

Finally, unlike benevolent gods, we would refuse to offer those who made it through the scourge an opportunity to get it right the second time around. All calamities, except nuclear Armageddon, offer the promise of a better age when the fires have been quenched and the survivors accounted for. Once our dismal mistakes may no longer be contained by feeble half-measures designed to forestall the inevitable, critical mass is achieved and our endless trespasses reach fruition. A purifying storm, the horrible measure of our sin, will then rise and rage out of control and out of the direction of clumsy mortal hands. Should we hold together and survive the effects of moral error, then suitably chastened, we may live on in a ravaged but quiet world, free from the grasp of former idiocies. Once the present has been rocked by epic disaster the future lies open—alive with tremendous possibility.

The future is also a better place, when the memory of past transgressions passes on, to those who have made it through a dreadful catastrophe, an explicit blueprint of what men and women should never do. A world-class disaster leaves the planet with holy scars. Able to remember how these scars came to be, we should be sufficiently motivated to forever avoid repeating our greatest misdeeds. For example, the Holocaust, an "unimaginable" crime, could, if not forgotten, prevent the reoccurrence of genocide.[2] To think otherwise would mean that Auschwitz and other concentration camps are maintained solely as remunerative tourist destinations.

Although we dutifully preserve the sites of our most egregious sins, concern with mass extermination and untold suffering is not marked solely with descriptive brass plaques and locked vitrines preserving poignant mementos. While the bomb laid the foundation for the Peace Memorial Park in Hiroshima, it also led to the production of an extraordinarily large amount of cultural work that did more than serve as an altar to the dead. Grim historical monuments have fictional counterparts that are also designed to prick the conscience and offer some understanding of what happens when humans are exposed to unthinkable terror. This work, explicitly concerned with how it feels to bear varying degrees of responsibility for bringing this world to a fiery close, is available in any medium (comic book, short story, sculpture, film) and in any language, from the sophisticated to the generic, so that all audiences have the opportunity to contemplate the brute force of the great atomic power. Under atomic influence, all representational practices have been irradiated, leaving no social group without its own portfolio depicting the great mushroom in a variety of settings.

Among the most common places, in number and status, to attempt an understanding of the enormous destruction suffered by Hiroshima and Nagasaki, and to face the possibility of an even more dire future atomic apocalypse, were theaters and drive-ins across America. Following the end of World War II, enclosed and open-air theaters were inundated with atomic product.[3] Paul Michael states that "on a sheer statistical basis, the number of fantasy and horror films of the 1950's . . . has not been equaled in any country before or since" (quoted in Lucanio, 1987, p. 1).

To the chagrin of more educated critics this work was vulgar, inordinately **stupid**, and dramatically flawed. As Vivian Sobchack (1987) writes, "The Creature cycle of the fifties and the Monster films . . . are often considered embarrassments" (p. 53). Lucanio (1987) furthers Sobchack's description of critical disgust by noting, "We can censure the films for their simple-minded reduction of events and characters to hackneyed and torpid formulas" (p. 131).

The sublime terror that accompanies the epochal failure of society and individual men and women has not, especially in the case of the 1950s creature film, been represented in holy enough language. The characters in most of these efforts are flat caricatures who bathetically spout maudlin clichés, mouth scientific mumbo-jumbo, and scream hysterically for far too long in the direction of monstrously large reptiles. These gross efforts, pathetic claptrap, answer the most significant question of the 20th century with tacky special effects, papier-mâché sets, and idiotic plots. How can lumbering dinosaurs spewing atomic fire, giant carnivorous plants, and implacable mutant insects approach the fiery chaos that engulfed Japan? The force that killed too many in a hellish firestorm, the force that poisoned thousands more with pestilent radiation, the force powerful enough to etch the shadows of unknowing pedestrians into the cement is not a fit subject for cheap Hollywood productions. We needed a responsible contemporary of Bosch or Goya and not Samuel Z. Arkoff or Roger Corman to render, in the proper proportions, our deadliest spectacle.[4]

In an astute passage from "The Imagination of Disaster," Susan Sontag (1979) explicitly defines why intellectuals have such trouble with the Creature film and its assorted offshoots:

There is a sense in which all these movies are in complicity with the abhorrent. They neutralize it, as I have said. It is no more, perhaps, than the way all art draws its audience into a circle of complicity with the thing represented. But in these films we have to do with things which are (quite literally) unthinkable. Here, "thinking about the unthinkable"—not in the way of Herman Kahn, as a subject for calculation, but as a subject for fantasy—becomes, however inadvertently, itself a somewhat questionable act from a moral point of view. The films perpetuate cliches about identity, volition, power, knowledge, happiness, social consensus, guilt, responsibility which are, to say the least, not serviceable in our present extremity. (p. 504)[5]

In cataloguing the lengthy set of important concerns that radioactive monster movies fail to explore, Sontag seems to be making the argument that worthy art, responsible art, is always ready to interrogate the world across an impossibly broad spectrum of extraordinarily complicated issues. Good and moral art (despite the offhand caveat that all art draws its audience into a somewhat suspect circle of complicity with whatever it represents) addresses a truly impressive slate of concerns—"identity, volition, power, knowledge, happiness, social consensus, guilt, responsibility"—without ever thoughtlessly repeating that which has been said once too often. Laudable art refuses to represent things as they are commonly seen; it will not adopt the easy cliché, preferring instead to offer new ways of seeing. When done well, art leads us to reevaluate our unexamined and oftentimes errant perceptions of all that lies about us. Art that does not push us to re-view the world neglects its most important duty: It fails to offer the possibility of changing the world. In so doing, in not enabling us to see ourselves and the world we inhabit in a new light, déclassé art becomes, at best, nothing more than gauche entertainment.

With this argument, Sontag is constructing something of a straw man. Obviously, we must champion art that scrupulously interrogates the vexing web of specious presumptions that run through our understanding of identity, volition, power, knowledge, happiness, social consensus, guilt, responsibility, and any other important area of inquiry. Any art that can work through even a small portion of the above without ever voicing a cliché is an achievement to be celebrated; yet the belief that there exists art that exactly fulfills these desirable criteria is made far too hastily.[6] High art, if it is not hectoringly didactic, is usually never as indefatigably responsible as Sontag suggests it is, and low art, that which harbors one cliché too many, usually fails to completely abdicate the compunction to question the world it represents.

It is also important to remember that although the atomic monster movies of the 1950s were no competition for Art they were, at least for the great bulk of the public, watchable. Most certifiable art is not readily enjoyed by the public. High art of the mid- to late 20th century has, in great part, purposefully left the untutored masses behind. Art, if it is to be recognized by the experts as such, must conform to a rigorous set of expectations that is well beyond the ken of the average untrained spectator.

Clement Greenberg (1985) is correct when he writes,

> In turning his attention away from subject-matter or common experience, the poet or artist turns it in upon the medium of his own craft. The nonrepresentational or "abstract," if it is to have aesthetic validity, cannot be arbitrary and accidental, but must stem from obedience to some worthy constraint or original. This constraint, once the world of common, extraverted experience has been renounced, can only be found in the very processes or disciplines by which art and literature have already imitated the former. (p. 23)

The world, or the world available to most, is thus rejected when respectable art must self-consciously interrogate itself and not common ground.

What is left for the masses when the majority of the public finds the modern work housed in hushed museums and austere galleries threatening or, as is usually the case, simply impenetrable? According to Greenberg, we get kitsch: an art that maintains some connection with the external world.[7] This style of representation is guilty of "using for raw material the debased and academized simulacra of genuine culture" (p. 25).

In this respect, the films of the 1950s are exemplary kitsch. They invoke scientific event, the arcane sound of scientific language (while never being remotely scientific), and very broadly appropriate real historical occurrences to profitably simulate experience.[8] Kitsch is also overly optimistic and ridden with cloying sentiment. That is, however, not enough of an indictment to dismiss such artifacts as useless tripe. Art may have reined in its baroque impulses, finding all sentiment distasteful, but the audience for popular films did not. For the masses, hope and a way out from the End remained more than an emotional trifle.

Although the monster movies of the 1950s are kitsch and cannot be recuperated as a misunderstood or underappreciated artform, it is still possible to avoid dismissing these films as totally inept or even immoral trash. If we return to Sontag, who maintains a deep fondness for monster movies despite the fact that everything she knows about art criticism tells her to condemn these works, we can find a way out of the confining definitions of the beautiful or praiseworthy offered by elite aesthetitions.

Without patronizing the audience, Sontag (1979) refuses to underestimate the fear these films addressed. They bear repeated viewing and will reward our attention because they so effectively capture the anxious tenor of the time. They show just how difficult it is for people to endure this

> age of extremity. For we live under continual threat of two equally fearful, but seemingly opposed, destinies: unremitting banality and inconceivable terror. It is fantasy, served out in large rations by the popular arts, which allows people to cope with these twin specters. For one job that fantasy can do is to lift us out of the unbearably humdrum and to distract us from terrors—real or anticipated—by an escape into exotic, dangerous situations which have last-minute happy endings. But another of the things that fantasy can do is to normalize what is psychologically unbearable, thereby inuring us to it. In one case, fantasy beautifies the world. In the other, it neutralizes it. (pp. 503-504)

When compulsive atomic concern became common sense it is difficult to consider obsessive worry as anything other than a sign of clear thinking. Existence got a little more difficult when, at any moment, everything could, without notice, be reduced to smoking ash. Each day could be a last day as the threat of nuclear annihilation added a dash of anxiety to even the most boring moments in life. Suspended in time, perilously balanced between banality and terror, fans made hits of films that slavishly catered to, if not global ill health, at least mass neurosis.

These, then, are films for panicky neurotics verging on paranoia; the product comes with no hidden transcendental message, as the audience demanded pictures that responded to the terrible things of this world. We knew who was ultimately responsible (us), but we did not know when the sucker punch would be thrown. What would go first, New York, Tokyo, Moscow, and what would annihilation on an unprecedented scale look like? Films like *Them!* (1954) and *The Cosmic Monsters* (1958) told us how it might look, giving us something tangible to build our nightmare around when dreaming of the End.

Even as she allows that monster movies of the postwar era have merit as markers of a culture's deep and widespread distress, Sontag still finds some significant problems relating to the reception that audiences accord imagery of the great atomic power. These problems fall along two lines. First, by allowing access into areas of which we had been thankfully unaware or forbidden to explore, we learn to navigate once unknown or formerly taboo arenas with too great a degree of comfort. The worst images may be loosed and we stand untouched and unbowed. In looking upon a never-ending series of end-of-the-world films, it no longer seems altogether obscene to reside in a world that may, at any time, be reduced to a noxious plane fit only for radiation-resistant vermin and mewling mutants. We lose the ability to be shocked and may encourage our own destruction by growing too close to puerile representations of scourge. Sontag does not use the word, but this process is usually called desensitization.

At the other extreme, we find a dangerously misleading succor in confronting what we should never have been damned to see. Thanks to "last-minute happy endings," audiences end up believing they can see their way through anything and everything. Whatever the danger, we can produce an image of it and end up believing no harm shall come because, at least in picture form, we have met the enemy and lived. Fears may be warily penned and gazed upon like dangerous and exotic serpents housed behind thick panes of unbreakable plate glass. In facing down potent imagery we believe, altogether mistakenly, that we will triumph when and if the real catastrophe occurs. The fantastic element of the 1950s monster movie is, then, not the beast but the idea that we can continue on after the atom has shattered.

The difference between these two perspectives is that we learn, or, more appropriately, think we learn, how to defeat the menace instead of just taking a voyeur's pleasure in gazing upon grim images that at one time would have left us profoundly shaken. Whether we consider these films objects of sick contemplation or an attempt of the imagination to encompass the end of it all, Sontag is right to underline the tremendous anxiety these films addressed. There were hundreds produced as Hollywood and large audiences conspired to create a mutual dependency that needed huge numbers of films as a fix. Individually these films lacked depth, but as a corpus there was extraordinary breadth. Only when we consider these films as one enormous text can we begin to see them as an important register of the vast reservoir of fear and amazement allotted to Americans lucky enough to live in the Atomic Age.

It is as if Darwin and Oppenheimer were fused and, as one, commandeered every major and independent studio in Hollywood to create bizarre exercises in evolution run amok. There was virtually nothing that went unaffected by radiation, although it took until the 1970s for a film to star giant rabbits drastically enlarged by exceptionally potent hormones.[9] A short list, a very short list, would include as representatives of the nuclear imagination alligator people, human flies, colossal man, transport man, she-woman, atomic kid, atomic man, atomic mutant, crab monster, 50-foot woman, giant leeches, puppet people, a beast from 20,000 fathoms, a beast with a million eyes, a blob, cosmic mutants, giant mantis, amphibian monsters, tree monsters, pod people, campus monster, mutant children, mutant parents, giant Gila monster, giant plants, man-eating brains, four-dimensional man, gamma people, giant squid, Godzilla, shrinking man, giant octopus, giant cucumber, killer shrews, magnetic monster, giant sea slugs, pterodactyls, giant tarantula, giant carrot, wasp women, and mineral monster.

The number and variety of things big and destructive highlight the incredible fear stemming from the fiery leveling of two unsuspecting cities. All the universe becomes a sight for danger. Things could erupt from the air, the sea, riverbeds, ponds, swamps, the desert, the mountains, the college physics lab, the high school biology classroom, the neighbor's house, the air force base, or garbage dumps, and it could happen while on a picnic, an archaeological dig, at submarine races, or when shopping for fishnet stockings or a new Buick—anywhere at any time, hundreds could die when the Earth turned against us. End follows end—through the food chain, through the ecosystem, including parts mineral and vegetable, and into every cell on Earth, like a personal cancer manufactured for each patient on the planetary ward. And all of it, the end of everything, would be our fault.

If these films neglected to propose political programs designed to rid the world of menace, just as they failed to present social concern over having a future with good taste, they nevertheless managed to depict the world in a fragile light. We are used to thinking of acid rain belched out from the Rust Belt crossing international borders, of profiteering Japanese whalers bringing marine species close to extinction, and of the shrinking Amazon rain forest replenishing less and less of the world's heavy air, but these are ideas that would probably not now be so easily comprehended had the 1950s films not existed. Rachel Carson, Ralph Nader, Earth First!, and others had their way partially cleared by big monsters stomping dozens and dozens of towns and cities to bits.

No other period in horror produced so many singularly dedicated films in so short a time frame. There was a common vision across filmmakers and audiences that never deviated from the idea that we are doomed.

The snappy solutions at the end of most 1950s films, freeing the world from certain disaster, were nearly always followed by a grim warning. We might live to see the dawn this time, but the day after is another question. Even if commercial demands not to commit cinematic suicide fostered technocratic solutions to the crisis, there was no way a smiling coda could annul the preceding 70 minutes of epic destruction. Neat and quick ends to such expansive woes never satisfied. No commercial film could end with the screen going blank; at the same time, not many commercial films could offer a convincing denouement that effectively counterbalanced the previous havoc. Narrative closure does not always mean the entanglements of the plot have been successfully resolved. It often only means the movie is over, with the nightmare continuing outside the empty theater. It is wrong of Sontag to highlight the last-second happy ending as if it were the only possible conclusion the audience could accept. These films were popular because of the way they pictured the Threat and not how catastrophe was narrowly averted.

The lemmings' rush to the films of the 1950s left the Universal monsters harmless nostalgic icons. They were finally dead, thanks to there being no life left at the box office. The emergence of an overpowering everyday terror, listening to the atomic clock tick, wiped out earlier incarnations of the monstrous. It is truly ironic that what superseded our vision of the worst beings on Earth was of our own planning. The atomic bomb dwarfed any monstrous vision ever previously imagined and killed a portion of our fantasy life. Not that it mattered much against the real deaths that took place, but our ability to envision a certain type of monster was eradicated with the deadly flash over Hiroshima.

The atomic bomb pioneered ground-breaking research in horror and transcendentalism. It directly put to the test whether or not our celebrated subconscious was totally responsible for producing screen terror. In counting the Universal stable among the casualties of World War II, we might consider how much of their makeup was taken from repressed sexual fantasies. If the Universal cast were lustful thoughts displaced to Transylvania, why did they virtually disappear from the screen? The atom bomb forced the Universal characters out of adult and adolescent collections of anxious moments and onto children's playgrounds. There they cavorted with Big Bird and offered safe passage into the rather more realistic torments of elders.[10]

On a cool spreadsheet, a couple of bewildered peasants and a frightened peer or two matter little against a formerly burgeoning metropolis now reduced to smoking ash. There is really nothing scary about vampires and wolfmen when our leaders might launch the world away while cowering in reinforced concrete bunkers far from the middling crowd. The new terror was impersonal, divinely destructive, and, until defeated at the last moment (without great conviction), an unstoppable juggernaut.

These beasts demonstrated no overt weaknesses; like metal-clad missiles, they went on about their business with no regard for human life. It quickly became apparent how tenuous our claim to rule the Earth was once radioactive monsters made their debut. They embodied the right to rule by virtue of their mammoth size coupled with extraordinary strength. Insignificant humans who got in the way were almost obliviously destroyed. We truly were nothing, and what would destroy us recognized, if such a word can be used for total disinterest, this petty fact. Even though these creatures tried to kill us, as a matter of course, such monstrous labor was done without malice. The beasts had a genetic program to follow, just as ballistic missiles were given a fatal arc to draw. Monsters exercised their natural rights, courtesy of the example set by contemporary technology.

Any city had to be our city—any body had to be our body—if we were to comprehend the effects of radiation. In this manner, national and international boundaries collapsed when Godzilla became a world-historical figure. The moment the great lizard became a star it was obvious that American audiences understood a bit of the horror our former enemies had experienced when Truman decided a toxic lesson was in order. Following closely on the massive propaganda campaigns against the alien Japanese, it was amazing that we could learn to appreciate their demons so quickly. It would seem, according to Noriega (1987), that the formerly inscrutable East was prey to some of the same night sweats as was all of the United States.

Terror ceased to be the province of an isolated group; in so changing, character became stereotype in the effort to achieve maximum identification across the social landscape. If we were to locate our place in the destroyed community, then actors and actresses had to be obvious members of the American polity.[11] If these films were to have any impact, then it must be our town that was leveled. The casts of sci-fi films were the social writ large in accordance with the need to understand something of what it meant when we were all reduced to nothing. The local precinct chief, our teachers, the guy down the block who was an aerospace engineer, and you and I were instantly available as banal caricatures. The great tragedy in such depictions lay in the fact that even such pitiful lives seemed worth living.

We need to look more carefully at the world given to us in these easily dismissed films if we are to acquire a sense of the enormous changes in the popular imagination. Horror, no longer staked to coffin and castle, left behind the Old World and came to the New. As a result of this drastic mutation, a new monster had come to lay claim to our world. We need to meet this menace; we need to meet *Them!*. *Them!*, an epic battle with desert-dwelling ants common to the Los Alamos area, contains all the elements common to the 1950s atomic monster movie, as it chronicles our struggle to survive in a radically new environment.

Them! commences with names of cast and crew wavily scrolled against a solitary silhouetted yucca tree standing forlorn against the withering assaults of the sun-baked desert. The immediate introduction of the American desert, before anything eerie is even suggested, signals a new meaning for horror as this is a previously unknown site for the presentation of terror. Not only are we outside, and it is not yet night, but we are in a distinctly American locale far removed from Eastern Europe and the familiar domestic and community settings of earlier eerie misadventures. Nothing projected on the screen has any association with horror's already rich tradition. The past has been totally rejected when an ostensibly scary film begins in the Lone Ranger's backyard.

The move into the desert makes explicit the break with earlier modes of producing horror. Unlike the haunted house or laboratory—metaphorical domains signifying household burdens and hubris, respectively—the desert and its flora and fauna are never used as metaphorical cutouts. That is, these films do not commit the pathetic fallacy and endow the arid spaces of the West with sterile attributes that rightfully belong only to human beings and the man-made spaces in which they dwell. These films make no attempt to animate the oppressive space of the desert with inappropriate emotion.

The desert is presented as bleak only because it is conceived of as a home for beings like us after the conflagration. As a place for hearth and kin it is really not all that inviting.[12] Were the desert not being assayed as our new neighborhood it would never appear as threatening or harsh. The desert, or deserted city streets mimicking the natural oven, is our future habitat. Whether we see actual tumbleweeds bounding across the superheated plain or balled-up newspapers sweeping across an empty main thoroughfare, the desert is the geographic norm of the soon-to-be-realized future. Hollow skyscrapers may replace erose mesas and asymmetrical rock formations, but the ecology is one and the same.

The nuclear desert was wildly out of synch with the future most often proffered in other American versions of what was to come. Disneyland, expositions, trade fairs, countless advertisements, and other commercial enterprises of the 1950s presented immeasurably more confident postindustrial versions of what the future held. Most institutional attempts to guarantee the future were extraordinarily optimistic, finding the time ahead to be rich with the promise of conspicuous consumption. The world of tomorrow was to be a domestic nirvana. As Thomas Hine (1986) writes, the atom promised

> that one day all drudgery would disappear and that almost every task that was dirty or dangerous could be carried out by unseen machinery, activated by the tiniest flick of a finger. Indeed, the adoption of push buttons for such mundane activities as adjusting the burners on the range probably grew out of far more remarkable feats that magazines and consumer products companies promised for the future. In these technological fantasias, always backed by the authority of a research scientist or director of product development, the push of a button replaced the wave of a magic wand in fairy tales as a tool to accomplish the unlikely. (pp. 124-125)

Both sites, the Jetsons' space-age abode and the squalid arid void, shared the broken atom as the source of future imagery. Disney and General Electric would give you luxury without end, all with the help of animated atoms. In lieu of the utopian home on the range, the Hollywood horror film offered only dead hot space.

In 1950s American horror cinema, humans hold a very precarious place in the desert. These exhausted sites do not carry scabrous titles like the Badlands and Death Valley with little motivation. This is landscape in extremis, where insufferable temperatures soar all day and drop precipitously once the torrid sun sinks, rain almost never falls, and life is made possible for hardier species only through extreme evolutionary shifts.

Our greatest national resource was reduced to hardscrabble. If the power of the opening to *Them!* is to register, then it must be read on the basis of the nation's immolation, as the fruited plain is transformed into scorched barren earth. Fantasies of manifest destiny are logically impossible when the future they were to make so glorious has vanished beneath waves of deadly heat and radiation. The verdant American landscape was denuded and plunged into the inferno. Lush greenery was replaced by forbidding barbed cacti. Animal life was reduced to the beaded reptile and the scurrying rat. Such ugly specimens might live here, comfortably equipped with fangs, poison sacs, and claws, but we would have to struggle mightily to exist unpeaceably with such unwelcome creatures. If this is the land made for you and me—you can have it.

Myths, which enable a culture to envision a glorious destiny, are rendered illegitimate pipedreams when the space across which they would take place can only be imagined as loathsome. The nation that had been settled as Eden by Pilgrims who thought they had found(ed) God's kingdom on Earth was replaced by the Frontier that in turn found itself overrun with shifting sands and scathing belts of choking heat. And while thoughts of New England as New Eden and the West as Frontier-land were largely fueled by metaphorical fantasies, the new desert was not a poetic reverie designed to provide solace like some comforting ideological quilt. The desert of these films was presented as probable reality. Should we survive the initial launch, the desert was where we were most likely to see tomorrow. No matter how tenuous the science that prefigured the death of America—just try to imagine giant tarantulas on the prowl—these films refused a priori truths that we were bound for glory as a country.

Where previous horror films had relied almost exclusively on the husks of earlier dramatic forms and inherited folktales for scenarios to enact, the 1950s horror film repudiated those conventions and began to work on American soil with contemporary dilemmas. Against the danger of real conflagration, these films had to move to more familiar environs if there was to be an audience for horror films. It would have been unlikely that horror films could successfully equal anything like the terror of tangible explosions had they remained in ancient mansions ornamented with hanging bats, musty cobwebs, and pungent wreaths of prophylactic garlic.

The conditions of existence shifted too rapidly for nothing less than a revolutionary change in the presentation of horror to take place. The unprecedented power that wiped out portions of Japan also inadvertently destroyed huge tracts of our mental landscape. The revitalization of horror took place only when the imaginations of the past suffered some losses. When the vast promise of the Frontier was exploded it became possible to experience real fear over future times in a theater seat.

Once the titles for *Them!* have cleared, the camera spies a wandering girl amid the threatening cacti and variegated rubble of the desert. She has been spotted from a police airplane during a routine flyover. Like the startling move into a bleak American wilderness, this is a new convention for the horror film. Children made few appearances in earlier films. That was the principle reason why the Monster's accidental killing of the girl in *Frankenstein* was so noteworthy. In films of the 1950s, children were threatened with great, even tiresome, regularity. The close-up of a child's gaping mouth shrieking in unmitigated terror as something gigantic stomps toward the little one became a signature shot for the nuclear horror film. As the scope of horror was enlarged by the atom bomb it became necessary to depict more victims of various stripes. No longer would the young be treated delicately, snatched to safety by loving arms before something really awful could transpire. They too would be reduced to poisonous cinder along with their elders. The guiltless child in peril offered a grim lesson: Relative innocence is no blessing. The pure will inadvertently suffer along with those who might seem more deserving of punishment.

The dazed child, clad in pajamas and clutching a ragged doll, is rescued by the police who cannot communicate with her. The girl is a catatonic cipher. She cannot voice the reason for her mysterious distress. Once we learn the girl's family has been besieged by mutant ants her catatonia becomes a symbolic silence as well as a natural reaction to terror. What has happened is unmentionable, impossible, beyond reason, and cannot be put into effective words.

Upon rescuing the girl, the puzzled officers soon chance upon her ravaged home abandoned on a highway shoulder. In the midst of empty plains, with no obvious source of immediate danger, lies a mobile home that has suffered a massive explosion. The police investigate and find some very odd clues. First, no money has been taken as there are crumpled bills scattered about the wreckage. There is also white sugar strewn around the debris, and outside the ruined hulk are odd depressions and weird bits of shell or shrapnel. Who or what would go to such trouble? The police have no answers and must wait for a higher authority to provide them with some rationale for this motley assortment of so-called clues.

On the heels of discovering the girl's shattered home a new battle site turns up. A general store has been plundered by some terrifically powerful assailant. In a nice sound effect, a radio is softly broadcasting news of recent developments in a European defense program as the queer evidence is being catalogued. Again, an impossible set of extraordinary clues lies before the police. A bewildered officer notes that the police, and perhaps some of the audience as well, are confronted with a scene where "nothing adds up."

The day's proceeds from the sale of fresh fruit and all-purpose flour lie untouched in the till. For unfathomable purposes, something other than monetary gain, the structure has been decimated. The store looks as if it were hit by a very localized tornado, as the wall facing out into the desert has been ripped to shreds. The body of the proprietor, discovered in the root cellar, has been torn apart as well. It is difficult to imagine any human creating this much havoc without a bulldozer or cache of grenades; yet there are no tracks from heavy machinery or burn marks indicating an explosion has taken place.

The mystified police bring in the FBI and even with the aid of such an august agency fail to come up with a roster of possible suspects. A routine check with area mental hospitals reveals no escapees. If they are under attack from a mentally disturbed maniac, away without leave from an asylum, then he is not a homegrown homicidal killer; still, the most rapacious schizophrenic would be incapable of doing this much damage without some very specialized equipment. The law begins operating under the presumption that the enemy or group of killers has enough ordnance to rival the state's militia as the destruction could only be caused by someone "armed like a battleship."

So far, the film has operated under the premises of a standard mystery. We are introduced to a pair of crime scenes and the trained personnel who are responsible for ferreting out unknown killers. The introduction of the FBI only enhances the apparent normality of the investigation. The appeal to a more experienced and prestigious force underlines the fact that for the local officers this is a big case, not an impenetrable crime. The hometown police need a hand up, and after all, a movie would not bother to investigate some easily solved misdemeanor.

There has been no indication that supernatural beings have entered the real world. The narrative has placed too much emphasis on police technique and the machinery of law enforcement for the audience to assume otherwise. The mystery began inside a police aircraft, as if we were a junior partner on the surveillance team; furthermore, the subsequent exploration of the crime scenes takes place under expert guidance, as the camera examines all the evidence with a police officer's careful eye. We follow along analyzing data as ill-suited puzzle pieces are individually accessed per police guidelines. The camera never adopts anything less than a straightforward position from which to view the scenes. There are no off-kilter shots or deviations from the point of view of an attentive thinker. The camera is positioned for inductive analysis, not wild speculation.

The rational camera, which almost never deviates from straightforward observation (no bizarre angles, special lenses, or other obvious distortion of perspective), is new. Previously, the camera would take all sorts of odd points of view to register a world not our own. In the 1950s, the camera rejects awkward angles of focus and adopts the stance of credible eyewitness in the attempt to document the future through the stylistic appropriation of newsreel footage and cinema verité.

The conundrum in which the varied representatives of the law find themselves immersed begins to clear with the delivery of a telegram from Washington, D.C., heralding the hasty arrival of the Drs. Medford, members of the United States Department of Agriculture. The USDA to the rescue—in a horror film! This, like the shift to the hellish desert, the harassing of children, and the abandonment of arty camera techniques, is another important break in convention.

The people who knew how to destroy the menace used to be either peasants, the learned Salt of the Earth, or highly intelligent men, well versed in the extensive literature of the occult and paranormal. Only the members of an ancient community, like peasants who maintained sacred roots or scholars who venerated the lessons of the past, had the know-how to confront otherworldly danger. No longer will those beset by evil, or those about to be eaten or squashed by an amoral bug, find answers in ancient texts providing ageless wisdom. The cultivated arcana of centuries, once an efficacious solution to night terrors, has been outmoded by the implacable advance of technological wizardry. The lore of the ages cannot compete against brainy physicists, their multi-million-dollar government laboratory, or the multiform creatures spawned there.

Collective outrage, expressed in the form of vigilante tribes, is a waste of time and energy when a solitary technocrat can depress a red button and blow up whatever seems to be the trouble. Organizing and carrying out responses to terror becomes the province of nameless bureaucrats when these same institutional minions make the future an untenable proposition. To participate in the war against beasts and other radioactive mutations, or conversely to conjure them up, now means going to college. One needs to have spent time in organic chemistry classes, taken elementary particle physics, or followed a parallel course of study in business administration and gone on to a prestigious graduate school before being qualified to engage/engender the enemy.

In these films, only scientists and their administrative colleagues kill, only scientists and pencil pushers can save, and only scientists and actuaries will determine our course of survival. What has occurred in the development of horror is that the dialectic between good and evil has been abridged to a contest between competing visions of institutional outcomes. Will our thinkers succeed and harness the atom for good, or will they trap us under Godzilla's scaly heel? There is no middle ground; either the scientific establishment will prevail and make everything right or the same corporate entity will err and we will die.

According to the 1950s horror film, the possibility of a future is not a question of moral or immoral choices but only the business of positive or negative research outcomes. Bad results from an experiment gone awry or mistakes in execution say nothing of the individual researcher's innate worth or that of the institution that subsidized the technological transgressions. Faulty research design and test error are not sins. The gulf that separates sin from error is the difference between describing an act as falling along the clear faultline between good and evil or within the hazy range betwixt good and bad. The use of either set of measures entails a vastly different set of expectations regarding the performance of certain actions and the personal responsibility one bears for the fruit of individual and corporate labor. The future for people like the Medfords, federal employees doing the best they can, is a matter of planning, not soul searching.

The entrance of the Medfords is just another pointed illustration of myth's demotion to the everyday in the 1950s horror film. It took particular screenwriting genius to have the USDA do battle with some of the very first atomic monsters to appear on our screens. Now the more mundane the position of the authorities who are dispatched to deal with menace, such as USDA representatives, the more probable the existence of such monsters seems. What should have appeared ridiculous, if we use earlier horror films for a baseline, instead looks natural and makes good sense. Just as the Department of Agriculture has experts on hand to deal with plagues of ravenous locusts and infestations of corn borers, it also has knowledgeable people to deal with huge desert ants. By lumping both sorts of disaster, the man-made and the natural, together, the film creates an equivalence that makes the ants seem as if they belong in our world. That is, the film presumes that man-made mistakes are no more unnatural than the exceptional, once-in-a-lifetime natural disaster. Whatever the problem, the government can send out assistance and attempt to preserve the future by binding it in reams of protective red tape.

The mad scientist, unwholesome intellectual, and possible necromancer has been superseded. The reformed scientist in these films is exquisitely rational—even those working within illicit or dangerous arenas have struck no deals with devils. There are reasons, usually good ones, for every experiment the 1950s scientist elects to undertake. The lone maniac, cursed with too greedy an intelligence, has been replaced by a lab-coated functionary. The scientist of the radioactive horror film only wants to methodically distill the physical universe into its constituent parts; he or she has no interest in becoming God or even godlike. These scientists may have an ego, but they are without profane hubris. Any ambition that drives these men and women is purely secular and commonsensical. They may want more of something (money, renown, power, etc.), but their goals are neither too large nor too distant from the wants of less educated individuals.[13] Science is merely another rung on the ladder to success.

It's just plain folks who happen to have earned Ph.D.s, who come to the desert to save the West from mutated ants. They are ordinary people in extraordinary times. A closer look at the new saviors reveals two people who could not possibly be more quotidian. First, the Medfords are old (the man) and young (the woman). Gone is the virile young man at the height of masculine physical maturity. Cleverly, the film subverts the usual cliché of worldly and academic success by virtue of machismo and adopts alternative images that topple commonsense notions of what a scientific superman, the *übermensch* of the whirling centrifuge and exotic reagents, should look like. In their stead, *Them!* gives us a codger and what the admiring police refer to as a "looker."

The senior Medford is a somewhat absentminded chap well past the age of mandatory retirement. This Dr. Medford should by now have left behind the many pressures of the working world. Instead of reeling in bass at favorite fishing holes or puttering about the bungalow, he flies cross-country and leads an ad hoc team charged with the immense responsibility of saving America. Medford has also acquired a nice little paunch (belly flab is uncommon among heroes of all stripes), and he carries himself in such a manner as to suggest that the self-absorption of unrepentant egoism and the thirst for power have been, if they ever existed, supplanted by gentle befuddlement in the face of a busy world. This is not to say the elder Medford is not an able scientist. He is still smart and capable of distinguished insights; it just seems he is always in his own slightly detached world, always a bit removed from his immediate surroundings. In the end, Medford is nothing more than an old man who knows a lot.

The younger Medford has been working under her father's tutelage since completing her advanced degree. She too subverts the dominant paradigm of how a scientist should appear; indeed, if she is to be considered a proper researcher, using earlier films as a guideline, there certainly ought to be testosterone coursing through her veins. Unfortunately, while her gender is used to reinforce sexist stereotypes, as the police seem to spend more time imagining what dinner with the Doctor would be like than they do listening to her professional opinion, the fact that she is a woman still serves to deconstruct even more dated conceptions of who is fit to be considered a scientist.

As soon as Dr. Patricia Medford deplanes, the waiting policemen resolve to date her. The welcoming committee are smitten by her comely legs and not in the least threatened by her brains. No one would have ever thought of seducing Dr. Frankenstein or even admiring his firm buttocks as he forthrightly marched up the stairs to his laboratory. The normal doctors of *Them!* are well-balanced people and, consequently, quite approachable. These scientists have descended from their more regal counterparts and are no longer remote savants. Their work is no more mysterious than any other career. They examine nature in the same way the officers investigate clues and they might even have time for a cold one at the local watering hole when the workday is done.

Once introduced into the narrative, the elder doctor quickly gets the silent refugee to unburden herself of what she has witnessed. As the girl emerges from her catatonic trance she screams "Them! Them! Them!" directly into our faces via a very tight close-up. The repetition of the title and the urgency with which it is delivered sets up a crucial binarism for understanding the film.

In the cinema of nuclear futures, the dilemma confronting our stand-ins is eminently simple—Them or Us. The utterance of these pronouns reduces every consideration in the film to an idiotically uncomplicated couplet: success/failure, continuation of our species/extinction of competing species, extinction of our species/continued existence of competing life-form, future/no future, ants/humans, and so on. When it comes to the End, nuclear cinema gives you relatively little to think about, to ponder, or to mull over—either the cast lives or the world dies. As the films never really touch on the validity of a negative response—might the world be better off if humans did not exist?—there is no intellectual quandary for the protagonists to debate. The choice, which is not really an appropriate word as there is never an opportunity to second the idea that maybe we deserve to perish, is always focused on what is the best way to successfully combat the enemy. Death is constructed as an impossible option against which humans fight all out for continued existence. Atomic films only toy with the eventuality that we could all be extinguished, as none of the nuclear beast films ever closed with the triumph of an oversized adversary. The dawn of a new day always broke with chastened allies gripping one another tightly. There was never a finale that showed the resplendent Earth free from noisome humans as the beasts were returned to supremacy.

It is the failure of 1950s films to fully investigate what it would mean for all to perish in a nuclear crisis that causes Sontag to term most films of this ilk fantasy. For her, they all too handily circumvent any serious examination requiring an assessment of corporate responsibility for the present dilemma; in addition, they neglect to inquire into new ways to deport ourselves in the future. We neither reevaluate the present mess nor dream of a future lived in ways fundamentally different from our current wayward path. *Them!* and its brethren allow us to playfully dream our death without ever confronting extinction as an imminent possibility. Our atomic peril is always shown with the reassuring sheen of unreality that accompanies the occasional nightmares that intrude on our sleep. When we must suffer from a periodic nightmare, no matter how bad the dream, we rarely, if ever, doubt that we shall eventually wake up and be restored to consciousness.

Nuclear films conjure up momentarily scary images of mass extinction without granting global death as a real possibility. This is especially true when the film pretends to evoke the death of our species. At these crucial moments, the nuclear horror film is most cinematic, most obviously a manufactured entertainment incorporating grand special effects that celebrate the spectacle of movie technology without unduly shocking the patrons in the seats with too realistic impressions of global slaughter. The end of the world is treated like an extension of a daredevil carnival ride and is therefore too pleasurably stimulating to effectively terrorize the audience. A more apposite strategy might have the world end in a poisonous whimper in lieu of Cinerama.

With the tormented cry of "Them! Them! Them!" defining our nemesis, the girl's simple response leads to the speedy discovery of the ants' busy colony. It is an immense nest far out in the barren desert wastes. Under these extremely harsh climatic conditions, the ants have had no trouble whatsoever creating an impressive base from which they may take flight and make the Earth their own. The desert, filmed with an eye for the ugly, presents no threat at all to the big insects. The mutations thrive where we would find ourselves in a mighty struggle to survive just for a day or even several hours.

Them! generates an interesting argument by first presenting the ants flourishing in a nuclear testing ground. At the time the film was sent to the theaters, we had very little idea of what our extremely aggressive technology was doing to the environment. If the film now seems to be offering a nascent argument for environmental responsibility it is because we are beginning to have a sense of global limits to growth. *Them!* seems an environmentally conscious text, aware of the damage we are doing, not because it was written as a warning tract but because we are now more knowledgeable of the noxious influence of radioactivity and other more common wastes.

The film might truly represent the first glimmer of environmental concern within the popular consciousness. The foregrounding of the ants' adaptability signifies a measure of equivalence between the ants' environmental successes and our own exceptional ability to adapt to changing ecosystems. The film may even go further; perhaps, if the ants can survive so well in the uninhabitable American wasteland, they are a species superior to our own delicate and dirty group. The ants might be more deserving of the land than we are. They are not bothered by the furious sun and, far more important, can survive and grow big under the influence of radioactive effluvia.

Given the ants' ability to prosper where nothing should grow large, what would happen if they migrate to more hospitable areas of the country? That is the Doctors' chief concern as the team begins to explore the vast underground colony. The ants must be stopped posthaste before the Queen gives birth to more progeny. If the little Queens escape, the Earth may be finished, or at least an Earth that can support sizable populations of humans.

The team eventually poisons the desert nest and discovers that several Queens have been birthed and taken leave of the mother nest. The new Queens have left with equal portions of the nest's original population to settle in as yet unknown sites. The team is now faced with an insect analog to the nuclear chain reaction. Each nest means new Queens, more Queens means more dispersed colonies, and on and on ad infinitum. The ant population will expand geometrically unless the new Queens are stopped before they too can conceive.

The ill-timed departure of the newly hatched Queens sets the boundaries for the film's awkward attempt at an optimistic, forward-looking conclusion. The clumsy finale, while failing to reassure the audience, does lead to new spatial possibilities for the enactment of terror. With *Them!* and its hundreds of near identical kin, the new horror became extremely mobile and, even more to our collective detriment, was random and unpredictable in its appearance. Ants or giant beasts of any sort—including thundering sea cucumbers—could rise up in any space that humans elected to occupy. There was no safe place to cringe and ride out an attack. Horror could no longer be considered a local phenomenon. Its depiction as a relatively isolated, geographically contained outbreak of evil or menace was a thing of the past.

In earlier ages, there were particular and difficult-to-reach locales to which unnatural menace was quite partial. For example, the Balkan outback had long held near exclusive rights to midnight werewolves and furtive vampires. Should these monsters emigrate to safer climes, leaving behind their native foraging grounds, they would still remain uncommon predators found only in tiny number. They kept to single sites and did not reproduce geometrically; in fact, these progenitors were always on the verge of extinction. Thus, even though Dracula could embark for Bremen or transform himself into a relatively elusive bat and outpace his pursuers, he could never appear anywhere at any time with tremendous litters following shortly upon his arrival. Under the aegis of the atom, monsters could sprout at all times, in all places, and were capable of producing exceptional hordes of dangerous siblings.

The menace had become global; it was inter- and intracontinental just like an ordinary nuclear warhead. For the monster, the entire earth was his/her/its stomping ground, leaving us heirs to a fragile globe that was "no more than a 'critical mass,' a precipitate resulting from the extreme reduction of contact time, a fearsome friction of places and elements that only yesterday were still distinct and separated by a buffer of distances, which have suddenly become anachronistic" (Virilio, 1977/1986, p. 136).

Once again, the similarities between the beasts of 1950s horror cinema and nuclear weapons are exceedingly obvious. These monsters can fly,

crawl, swim, or burrow wherever they are instinctually guided; consequently, they may strike any sprawling city, protected hamlet, or strategic
military outpost that falls in their path. Very little can be done to protect
anonymous victims who, simply by chance, fall under the monsters' flight
plan. Civil defense preparations are a black joke, a laughably absurd
impossibility. There are no precautions an individual or a country can take
when an 18-foot-high ant decides to feed on civilians in your backyard. They
are not easily diverted.

As a result of the monsters' imperviousness to human obstacles, the army
in *Them!* is somewhat disorganized and unable to respond with a surgical
strike. Its soldiers are forced to wait impatiently for the crotchety bug specialist
Dr. Medford to tell them what needs to be done. Such leadership, from Patton
and MacArthur to Mr. Peepers, does nothing to suggest our national defense
will be heroically marshalled in the face of an awesome enemy. And if the
nation's defenses are paralyzed, then what of individual initiative? Can the
exceptional man or woman rise to the challenge? The answer must be no. For
when entire nations quake and the horror easily involves more than a domestic
pair like the Harkers or even a small tightly bound rural collective as in
Frankenstein, individuals are cheap and disposable. Under the threat of mass
extinction, there are no lone responses that may be called efficacious.

Terror has been made brand new. There is no past to examine for lessons
about *Them!.* No wise men can be counted on to come forth and save the
world. Any quick-fix solutions are a matter of hit-or-miss fumbling. With
the passing of dated myth, now reduced to the status of retrograde children's
amusement, we tell one another terrible stories that, unlike earlier narratives, harbor no real possibility of producing a happy or even survivable end.
No longer will we live happily ever after. Global mass extermination robs
us of older and more comforting systems of belief regarding the success of
human effort in the face of incredible power. Resistance seems impossible
when opposing forces are measured in rads and megatons. At the same time
as the possibility of resistance is diminished, death has acquired another
more stinging meaning. When death is forced on everyone at the same time,
as opposed to an individual destiny that arrives differently for each human
being according to the quality of life each has lived, then we learn to reject
many of the useful fallacies that made life resplendently meaningful.

A long time ago,

> individual death founded all of religious, mystical and magic thought. From
> the recognition of the death of the tribes, of the group, they then arrived at

the idea that civilizations, too, are mortal. With nuclear weapons, the species is now reaching the possibility of its own death. (Virilio & Lotringer, 1983, p. 37)

The possibility, however remote, that we are all to be denied individually meaningful deaths and instead perish in an anonymous slaughter is one of the things that makes jaded slogans like "Life sucks and then you die" become common fare.

When *Them!* concludes, we may live and our world endure—but at a cost that reduces all triumphs of goodwill and resilient spirit to pathetic dreams. We could not win these atomic battles if the hour and a half preceding the last-second victory was convincing to the audience. If the films were able at any time to threaten the audience, then their idiotic endings must be dismissed as false codas attached by blanching studios and calculating film producers unable to finish a tragic vision in the suitably bleak fashion it deserved. Sontag (1979) is correct: These upbeat finales made death impossible and plunged the film into the safe embrace of fantasy; however, this magical solution could only work if the smiling epilogues were considered equal to the rest of the movie. All 1950s closure was ad hoc and, like most jury-rigged solutions, unsatisfying. In later films, so negative that many older viewers are absolutely repulsed, all happy endings are pathetic illusions. The films to come will remember these cloying endings and, as if in revenge, erase the last scintilla of hope that even the most depressing 1950s horror narrative could offer.[14]

As *Them!* draws to an end and the ants make an abortive attempt to claim the world, they are driven by sure instinct to colonize two brilliantly selected sites. With their success in the desert, it is time to move on to more inviting spaces. Just as the bomb was tested in the wild and then moved to more populated areas, the ants follow the same course. Early positive results in the empty wastes mean later assaults on men, women, and children.

The first Queen homesteads on a naval ship, the U.S.S. *Viking*, sailing offshore Acapulco. Although the inconvenient visitation ends with the death of the young mother, the episode points at some dangerous possibilities for our future: evidence that belies the rosy conclusion to come. The ant has mistaken the military vessel for a small island and landed in an empty cargo bay left uncovered by a sloppy sailor. She is subsequently beset by an astonished crew who cannot defeat the unbelievably strong enemy in an acceptable manner. The Queen is eventually destroyed but only after the ship is scuttled. For the navy, it is a pyrrhic victory. If the ant must perish, then all hands go down with her, drowned as newly minted Medal of Honor recipients.

The magnitude of what terror can do reaches incredible heights in comparison with the power of the ant's forebears. Dracula did kill a small sailing crew on his trip to Bremen, but he did not bring down an entire frigate or man o' war. He killed a seedy, bedraggled crew, which is something other than sinking a World War II warship captained by strapping young men armed with the finest military hardware a superpower can furnish. The end of the crew is really extraordinary; in *Them!*, more people die than were probably killed in all horror films preceding the arrival of nuclear power.

The death of the crew directly puts in question horror's status as an immutable transcendental object, safe from the vagaries of the moment, able to transmit the same message whenever it is encountered. If the meaning of horror was invariant, why the acceleration and escalation of death? The transformation that is highlighted by this unprecedented attack recasts what it means to be a victim. When the monster selects anonymous sailors or, as *Them!* will later show, a bustling city full of unknown faces, a victim is a stereotype, a bland caricature of the unfortunate. We learn exceedingly little of the departed when people are extinguished on such a large scale. To accept mass slaughter, to comprehend such large numbers of vanquished, we need to reduce them to a lowest common denominator. The dead lose all trace of individuality as they are labeled sailors, young men, or simply Americans. When this happens, when loss is reduced to collective tags, death becomes easier to take. The individual memories that make personal loss so painful disappear when many perish.

The navy is not society or a family group; it is however, a necessary institution without which modern society is unthinkable. The ant selects not a couple nor an isolated community that unwittingly supports an overeducated egomaniac; it randomly assails one of the principle supports for a nation and tears it asunder. All the anonymous deaths on board the battleship stand in for our own diminutive stature in mass society. We could just as easily number among the numerous faceless dead.[15]

The other telling locale to which a Queen flies is Los Angeles. What became the center of American life west of the Mississippi, once the frontier closed, is in danger of a hostile takeover from a newly reconfigured species. The city of Los Angeles is a wonderful spot to test shared assumptions of inviolability and the manifest right of American men and women to rule with impunity over the Earth. With the move to Los Angeles and Acapulco, the ants operate along vulgar Darwinian assumptions. For the victorious species, might makes right.

Once the ants are known to be in the area, the citizens of the city become frenzied, and martial law must be declared to prevent the good people of L.A. from destroying their town in a panic. No one is immune from the influence of the unwanted invaders. Even if a citizen never sees or hears the insects, he or she has been contaminated with their presence—every section of the social fabric is unwillingly involved. To demonstrate the tension produced with the widespread knowledge that the city is endangered by gigantic vermin, the film cuts in newsreel-like footage of people nervously going about their tasks. The stuff of the everyday—heading to work, returning to the nest after a difficult day at the office, and shopping for milk before dinner—acquires an aura of unreality when normal chores and duties are accomplished under the threat of imminent annihilation. It is just when people are doing something normal in periods of absolute calm that they will be attacked.

This was not always so; Frankenstein, Dracula, and werewolves usually besieged humans at predictable times, such as when night fell or when the moon was full. The behavior of earlier monsters could be predicted with a high degree of certainty, but because the ants are nuclear, their scattered movements are Brownian. They circulate randomly without creating detectable patterns. Obviously, the ants can eventually be found, but before they are detected in Los Angeles and aboard the *Viking*, the army spends a long and fruitless amount of time trying to track the migrating insects. In the end, the army must bide its time and wait for the ants to reveal themselves.

When the ants arrive in Los Angeles they take to the sewers. In the maze of reinforced concrete tunnels lying below every inch of the vast city, they establish a burgeoning kingdom. The sewers allow for concealment and also give them access to all parts of the metropolis where humans used to feel secure and in control. Should they feel like it, the ants may forage for sugar and other foodstuffs in any sector of the city. The ants have, in colonizing waste pipes, undermined the entire city.

The sewer is, however, more than just the only available space for the creatures in an already overcrowded environment. It is true the sewer offers cover, but the sewer also seems to allow the ants to prosper. If the desert is, to our eyes, nature's most undesirable ecological niche, then the sewer must be the worst man-made environment in immediate proximity to our homes. Of course, we have done greater harm to the Earth, but the sewer is the foulest ground we let penetrate our pristine living quarters. The ants seem more than just immune to our worst excesses; they are strengthened by whatever horrendous environmental destruction we might create in our disregard for all life.

The last battle in *Them!*, once it is known the ants have taken refuge in the sanitation system, is particularly noteworthy for the mismatched people it brings together as the menace is, only for the moment, defeated. The scientists believe the ants are in Los Angeles because a freight train has been ravaged and a multi-ton load of cane sugar hijacked. It seems a sure thing that only huge ants would bust up a boxcar for sugar, but the location of the elusive pests remains a mystery. The fact that large numbers of 18-foot-high ants are not immediately obvious is another example of how stunningly inefficient the authorities have become. How can you not find ants the size of midsize cargo vans in an urban environment?

The ants are finally located not by expert sources but by a street alcoholic whose fabulous tale is not immediately believed. Pink elephants or big ants, it's all the same to the drunk's deaf Doctors until one of them decides the sot just might be telling the truth. Where the army proves incapable of the task, a street lush triumphs. The alcoholic tells the authorities that he has seen the ants troop in and out of the sewers in a nearby culvert. His observations are finally given full credence when a hysterical mother, a figure nearly as disreputable as the wino, tells of her missing family who were flying model planes near an entrance to the city's labyrinthian sewer system. Once the highly unreliable witnesses are allowed to direct the search, the authorities fall upon the children's plane and the husband's splintered remains.

Because *Them!* will only go so far in offering a negative vision of the future, the missing children will be allowed to grow into adults. *Them!* cannot go so far as to have the children eaten or trampled by the beast. As a compromise measure, the film will threaten children but not kill them. The films of our time regularly destroy kids, as the failure of nerve exhibited by earlier films, or what now seems like hesitation for fear of serious offense, helps drive contemporary films to new nihilistic depths.[16]

As in the beginning of *Them!*, the depiction of children as victims, even if they will live to play another day, moves us all closer to the place where victims stand and fall. The placement of "unthinkable" victims in the opening and closing of the film makes firm *Them!*'s commitment to reshape horror and leave antiquated forms behind. The fact that all the newly victimized survive also serves to indelibly mark the film as a nostalgic exercise in the production of fright. At the time of *Them!*'s original release, the shift to more innocent prey was a signal turn. To contemporary audiences, who dies in a horror film is not all that meaningful. We know that anyone can get killed without reason.

The ants finally found, the armed forces converge, laden with flame-throwers and assault rifles. Individual acts of sacrifice, soldiers giving up life and limb, are common as the fight is waged. Clearly, these are good men fighting in the tunnels. They are shown to care for one another **and** us, as their principal reason for being in the tunnels is to preserve society and not just their fellow comrades.

The fight is a strategic nightmare, for our team has a number of objectives that are at odds with one another. First, and most important, the ants must be destroyed; however, the children may be alive somewhere in the depths of the extensive warren. This means that the men cannot go ahead and poison the nest. If they flood the formicary with insecticide, the children will die. They cannot blow the ants to smither-eens as the colony is directly under the city. Were they to detonate a smaller charge of explosives and not bring the city crashing down, they would still harm the potential survivors. The fight must be fought in the most inefficient manner possible: at close quarters with minimum fire power.

It is at this point that *Them!* begins to actively renege on the promise it made throughout the rest of the film. *Them!* rapidly devolves from a relatively innovative atomic horror picture into a routine war movie. The previous portions of *Them!* made fighting the ants a comparatively high-tech, anonymous affair conducted from research labs and field sites. Now it is a matter of sending in the boys and mopping the place up with Them.

To completely eradicate the ants should take a corporate effort on a par with the atomic mission that led to their creation/mutation in the first place; now, however, when the ants are found, the film begins to radically refashion the demands it has so far made of the human protago-nists. Instead of a full-scale technological assault, the fight will be personal and low-tech. The film collapses into preatomic clichés by having good tough men beating a nuclear menace with the tired combi-nation of guts and altruism. The conclusion of *Them!* is regrettably unconvincing. Later films will not make the same mistake. Unwitting optimism will not be a plot development audiences long suffer gladly.

The missing children, adorable even when terrified, are heard screaming as the conflagration heats up. The agitated ants begin to defend their threatened complex with previously unmatched ferocity. The film has now fully left horror and become something akin to an atomic *Perils of Pauline* in army battle dress as one of the warriors, in a last-second attempt to rescue the kids, gives his life to help spirit the children to safety. In a medium close-up meant to evoke some powerful combination of awe, sympathy, and respect, we see the ants' scythelike mandibles join about the noble soldier's soft belly and crush him to death. As if to demonstrate the higher level of evolution our species has achieved, this act of courage is especially selected to underline our ability to reach virtuous heights lesser species have no hope of scaling. Of course, the film neglects to also underline the fact that this apparent sacrifice is a result of the officer's rigid training. He may not have a choice about whether or not he should surrender his life in battle. It might have made for a stronger horror film if the director had remembered that programmatic acts of behavior mimicking virtues are not virtues at all but automatic reflexes. The film will note other such courageous acts as the ants are eliminated in a furious celebration of ersatz human virtue. When we win so easily, any sense of frisson from earlier scenes is lost. In erasing, or attempting to wash away, real doubt over the possibility of a future, the film is finished.

The ants are slowly eliminated as the stout fighting men converge on the birthing Queen. If any new Queens have escaped the colony, we are in real trouble. The aforementioned little exercises in heroism will mean nothing if new colonies are founded. Developing Queens, still sequestered in the nest, are discovered. Their wings are immature, making them too young to take leave of their mother. The mother fights mightily for the lives of her babies, but she is soon dispatched.[17] The plaintive baby Queens, who almost look cute, are caught in the burning spray of a flamethrower and summarily executed.

The trouble is over. We are safe from evil or the bad aftereffects of inspired invention. Men can pull together as one and make up for past errors. Teamwork, altruism, and indefatigable hope are all it takes to save the children and rescue the Earth. Never mind that all this now seems like State Department or Atomic Energy Commission propaganda.

We have triumphed and live to see another day. When the question comes down to Us or Them, the answer must be Us.

The films to come will disagree.

Notes

1. Some Christian soldiers on the religious right would disagree, arguing that turning plowshares into nuclear swords is doing the Lord's work. Any event of this magnitude would have to be divinely inspired no matter how much evidence of human fallibility is available to the true believer. After all, Ronald Reagan, the most popular president of the past 30 years and a self-professed Christian, was certain we would soon exit the doomed Earth in a divine conflagration. Thus the man who would start the ball exploding and order the missiles away found common comfort in looking to God for a reason to start something.

2. The latest use of images designed to trigger Holocaust memories comes from Bosnia-Hercegovina. Videotape of emaciated prisoners stripped to the waist, with spindly chests drawn to the bone, standing behind lines of barbed wire, reawaken fears that genocide has returned. It is the combination of wire and flesh that calls us to act with alacrity. Starving bodies are, in and of themselves, often not enough to call into play the need to do something with haste.

3. Andrew Tudor (1989), in his recent survey of shifts in the horror film, points out "the unique contribution of this period: a body of films in which the threat is firmly beyond our control, but still entirely secular" (pp. 42-43). The supernatural has virtually disappeared and been replaced by a threat that cannot be considered paranormal. In examining this turn, which he breaks down into several subgenres, Tudor argues that "the fears articulated here, compared to those of earlier periods, are firmly this-worldly, an expression, perhaps, of collective concerns with invasion, communism and the atomic bomb" (p. 47).

All of Tudor's terms, "invasion, communism, and the atomic bomb," are part and parcel of the same reconfiguration of the political realm that occurred when the bomb blew. National anxiety over the threat of communism and a possible Soviet invasion cannot be considered apart from the atomic bomb. Had the Soviet Union not elected to keep up the pace in the arms race, it is unlikely that we would have let the dangers of the Red Menace occupy us to such a great degree.

4. An appropriate response to the technological advances which endangered and continue to threaten us all would follow along the lines of *Hiroshima Mon Amour* (1959). This painful film addresses memory and responsibility, as well as genocide, across two disparate fronts and is both aesthetically rigorous, if one has the right sort of upbringing to tackle the film, and witheringly depressing. In comparison, the Creature from the Black Lagoon, or any other oversized scaly monster, does not bring the desired level of gravity and sense of occasion to the problem of mass extermination.

The audience for creature films does not all too often overlap with the avant-middlebrow group that embraces difficult films like *Hiroshima Mon Amour*. The far vaster audience that enjoys big beings from space and mutant grasshoppers menacing the Southside of Chicago wants something entertaining no matter what the immediate subject at hand. Leisure time is too dear to be invested in the wrong sort of cultural capital. They were not willing to suffer for art.

Like the work for elites, the films of the mutants investigated the issues involved with radioactive slaughter, but they also provided some sort of diverting spectacle. The rarefied word games and unsettling pace of *Hiroshima Mon Amour* were too uncomfortable and forbidding for the demotic horde. And while *Hiroshima Mon Amour* may approximate what hell is like for the creature film audience, such films also left the larger public almost as dazed as the real events that led to the creation of bitter and inaccessible art.

5. It is worth noting that this excerpt belies Sontag's (1979) deep appreciation for such films. In earlier lines, she could be a "fanzine" writer reveling in the thrills and ideas provided by commercial films concerned with the apocalypse. There is a schizophrenic quality to her essay that suggests she feels quite ambivalent toward her well-regarded position as a first-rank intellectual who was reading Plato and Nietzsche as a preteen. This out-of-character coda, a **real** return of the repressed, comes as a shock after 20-odd pages of observation marked by a high regard for what she has seen on the screen.

6. What do Picasso's venal female nudes say about women? Is the *vagina dendata* so prominently featured in many of his works an original or truthful statement about the female sex? Are Celine, Acker, O'Connor, Burroughs, and Walker responsible writers? Are the Impressionist trainscapes of industrial Paris an accurate reflection of metropolitan views on the emergence of a modern city? Did Dickens's busy novels contain all the varied tones of Victorian repression? Obviously, this list could be extended ad infinitum to find fault in all artistic "triumphs."

7. The most spectacular contribution of American high art, the type Greenberg (1985) championed, has been its incredible ability to outperform inflation. Kitsch may be insipid, but nearly everyone can afford it.

8. It is, however, somewhat difficult to imagine what form metascientific thought, as it relates to nuclear extermination, would take when displayed on theater screens. How does one comment self-reflexively on the scientific method and the Atom Bomb? What crafty language could be concocted to abstract science from its horrible effects on humanity and how could we ensure that more than just a few art patrons understood it?

9. In the early 1970s, there was a small onslaught of horror movies that bore an exceedingly strong resemblance to the monster films of the 1950s. The plots, characters, and last-minute end to the threat were identical to those featured over a decade earlier. The only difference between these films was the origin of the menace. In the 1970s, the source was man-made environmental damage. The effects of widespread pollution, a new threat in the public consciousness, were now dramatized via a model that had already proved its worth as a way of examining the consequences of technological disaster.

One of the worst environmental films, *Night of the Lepus* (1972), also featured the best line ever delivered in a creature film. Sheriff: "I don't want to alarm you folks, but there's a herd of killer rabbits on the way."

10. Frankenstein and the rest of the gang do, of course, reappear from time to time; however, most attempts to resurrect the Universal undead are usually markedly unsuccessful. There has only been one studio that was able to bring the Universal cast back and have some luck in keeping them breathing for more than just an appearance or two. From the late 1950s until the early 1970s, Hammer, a British studio, released a large number of films and sequels featuring monsters who were obviously drawn from Universal releases.

These films were not, however, as adept in creating monsters who were as lovable as those in the original source material. What made Hammer films successful was that they introduced a new level of violence, gore, and nudity into the Universal canon. Each new Hammer film seemed to go further than the last. These films are memorable, then, not because they kept the Universal cast alive but because they introduced explicit violence and bared flesh into the horror genre. As *Village Voice* film critic Manohla Dargis notes in a roundtable discussion of movie violence: "I was so impressed as a child watching Hammer films because it always had the best gore spurting out of the vampire's chest" (quoted in L. Kennedy, 1992, p. 10). No one has ever watched a Universal film and been similarly impressed.

11. Unless you are a truly devoted horror fan, it is difficult to name many memorable actors from this era in horror film history. For this type of film, memorable acting is a positive hindrance. "Good" acting calls too much attention to itself. When a good actor owns a role you remember not only the part but the man or woman who played the character. When we see *Frankenstein* we think what a marvelous job Karloff did as the Monster. The movie works better when we think of the Monster as an individual who cannot be brought to life without the skills of a consummate actor. Conversely, for a 1950s movie to work you should not leave the film thinking what a good job James Arness did as the Thing. We need to think of these monsters as beings animated by radiation—not the Method.

The same is true for the actors portraying ordinary people. The 1950s monster movie needs stereotypical performances if the audience is to identify with the characters. They must look and act like us, even if the performances are a bit wooden, so that we think of them as us. Finally, good actors also run a little more than mediocre ones. Given the fact that these films were made on very small budgets, stellar acting was not a priority.

12. For a different view of the desert, look at the westerns. There, the desert is treated metaphorically as a distant moral host overseeing the epic struggles taking place across its austere purview. Westerns' lands are spaces endowed with the glacial clarity and sculptural rigor to be found only in geography fashioned to make the presence of God obvious. In addition to carrying a metaphorical burden, the desert of the westerns is most often a starkly beautiful locale in which to fulfill uniquely American destinies. The desert of *Them!* offers no beautiful visions, spiritual aid, or quiet commentary. The desert of the 1950s horror film is just hard.

13. As Tudor (1989) notes, "The inhuman ambitions of individual scientists are far less to the fore than they were in the previous two decades. Though there are still cases of science used for evil ends, as well as one or two traditional mad scientists, the sub-genre's major emphasis is on unintentional and often accidental threats" (p. 147).

14. *Popcorn* (1991), an otherwise forgettable horror movie, features several parodies of earlier films in the genre. One of the best of the films within a film is *Mosquito*. *Mosquito* perfectly articulates the reasons why latter-day fans are so contemptuous of 1950s films.

15. It is quite possible that our films are not intrinsically more violent than those of earlier eras. City upon city was leveled in the Atomic Era. It is open to debate whether the explicit gutting of a baker's dozen witless teenagers is all that far in excess of the spectacular demolition of an entire city. If mainstream film critics behaved like bonded actuaries, then the immense destruction of property accompanied with the anonymous deaths of manifold citizens in an atomic horror film would not be a preferable alternative to the close-up deaths of a few youngsters.

The distaste for explicit death when older, more responsible films depicted mass destruction from a distance presents a unique contradiction for a capitalist society. Why shouldn't a smattering of gory deaths be judged vastly preferable to the huge financial write-offs and immense human distress following widespread property destruction involving hundreds of thousands of people?

16. In *Body Snatchers* (1994), the latest remake of *Invasion of the Body Snatchers* (1956), one of the few truly respectable 1950s monster movies, an infected and infectious child is unceremoniously pitched from a helicopter because he represents a threat. There is no equivalent scene in the original.

Along similar lines, *Mikey* (1992) stars an ingenious and ambitious child serial killer. The advertising for the film states that "Jason and Freddy were little once too."

17. The mother of the young Queens might have as much right to see her young develop as the mother whose children are held in the nest does. The idea of unnatural others having as much maternal concern for their offspring as we do will later be developed in a far more rigorous fashion in *Aliens* (1986).

6. JASON

*They who assert that a blind fatality produced the various effects we hold
in this world talk very absurdly.*
                                    —Baron De Montesquieu (1949, p. 1)

The Atom Bomb is a worn-out icon. Once capable of sparking horrible fantasies of world destruction, the Bomb is now, at least to the enervated imagination, an empty threat. Of course, good citizens continue to march against the deployment of penultimate nuclear weapons (the defense industry is unlikely, no matter how bloated the deficit, to ever cease tinkering), scattered atolls are still erased from the South Seas, and underground testing in poisoned deserts goes on, but the ability of the Bomb to evoke instantaneous and involuntary shudders is no longer possible. It has lain dormant for too long to inspire the masses in the same anxious fashion that it once did.

In a perverse double bind, the Bomb remains exceedingly dangerous and also staid. Its enforced captivity (to date) and extraordinary capacity for harm make it a unique item on the cultural/political landscape. Exiled for years to lonely Colorado silos and wandering submarines, the Bomb has suffered a significant degradation in status: It's deadly and boring.

This new relationship between terror, the imagination, and atomic power is highlighted in the third edition of *The Emergency Public Relations Manual*, a guidebook for the people and institutions who tell us how to conduct ourselves in troubled times ("Axis of Fear," 1988, p. 31). To help public and private officials carry out their appointed duties, when all about chaos reigns, management experts assessed public apprehension over a variety of possible mishaps. Included in the survey were a wide assortment of snafus, ranging from the minor accident to the apocalyptic disaster. If the consultants are right, we have found other things to worry about.[1]

The ready PR mavens plotted our reactions to possible catastrophes across two axes. Along the vertical axis, emergency planners have charted how well informed the public is as to the nature of risk presented by a particular hazard; consequently, the havoc created by dynamite is extremely well known while electric fields are a relatively mysterious and indeterminate source of alarm. Along the horizontal axis, the public relations authorities have plotted dread (how scared do we feel?). On this axis, caffeine falls on the light side, and nuclear weapons (war), nuclear fallout, and nuclear reactor accidents inspire our greatest fears.

What is interesting about the chart is that while nuclear "accidents" of all stripes are what we seem to dread most, they are also possible mishaps that hold little unpredictability. The American public claim to be as familiar with the aftermath of a nuclear reactor meltdown as they are with the results of inappropriate tranquilizer usage. Nuclear fallout is as predictable a danger as the troubles which arise from heavy industry. Public confidence in their ability to accurately predict the end result of a farming accident, radioactive warfare, or the errant plunge of an inexperienced swimmer into the deep end has nuclear weapons (war) falling between tractors and home swimming pools. The idea of widespread radioactive alarm is much scarier, of course, than contemplating the harm that can come to a passel of unsupervised children playing around the swimming pool, but neither scenario requires much mental effort to fully imagine the exact nature of harm delivered to unwitting victims. Nuclear catastrophe is no longer an **unthinkable** event, no longer a disaster of such epic proportions that the consequences are **unimaginable**—the very dullest of minds have a clear and well-detailed picture of what will pass should the atom be loosed.

The most obvious reason why we have come to consider the atomic bomb a run-of-the-mill threat is that we have been subject to images beyond number of unleashed atomic power. We are inoculated from birth with vivid pictures of the ordinary apocalypse, having seen mushroom after poisonous mushroom blossom on television and in the movies. Just as those living next to airports and railroad tracks become inured to the scream of jets and the rumble of freight, losing the ability to notice the passage of heavy traffic, we too have become used to the sights and sounds of atomic explosions.

The most spectacular exhibitions grow dim with too frequent exposure. Far too many identical images have flashed before our eyes for the Bomb to retain its original impact. If the threat of annihilation is to carry any weight, we need images that carry a bite. Watching the toxic cloud explode yet again is like turning on the television, zipping through all the channels, and finding nothing on other than syndicated reruns that are no longer of interest to even the least demanding audience member.

The problem with atomic burnout is also caused by something other than just image fatigue. We are more than simply bored with pictures of gigantic fireballs. Along with lacking the energy to be moved by atomic imagery, many of those who have grown up with the Bomb have lost the ability to believe they can exert some control as to the direction power is used. Real power, whether evidenced in international accord, presidential fiat, state and federal legislation, or corporate decree—in fact, any expression of institutional authority whatsoever—is power expressed without our consent. The world may be getting safer as a few warheads are dismantled, but it is still extremely difficult to believe we can make the world a better place. As Lawrence Grossberg (1992) writes,

> For those generations that have grown up after the war . . . it is increasingly difficult to locate places where it is possible to care about something enough, to have enough faith that it matters, so that one can make a commitment to it and invest oneself in it. . . . The result is that it is ever more difficult to . . . put any faith in the taken for granted interpretation of the values of our lives and actions. . . . We are condemned to constantly try to make sense of our lives in structures that clearly contradict our experiences, and to invest in structures without any clear faith or even ability to distinguish their merit. (pp. 221-222)[2]

Paul Loeb (1986), covering similar territory, notes that

> the cynicism of the young . . . trusts neither experts nor truths. Rather, it denies the possibility of worthwhile human action and denigrates even attempts to link moral vision to day-to-day choices . . . bitter proof that nothing can be done. And by denying or trivializing consequences . . . it destroys links between individuals and the sense of continuity and meaning which might sustain risk and dissent. (pp. 252-254)

The virulent cynicism of the young becomes especially obvious when we return to the reception that youthful audiences accord the postwar films generated by unrestrained atomic energy. For this jaded group, the end of the world, as the bombs lay it all to waste, is a joke. It is difficult to imagine any contemporary audience entertaining the utterly perverse idea, the idea that drives almost all atomic films, that the world can be rescued from the brink by ordinary folks with good hearts.

What a deliriously insane counterpoint such films offer to contemporary attitudes about the power of ordinary people to effect change for the better. The more ingenuously such campy artifacts try to convince the audience of the possibility of moral success, the funnier the film. Perhaps the most laughable notion, the most ridiculous sentiment in the atomic horror film, is that not only can ordinary men and women find themselves in positions of real consequence but that we will, given this magical moment of civic opportunity, act in a morally and logically responsible manner to the benefit of all. Imagine imagining we can harness nuclear energy, bureaucratic power, unchecked scientific sovereigns, and the might of the armed forces and, having all the power in the world, actually make the Earth a better place.

Our inability to take control of the powers that be, our incapacity to believe we can make a difference, goes well beyond simply feeling cowed by hegemonic institutions that seem to owe us no fealty.[3] Even if we lived mercifully free of the possibility of exploding the planet, we would certainly continue to exist with extreme and debilitating doubt. Most of the stories we tell each other to make sense of our common situation are no longer all that credible. They have fallen apart as the world is continually being called into question, and the answers we half-heartedly exchange with one another in response to grand queries are usually found wanting.

Across a nearly infinite variety of discursive positions, from that of the academic elite to the spaces maintained by multitudinous fans of heartland rock, one can find endless signs of meaning's exhaustion. This is the age of credicide, or bardicide if one maintains a membership in the Modern Language Association, in which "nothing matters and so what if it did?"[4] To cope with life in a sea of disbelief, "it becomes almost a principle of survival there to hack up one's own moral substance so as not to be tempted to believe in some sort of 'one's own cause' " (Sloterdijk, 1983/1987, p. 302).

What almost anything of importance means is up for grabs. All master narratives, those touching stories we concoct in order to have mythic facts and factual myths we can trust and believe in as a collectivity, are under assault in nearly every quarter of the public arena. Unfortunately,

one of the hallmarks of this chaotic process of near universal deconstruc-
tion, wherein cherished beliefs fall apart or are torn asunder, is unrestrained violence.

The consumption of stable signifiers occurs under conditions that
approximate physical battles as once certain meaning systems are brutally
transfigured into vaguely memorable clumps of uncertainty. In these
perilous times,

> we live in the era of the double refusal of the beginning of philosophy: the
> refusal of the logocentric world of speech and reason; and the refusal of the
> deconstructed world of difference: Neither Socratic wonderment nor
> Derrida's *ecriture*, neither the dialectic nor the dialogue, but rather the
> pleasurable voyage under the sign of "viciousness for fun." (Kroker & Cook,
> 1986, p. 27)

There is no longer a single privileged site, resistant to the catastrophic
degradation of the signifier. Meaning leaks, like vital fluid, from all
objects. In a world of fatal indifference, the only important distinction
between signifiers is how rapidly each is being eviscerated. As all signifiers suppurate, the world becomes an increasingly difficult place to
endure. No meaning is safe from being gutted of significance, and we, in
turn, are left scrambling—incapable of locating a patch of secure ground
on which to stand. Collapse is inevitable; it is only a question of how
quickly loss of function is attained.

The traditional methods by which we attempt to reconcile men and
women with the world and one another do not work. Dialectic is
impossible when *aufgehoben,* the transcendent reconciliation and creation of new meaning, is as illusory a prospect as building architectural
marvels from bricks of water. As there is only debilitating difference, the
endless and fatiguing deferral of meaning, there can be no place or time
where meaning can exist free from assault. Dialogue is reduced to
nothing more than the exchange of equally pernicious counterargu-
ments—an act of mutually assured destruction.

There is no surcease from meaning's deflation. The only way to call a
halt to this process would be to impose agreement by irresistible force,
an action that makes one choose between fascism and terminal exhaustion.[5] If we are to survive in a world drained of life, it only seems
reasonable to act as enraged vandals and smash those few objects that
have not yet completely imploded. We are bound to be disappointed and

deceived by any set of symbols or individual signifiers that offers itself up as a stable reservoir of meaning—better to get them before they get us.

The need to destroy is readily demonstrated in the contemporary horror film where no venerated narrative truth or inspirational signifier survives for very long and none are allowed to expire quietly. Recent films do more than serve notice that these times differ in tone from earlier epochs. They murderously mock what has not aged gracefully. Meaning is throttled unmercifully—not left to peaceably slip away in a dignified manner—as horror films bloodily extinguish useless truism after useless truism.

In the latest horror film, humans are bumbling know-nothings who act with incredible stupidity. They really cannot succeed at much of anything. The easiest tasks are far beyond the capabilities of nearly everyone in the hapless cast. For people who do not like contemporary films, this is one of the signal breaks with the past that is particularly grating. The characters act irrationally, or if they perform logical actions with some seeming expertise, the film erupts in irrational mayhem that instantly and effortlessly cancels the pains taken by a logical protagonist.[6] The impossible is easy for a killer, and the logical practically impossible for everyone else.

The 1982 remake of *The Thing* is a perfect example of a film designed to disturb former audience members who still want to watch decent men triumph over evil in exciting but utterly predictable showdowns. *The Thing* is exquisitely constructed to deny every attempt, from the pathetic to the brilliant, on the part of its supposed protagonists to master their world. Every moment that would have assured success in earlier eras is marked by total failure. The film refuses to allow humans any success no matter what they do. The erstwhile protagonists still perform certain actions based on good reason, but they have no effect on their material circumstances as things get worse and worse. When they perform superbly, they die. When they screw up, they die. Whatever happens, they die.

Logic, or, more broadly, knowledge, refuses to operate the way it used to. What has occurred in the horror film is part of a more extensive deterioration of understanding. Knowledge as it is most widely conceived

is not only a set of denotive statements, far from it. It also includes notions of "know-how," "knowing how to live," "how to listen," (*savoir-faire, savoir-vivre, savoir-ecouter*), etc. . . . Knowledge, then, is a question of competence that goes beyond the simple determination and application of the criterion of truth, extending to the determination and application of the criteria of efficiency (technical qualification), of justice, and/or happiness (ethical wisdom), of the beauty of sound or color. . . . Understood in this way, knowledge is what makes someone capable of forming "good" denotative utterances, but also "good" prescriptive and "good" evaluative utterances. (Lyotard, 1984, p. 18)

If we follow Lyotard's expansive definition, we can begin to grasp just how much territory the contemporary horror film disrupts. Whatever we once considered useful, doable, or understandable, the horror film considers fair game. Nothing is spared in these harsh examinations. It cannot be overstressed that earlier eras took for granted and found security in types of comprehension that today's films dismiss with unprecedented malice. In comparison, previous films are amazingly sanguine about what humans are capable of doing. Our horror films regard the concept of efficacious knowledge, however it may be conceived, as a quaint chimera; they work, like deadly and incurable epistemological viruses, to destroy all we once took on faith.

The films of the 1950s were plainly devoted to asking the "question of competence" in relation to scientific inquiry. They critiqued, to a degree, the scientific establishment as well as the military-industrial complex while arguing for the inevitable successes of good men and women as evil and danger were driven from our land. They narrowed doubt to the sure question of whether or not we would successfully fetter the un-leashed atom. Frequently, the question of vanquishing the enemy was even more rigidly constrained to asking only how long until victory?— and at what cost?

No matter what terrible havoc a monster caused, normality would be restored in a couple of minutes as "a crazy plan that just might work" was miraculously realized. The easier it was to beat tremendous odds, with schemes derived from Rube Goldberg, the more apparent it became that all the films wanted to prove was that the answer to public misgivings was always a comforting affirmative. We only needed to venture more cautiously into the unknown and plan more intelligently as we seized the bright dream of tomorrow.

In Universal films, the cause of trouble was always some lone soul who learned, whether through accident or on purpose, horrible secrets and esoteric mysteries not meant for the general run of mankind. You could not blame innocent townsfolk for the damage caused by Dracula or the Wolfman. There was no mass accountability in Universal films when a monster's shadow was cast upon the land. Taboos, not all of a sexual nature, were trespassed as humans either blundered into peril, as in the Wolfman films, or heedlessly violated sanctuaries, as in the Mummy series. Only errant outsiders or community misfits who imperiously believed they were better than the rest of the community were to blame. In Dr. Frankenstein's case, he thought the rules meant for his inferiors in the medical school could not possibly apply to him. Had he only obeyed his unadventurous mentor, nothing remotely troubling would have happened.

When monsters appeared, it was up to the people to rid themselves of the beasts. No bloodless technocrats, bearing expensive leatherette attaché cases crammed with foolscap, or exceptionally humane bureaucrats, who knew when not to go by the book, would answer the prayers of besieged villagers. The people themselves, or a wise representative of the folk, laden with ancient lore, must extinguish the unwanted visitor. The means whereby these capable protagonists routed evil were always drawn from the past. No one had to do any last-minute guesswork to save the town and its worthy citizens. Follow ancient wisdom as you bond with brothers and sisters and the world is made safe. No monster could survive for long when people got organized and appealed to the lore of the ages for an expedient solution. In showing how people could save themselves and their close-knit communities, Universal films cautioned us to preserve the past if we wanted to preserve the future. The times ahead would be safe if we only remembered from whence we came.

In *Nosferatu*, what characters do when threatened is determined by the inner resources they possess. Sinless heroines like Ellen Harker were sure to save the household from dangerous guests. Jonathan fails because he is a weak and vain creature unable to muster up the self-reliance it would take to confront the vampire and save his family. He cannot be a divinely inspired hero or even a manly man as his bootstraps lie abandoned. His wife, mirroring Jonathan's faults with exemplary virtues, is an angelic heroine quite capable of making the necessary sacrifices. As in Universal films, the lore for exterminating the demons of the night is passed down from generation to generation; however, it is up to individuals to make their heritage work. The community is only peripherally involved in the struggle between good and evil.

When Jason comes to our town, what we gleaned from past experiences with horror films proves of little worth. The precepts that used to work and made our history a valuable reservoir are proven to be, in the very best light, wholly insufficient guides for further action. We cannot trust in the efficacy of fundamental truths bequeathed by our predecessors. None of the strategies previously examined in the history of horror work any longer. Individual virtue, collective endeavor, and scientific progress come to absolutely nothing. If you learned about horror films in a different age, what you see on the screen now is almost unimaginably depressing. The level of violence, staggeringly vicious cynicism, and withering prospects for the future are truly shocking.

None of these things bother today's audiences. They understand, even revel, in bloody demonstrations of just how utterly without value any sort of knowledge truly is. Today, knowledge of how things work may help you become champion in an inconsequential game of Trivial Pursuit®, but it will only leave you frustrated if used for greater gain. Knowing what is, having a clear picture of the world, and making appropriate and necessary changes in how the world is run based on that knowledge is a herculean task of fearsome difficulty. The more you learn, the more likely you are to become depressed in the face of your own overwhelming impotence.

As horror accelerates in its savagery, finding no barriers to absolute pessimism, and the camera moves closer to examine the kill, our fascination with extinction and the extermination of the future grows ever more obsessive.[7] All doubts are voiced, explored, and verified with monstrous precision. There are no limits that a horror film may not trespass, nothing deemed so unfit no body could bear it. In a culture in crisis, there is no refuge for platitudes; impregnable truths, once assuredly permanent cornerstones of social wisdom, crash and burn in films that are shockingly profane.

Accordingly, to fully appreciate cinematic terrorism, the audience has resigned itself to the rarefied pleasures of horror without hope. We need to cease trying to read hacked torsos for conventional morals, like nattering seers perched over chicken entrails, and embrace the surcease of life with meaning. Along with forgetting to interpret too deeply, we need a liberal dose of schadenfreude (better those unlucky stiffs than me) to understand mass pleasure in excessive destruction.[8] Audiences have dropped the once conventional taste for significant struggle (death with meaning) and taken up certain extermination as fun. Since the end is inevitable, one may as well buy a jumbo box of buttered popcorn and herald its arrival with like-minded strangers.

The spectacle of death, a uniquely brutal conjunction between lack of faith in knowledge and the special effects machinery that can make any vision a marvelous screen reality, only confirms common experience.[9] The further special effects technicians go in their work to realistically abuse the body, the closer they come to flaying real flesh, the more appreciative the audience becomes. Not only does the center no longer hold, nor do inviolate beliefs survive in this world, but even the body, the form with which we are presumably most familiar, cannot hold itself together.[10] Thus the human body, our most precious sac, achieves a pittance of worth only when it is reduced to a weeping pile of scattered exuviate.[11]

Splatter aims to unfold the body in exacting surgical splendor and render the human corpse in toto through the indecency of unremittingly refined detail. Here, under this new regime of horrific representation, the exceedingly realistic construction, the perfectly broken body, is the most interesting and most vital special effect in any contemporary horror film. The captivating confrontation with the resplendently appointed corpse, all but indistinguishable from an actual dead body, provides the horror film's moment of truth, the instant when we decide, if the blood and bitten flesh are real enough, that this is a "good" horror film.

To paraphrase French philosophe Jean Baudrillard, who describes a similar encounter with hyper-real sculpture of the human figure in "What Are You Doing After the Orgy?," the scrupulously well-detailed object, the thing that can easily be mistaken for the real thing, is an object of endless fascination that collects, in its infinite detail the grain, or feel, of reality itself (Baudrillard, 1983, p. 43). And, in a horror film, if the represented flesh is real enough, then it forms the ground from which to experience the horror film as the encapsulation of everyday life. The incredible viscerality of insulted flesh is, like Baudrillard's human dummies, "a frozen moment when everyone sees what is on the end of every fork" (Burroughs, 1959, p. xxxviii).[12]

Certainly, there is some measure of public censure for these vicious displays; not everyone is convinced this is fit mass entertainment. Yet the longer and louder horror's detractors lament popular taste, the more evident it is that gore is an entrenched cultural pleasure.[13] In a nation that buys Charles Manson CDs, pays art patron prices for John Wayne Gacy clown paintings, and makes television hits of real-life crime shows detailed as autopsies, the popularity of the slash-and-hack film is neither irregular nor surprising.[14] Those who would dismiss this turn as an isolated moment of barbaric indulgence are testament to the fact that all cultural movements have been tailed by some nostalgic laggards clinging hardily to retrograde impossibility.[15]

To more fully grasp just how bad things have gotten, to reach an adequate understanding of how ruthlessly negative contemporary horror films are, we need to examine one of our most disparaged and beloved cultural contemporary icons. We need to meet Jason.[16] The indefatigable nightstalker and mass-cult star has, along with a select handful of other worthies, dominated the horror genre for the past 15 years. His star vehicle, the *Friday the 13th* series (totaling nine identical films), featuring our hero monomaniacally slaughtering countless anonymous teens, has brought in millions in ticket receipts and video rentals while producing many, many inferior and superior spin-offs.[17]

With nothing more in his favor than gutting teens in enormous multitudes, Jason has become an American institution. What is exceptionally interesting about Jason's stardom is that it is the persona who is popular and not the actor or a combination of actor and character.[18] Any large human who can don a goalie mask and wield something sharp can play Jason. Jason is a cipher; a stumbling mute who lurches through his appearances without benefit of voice or personalized gestures. He is a murderous blank, well-known and well-regarded for killing in great numbers, and being in turn unkillable. That is all.

Plucking an axe murderer from a cheap B-movie and transforming him into a worldwide icon of human futility is more than just a little shared black humor among the simple minions. Jason, as well-known as any prominent American personality, ranks among the foremost of all popular signs embodying meaning's demise.[19] It should be clear that as Jason sweeps his way through human detritus (and is made a megastar for his trouble) the audience appreciates him in ways other nasty creatures previously examined were not. When his star radiates more intensely than other stellar worthies, its brilliance is stoked by conventional notions of instrumental knowledge, group survival, and a livable future.

Jason's first feature commences with a standard Universal opening shot. The full moon hangs low and bright as ominous clouds, ostensibly dire portents, flow across the face of the luminous icon.[20] The camera descends from the clouds and falls upon a group of freshly scrubbed and well-groomed camp counselors singing "Tom Dooley" and other cheery folk songs around a communal fire. A subtitle informs us the place is Camp Crystal Lake and the time is 1958. The teens' too comely appearance (they could have been the models from whom Ken and Barbie were sculpted) underlines their status as stale clichés. Clearly, by starting in the late 1950s with this trite picture of teenage relics at the end of the Atomic Age, *Friday the 13th* is ridiculing scenarios created following the leveling of Hiroshima. The characters are thin, even by the standards of the postwar era, and the events that ensue would never have appeared in an atomic horror film. Such displays would have been literally unimaginable for the audiences and producers of those passé efforts.

Two of the advisors leave the hootenanny for a petting session. The duo rush into a nearby loft, begin kissing, and die. The boy is killed first, stabbed deep in the lower abdomen. The terrified girl is then pursued briefly about the tight loft as she tries to evade her adversary. She is soon caught in a death's-head close-up that goes white with her piercing last scream. We do not get to see where the fatal blow fell as her image fades to nothing.

A new age has begun. One minute or so of brutal death within a known locale, presaging the endless carnage to come, is all the meager exposition necessary to a contemporary shocker. As soon as audiences are familiar with the everyday arena in which violence is to fall, the blood can begin to flow. Considering how heavily such films rely on generic locations, banal and overly familiar icons signifying the homogenization of space, it does not take long for the axe to drop.

Following the deaths of the dated teens, the film moves to the present. The first contemporary victim is a sweet young woman named Annie who has come to Camp Crystal Lake to take a job as the head cook of the kiddie resort. Annie has hitchhiked to Crystal Lake and is either rather stupid or naive beyond incredulity for depending on the specious kindness of strangers. Not many women, excepting those with impaired mental faculties, are unfamiliar with the innumerable dangers facing unescorted females who thumb for rides along the nation's hazardous interstate transportation system. Inexplicably, Annie must not have heard that giving rides to lone women is a favorite pastime of industrious serial killers. And if, contrary to all appearances, Annie is aware that she makes a promising target, then she lacks the uncompromising hard edge necessary to survive as a hitchhiker. She is too pleasant a passenger, ready to converse, eager to share her thoughts, and learn a little from her fellow wayfarers as she journeys along life's winding path. In a less brutal genre she would have been a Madonna figure or Innocent, too good for this harsh vale of fears.

We never learn for certain if Annie is intellectually suspect or a tough kid who masks her resilient interior with abundant common courtesy, as her ruthless destruction follows close upon her introduction to the audience. There is, however, a strong possibility she is stupid, as a friendly truck driver tells Annie that she and people like her have "heads full of rocks." He knows that anyone who would venture out to Camp Crystal Lake is a "dumb kid." Annie refuses to listen, calling him an "American original" when she hears him tell of the Camp's infamous history. For Annie, his blunt warnings of sure trouble are a welcome sign that the backwoods locals are still superstitious folk untouched by urban cynicism. His queer alarm goes blithely unheeded, read simply as an authentic experience of real Americana by a doomed child.

Annie is also warned not to venture out to Camp Crystal Lake by the aged village idiot/alcoholic, Ralph.[21] She opts to neglect this bit of advice as well. Finally, after two calls to abandon her journey, Annie is killed when a free ride, a little uncommon courtesy, turns costly. She is mindlessly chattering to her unseen escort about the deep love she feels for little children, summer camp, and other inconsequential matters that make a short life pleasurable when she notices the driver has sped past the Camp Crystal Lake turnoff. In a futile effort to preserve body and soul, Annie throws herself from the speeding vehicle, and, slightly injured, runs pell-mell through the woods. The dogged killer pursues her, listens to her beg for her life, and slashes her throat. Annie's eyes bulge with terror and disbelief as her life quickly dribbles down her shirt. The camera holds fast throughout the attack, in a medium close-up, as the skin across her pale throat noiselessly parts and precious blood issues forth.

The rest of *Friday the 13th* is devoted to the collapse of community as Jason mows his way through the remainder of Camp Crystal Lake's new employees. Up until the moment the focus of the film shifts from Annie's drained corpse and the bodies of the dated teens to the annihilation of the recently assembled camp staff, it might have been possible the first murders were a singular moment of cinematic excess; however, when brilliantly outlined death follows luminous death, the audience learns that Annie's erasure and the deaths of the 1950s kids are not horror faux pas made by overenthusiastic filmmakers dizzied with the possibilities afforded by breakthroughs in special effects technology.

In earlier moments of horror history, a singularly grotesque death would have been the linchpin around which the entire narrative was organized. A monstrous murder would have set the central mystery in motion. Today, death is no longer the opening bit of film excess that provides a horror narrative's initial impetus. We know that death is all around us, that there is nothing mysterious about death; however, the manner in which untold victims perish is of some interest to the audience. Today, the spectacle of endless death, the form of death is, in and of itself, the story.[22]

Following the knifing of Annie, we are summarily introduced to each member of the Camp Crystal Lake staff. They are busy getting the time-worn facilities into shape before the summer season commences. As each employee goes about his or her assigned chores, we are witness to a counterfeit performance of teamwork. The progress the happy campers make as they refurbish the run-down site is a terribly misleading display. Teamwork and community mean nothing if all you are capable of doing as a bonded group is restoring a couple of weather-beaten shacks and pruning an overgrown archery range. Once forced to respond to an attack, our erstwhile protagonists are subject to an "almost complete breakdown of even the most minimal forms of social solidarity. With charity for others guaranteeing only one's own death, friend shunned friend, neighbors acted towards one another on the basis of a ruthless calculus of self-interest" (Kroker & Kroker, 1987, p. 13). At the first sign of danger, the crew is fractured into a bunch of helpless and weak individuals who have no hope of survival.

As the audience impatiently waits for Jason to get busy, the cast is allowed a brief reprieve and given a moment to distinguish themselves via the exhibition of some superficial character traits. In tiny fragments of inane dialogue, cast members lay some tenuous claim to one or perhaps two of the following broad qualities: They are funny, sexy, shy, artistic, and so on. Like World War II flying films featuring a Detroit Black, a Brooklyn Italian, a Peorian WASP, and a Bronx Jew piloting a B-52 on a dangerous, vitally important mission, anonymous ensemble casts divided with broad demographic or psychological traits are pasteboard constructions designed to rapidly orient the audience within a compact circle of well-known dispositions. Everyone holds something in common with the group on-screen even if we cannot, with any precision whatsoever, demonstrate what glaring qualities we so obviously share with the clichés projected before us.

Long ago, the hurried establishment of phantom identities was forgivable as soon as solitary persons forged unyielding links. They consequently triumphed as a melded unit in uplifting films where the group endured through the exploitation of individual skills made immeasurably stronger when synergistically combined with the expertise of other members. An unshakeable unity, a vastly reassuring solidarity, underwritten with a conscious appreciation for communitarian values, allows stereotypical characters to survive any assault propagated by outside agents.

Friday the 13th operates along identical lines until it comes time for the group to emerge triumphant. The film takes the nascent community, the one we have assumed through years of similar cinematic experiences must of necessity prevail, and crushes it. Victims, gifted or without special talents, number so many bags of muscle and viscera for Jason to slash to pieces. Where we had expected to see bonds gel and unbounded love for the unit develop, only hot blood runs as the impotent community's guts and brains are sprayed across Camp Crystal Lake. Jason does more than prevent individuals from coalescing into communal regiments; lowly individuals cannot even keep skin on bone. Gristle and bits of bone-speckled flesh are capable of nothing more than falling to the floor, to perhaps find some measure of utility in providing food for passing insects and other hungry bottom feeders.

Even though the bodies of the counselors are slated to be treated as animated litter, the film makes a slight attempt to assay the moral nature of those about to be cut and to, perhaps, justify their foregone obliteration. Has the accursed community earned Jason's attention? Have they, like Jonathan and Dr. Frankenstein, committed dubious acts for which they must now suffer some great expiation? And if the camp counselors are guilty of some malfeasance, is the particularly vicious punishment meted out to them deserved?

The film's cursory evaluation of the moral mettle of the cast is critical but not unduly condemnatory. The majority of the kids are portrayed as vapid and selfish, but most ethical systems would leave such foolishly egotistical subjects corporeally intact as their irksome, but relatively insubstantial, sins do not seem to merit the final penalty of death. And even as we watch some of the cast go about their lives with less than Christian charity, many of the murdered were exemplary in their behavior toward others. Annie, for one, was a kindly soul who (before she had her delicate throat slit) did no wrong and was, moreover, an altogether delightful traveling companion. Ralph, the dipsomaniac oracle (killed by Jason early in the following sequel), did his best to help the beleaguered staff, going so far as to laboriously peddle an antiquated bicycle out to the distant camp and alert the disbelieving counselors to their terrible lot. The good are dismembered along with those who are weak in the face of temptation, as cast members who do not commit venal little torts find a falling hatchet cleaving their fragile skulls.

The notion of justice, however stern, presumes a rational and orderly dispensation of punishment. One might be able to manage the argument that there is a steep price for sin, if only the heavy penalty of savage death were limited to those whose actions are in significant conflict with religious or civic doctrine; however, the acts perpetrated by the errant counselors are at once too banal and Jason's activities too ferocious to be equated on any scale of judgment. No religion, order of law, or exacting system of ethical conduct treats each and every wrong with a knife to the head. You cannot attempt to read Jason and the extensive damage he does to his unwitting victims as if he were a particularly zealous reformer and his handiwork the serious toll levied for being bad. *Friday the 13th* has sloughed off all moral strictures: There are no lessons to learn, no terrible sins to avoid, as black violence splatters across the screen subsuming everything and everyone to come in contact with irrational menace. Jason is not a potent reminder that we should scrupulously avoid all sin—Jason is a random event.[23]

The counselors bear no responsibility for their gruesome passing. They have not been tempted by secret knowledge. They have not acted rashly and gone where no man or woman should tread and they have not really committed any cardinal sins. Their fatal mistake lay in occupying the wrong space at the wrong time. Unfortunately, there are no unmistakable signs informing the protagonists how to recognize what constitutes an inappropriate space or time. In effect, *Friday the 13th* demonstrates that any place in the world may be transformed into the wrong place at any time. The many dead had no choice but to perish having, through no fault of their own, come to Camp Crystal Lake at an inopportune moment.[24]

Life, whether lived in good faith or bad, does not have a chance. Nothing the counselors do will have the least effect on the ceaseless flight of Jason's gigantic blade. Accordingly, feeble human lives and inconsequential escape attempts are experienced as so much tiresome screen filler. When all individual lives are fodder, it is, of course, ludicrous to even bother wondering how the on-screen community will manage to battle the monster. The only thing that counts in such films is how Jason will dispatch the next victim. Will it be a pitchfork to the gut, sledge to the head, or rusty wire to the neck? How did they live? Who cares? Life this cheap cannot be examined too closely, and the whole enterprise is damned from the start anyway. How did they die? Now **that's** an excellent question![25] Jason drove an enormous stainless steel trident through his skinny neck and pulsing carotid artery—it was an incredible effect.

The question of whose neck that arrow pierced is of interest only to the horror film tyro. Personality, the unique matrix of individual identity, is an insignificant trifle. To enjoy contemporary horror, it is best to divest oneself of any hopeful interest in character as all extant protagonists are nothing more than thinly drawn stereotypes whose time is soon. Only when inscribed with Jason's signature do bodies acquire any meaningful or notable mark of difference. Only in death, reduced to shattered viscera, do the victims become truly worthy of our undivided attention.

In the end, when these simple characters are destroyed with utterly realistic and ultraviolent special effects, when these insubstantial collections of entirely fatuous traits are driven to worthless dust, they decompose as completely convincing representatives of select victims drawn from the faceless masses. One of the ways *Friday the 13th* and many other slasher and gore films work to make us accept empty characters as veracious representations is by denying the victims last names. Failing to write out entire names for the dead, an oversight we could attribute to laziness, ineptitude, or cheap cynicism on the part of the screenwriters, actually works to make a stronger film. No complete names, a positive signal of inauthentic, low-budget filmmaking (authentic fictions always draft complete signatures), helps to consolidate the commonalities between the seated bodies and the bodies displayed before them.[26]

Fingering the dead, on a first-name basis, makes it impossible to avoid the presentiment of knowing the characters.[27] The film pressures the audience to presume they know these people quite well, so that when Jason strikes it is Annie, Ned, Bill, Alice, or Ralph who is killed and not some made-up character with a fictionalized name propped up by a deep narrative cover. When you may only refer to them by Christian names, you are forced to use language appropriate to close social settings. Of course, these are not real people but simply a small set of shallow character traits wound together by a common proper noun. With just an informal appellation, the practically anonymous dead are transformed into close companions and the writers do not even have to bother with constructing a convincing backstory.

Still, the notion of unworkable community is too theoretical at this juncture. We need to peer closer at what the audience so enjoys in new horror—the visceral end of the contemporary community and the resplendent generation of dead meat.

Victim 1—Annie. Annie, as previously discussed, is relentlessly pursued through the claustrophobic woods until cornered against a mature tree and slashed across the throat. The severed skin slowly splits, as Annie takes her last gulp of air, disgorging life in a spectacular shot that nicely captures Annie's stricken throat vomiting forth a wave of crimson gore.

Victim 2—Ned. Ned's ashen corpse is disclosed in a slow upward tilt away from a pair of distracted lovers. In a move that showcases just how close death is to unknowing protagonists, we are privy to a mutually satisfying carnal embrace between two future victims immediately prior to the shot of Ned's gaping throat. He has been left displayed atop a soiled mattress on a cheap bunk bed above the engrossed lovers. When the camera ceases to rise, we are granted a medium close-up of Ned's broken larynx. The camera stays fixed until we could furnish an anatomically correct description of Jason's meticulous handiwork.

Victim 3—Jack. Jack lies in the bottom bed, unaware of the gruesome mess above, lazing in postorgasmic rapture. He lights a cigarette or joint and inhales deeply with great pleasure. As Jack relishes his smoke, a hand springs from underneath the bed and holds Jack's head immobile. A shifting bump in Jack's skin appears just above the breastplate as his eyes bulge from their sockets. The mound erupts, and a barbed hunting arrow surfaces from Jack's throat. Dark blood leaps about the exit wound, creating a gory fountain. The arrow twists in the hole, a final gratuitous exhibition, before the film moves on to examine more bodies.

Victim 4—Marcie. Marcie is in the counselors' bathroom, voiding her bladder after making love to the presently deceased Jack. She beams with happiness, smiling to herself as she appears to recollect her recent erotic encounter, before reading aloud a moronic line of scatological graffiti scrawled on the stall wall. She washes up and, while performing her ablutions, does a remarkably poor impression of Katharine Hepburn in the mirror above the sink. Clearly, Marcie could not be more content as she amuses herself with weak humor that could only appeal to an already very elated individual.

She hears something and assumes Ned or Jack is teasing her. Mistakenly believing she is involved in a harmless game of hide and seek, Marcie tears open plastic shower curtains, gleefully shouting "Ollie, Ollie, Oxen Free." She spins away from yet another empty shower stall and an axe threatens to come crashing down into her upturned face. The weapon, of course, creases her head from hairline to nostrils.

Victim 5—Brenda. After washing up in the same bathroom where Marcie died, Brenda hears some faint noises. The nondescript noises are finally resolved as tiny cries for help. In the teeming rain, Brenda selflessly traces the mysterious voice to the archery range where she is paralyzed by blinding lights. She screams, and the last surviving counselors, Bill and Alice, go to look for her.

We will not see Brenda's riddled corpse until it is thrown by Jason through a window behind which Alice has barricaded herself. This may be the most ignominious abuse of human flesh in the entire film, as the body of one victim is used to further an attack on another companion.

Victim 6—Steve. Steve, the smug camp owner and ostensible authority figure, who refers to his (now mostly dead) employees as "babes in the woods," returns to Camp Crystal Lake to tuck the crew into bed after a night in town. He is slightly worried about the safety of his tenderfoot charges as a violent thunderstorm has pummeled the area all evening. He forthrightly strides into camp, believing himself master of all the diverse recreational facilities arrayed before him, and has a knife thrust into his unprotected belly.

Victim 7—Bill. Bill's corpse is discovered by Alice, the last remaining camp counselor to still respire, mounted on the inside of a cabin door fashioned with weathered planks. Bill has been nailed to the door with arrows running through his neck, left eye, abdomen, and groin. Drenched in blood, the camera moves in on the wet corpse for a very tight close-up, enabling the audience to estimate just how much blood has flowed from the multiple entry wounds located throughout Bill's posted carcass.

Victim 8—Mrs. Voorhees, Jason's Mom and Jason's malevolent agent in the first *Friday the 13th.*

Throughout this chapter Jason has been referred to as a he. I have used the male pronoun as Jason is a male name and the narrative compels us, until the film concludes, to identify Jason as a male. Except for a few scattered shots of unsexed hands guiding a variety of weapons through vulnerable flesh, we never catch a glimpse of the killer's face or body as the first nine teens are butchered. Without a good shot of the monster it seems natural, following venerable tradition, to assume the killer is a male.

Only in the penultimate climax does the audience discover that Jason's spirit has used his mother's body to cleanse the camp of human beings; yet it would be wrong to call Jason a she—especially when, after *Friday the 13th* concludes, Jason will do most of his lonely work with his own form, although other bodies will, from time to time, don the enigmatic mask and be transformed into a murderous black hole.[28]

Jason is neither male nor female: Jason is really an it. He has no identity beyond the blank hockey mask that carries no gender markings. A hard plastic shield with nothing more than black ports, empty cavities that allow the thing to see and breathe as it kills, is not truly a face. The faceless mask, equipped with tiny circles for selecting targets, small dots for nostrils, and a thin rectangular slit representing a mouth, is the human face horribly reduced to a plane of purely vicious instrumentality. No humans, even the most horribly scarred burn casualties, have such blank faces. The most afflicted of medical patients retain recognizably human features that can form a host of complex expressions. The antihuman mask, so denatured from an actual human visage, is a wholly vacant signifier that completely absorbs anything that speaks of human understanding. Jason can express nothing and his mask hides nothing, as there is only meaningless death behind the blank holes.

Humans finally get a crack at Jason when Alice and Mrs. Voorhees, animated by the spirit of Jason, face off. Knowing Jason's mother is responsible for the evening's carnage, Alice bludgeons Mrs. Voorhees in the arm with a handy fire poker. Mrs. Voorhees, momentarily disabled with a minor flesh wound in her upper right arm, collapses to the floor. Alice whacks her on the back for good measure, drops her trusty club, and flees.

These little blows are not enough to bring the night's festivities to a close as Mrs. Voorhees returns to consciousness and chases Alice about the bloody camp. Mrs. Voorhees gets clobbered with a blackened iron frying pan (shades of a Warner Brothers cartoon gone wrong) before she is finally decapitated in slow motion. Alice wrestles Jason's machete away from the possessed nurturer and removes her head in the most dramatic murder in the film. As the slow blade cuts from left to right, Mrs. Voorhees' head leisurely takes leave from her neck providing as detailed a picture of the various parts that comprise the area between torso and head as can be found in any edition of *Gray's Anatomy*. The loosed head describes an easy arc through the air and plops gently in the soft sand.

The final indignity of *Friday the 13th* leaves the audience with the image of the single surviving "protagonist" committing the most graphic act of violence in an already exceptionally violent film. Alice is, after her overlong evening of torture, completely justified in handing out the worst punishment she desires to Jason's envoy; yet there is something troubling in having the protagonist seem to conquer in an action more barbaric than any killing stroke taken by Jason. In filming the momentary victory of Alice with the vivid clarity only advanced special effects can provide, Alice not only seems to defeat Jason, she becomes more bloodthirsty than the monster. Jason killed more people than Alice, but Alice wielded her weapon as if she were the champion of excessive force and the end of Mrs. Voorhees merely a self-aggrandizing demonstration of the most spectacular way to eradicate bodies.

This situation is, of course, temporary; Alice's elevated status will quickly plummet. The end of Mrs. Voorhees is a terrible joke. Alice is not worse than Jason, despite the grand beheading—and she has not defeated the menace. Fans know that, howsoever a victim may avenge her- or himself, Jason will return and make any protagonist regret she ever put up a struggle. Alice probably would have been better off trading places with the late Mrs. Voorhees and dying free from impossible hope. Instead, she will live long enough to learn hope again and find her renewed trust in the future brutally vanquished.

Victim 9—Alice. Alice blanks out and enters an implosive fugue state occasioned by suffering an extended period of too much stress. The film lenses have been draped with gauze or smeared with Vaseline® to underscore that for the time being Alice has sought retreat in some quiet corner of her mind. In her lovely dream, a brilliant new day has dawned and Alice has escaped the bloodied land by taking refuge in a canoe that has drifted to the center of Lake Crystal. She mindlessly dangles her hand in the calming waters far from the black ground of the camp. The world has been restored to normality until the quiescent waters break and Jason doggedly attempts to bring Alice down to the lake bed. Despite the diversion of misted lenses and the recognition that a flight from reality might not be such a bad idea, at this point the final climax is not really a peaceful meditation turned nightmare. Jason is alive.

When Alice next awakes, in a secure hospital bed, surrounded by the hapless authorities who failed to rush to her side and, in reality, could never have come to her aid, she asks the Crystal Lake Chief of Police about the butchered others and Jason. She knows her companions are all dead but cannot yet bring herself to acknowledge the vast dimensions of the destruction in which she has played such a central role. They tell her the staff has perished and there is no Jason. *Friday the 13th* is now over, although in a rushed release, *Friday the 13th, Part II*, Alice swiftly joins her condemned co-workers.

After a brief reprise of *Part I*, the sequel begins with Alice sleeping. Her nap, punctuated with unsettling dreams of Jason, ends when she receives a phone call from her concerned mother. In an action that speaks of taking responsibility for her own well-being and mental health, Alice tells her overwrought and possibly domineering mother not to fret. She merely needs healing time alone to recover from the turmoil and bloodshed she inadvertently witnessed.

In reassuring her mother, it is immediately apparent that Alice has not learned from her dreadful experience at Camp Crystal Lake. Alice has failed to realize she has no control over her destiny when Jason wants to destroy another body. In a few minutes, her head will be pierced with an ice pick driven through her skull just a bit above the right temple.

Upon ringing off with mother, Alice senses something is out of sorts. Obviously, she does not think it could be Jason redux or she would be quick to abandon the house. Suddenly, Alice is surprised and relieved when her hungry orange-and-white kitten leaps through an open window into the kitchen. Freed from worry, Alice opens the packed refrigerator to feed her famished pet. She cracks the door and screams as Mrs. Voorhees's severed head greets her from inside. Jason steps up behind Alice and kills her, proving that no one can escape and no one can learn anything from an encounter with present-day visions of the horrible. Momentary survivors are still doomed, and the future lasts only as long as it takes an unconquerable killer to decide who will be the next victim.[29]

While the new horror rips the flesh from our bodies, it also takes something else once vitally common to feeling human. Once upon a time, we were certain life had some precious value: no longer. Once upon a time, we were certain the grotesque forms on the screen had no connection to the lives we lived away from the theater: no longer. Under the transcendental model, we could encompass the meaning of our monsters within a carefully policed preserve. The transcendentalists kept us blissfully free from the horrible realization that the worst monsters are created under monstrous conditions of existence.

When *Nosferatu* argued for the preservation of life, within the context of unquestionably valuable domestic arrangements, the audience did not disagree. When Universal films examined the meaning of good, all the while never presuming that the entirety of human experience lacked worth, few found their conclusions wanting. The Big Beasts of the 1950s left us mildly shaken, without undermining our faith in the possibility of good works arising from any sector of human endeavor. Errors, even on an unprecedented scale, might be made, but in the end we would see our way clear. Today, the audience for contemporary horror films lies bereft of such pitiful fancies. Every response made in the face of trouble is of no value. Life only achieves a miserable pittance of worth when destroyed as part of a special effect. All that really matters is how much visual interest a foul, dismembered corpse (our body double) provides splattered across the big screen.

We are idiots living only to perish in deaths made memorable by their sound and fury. Thankfully, horror films keep us secure against the threat of hope.

Notes

1. In fall 1992, the Fox Network, whose only concern seems to be cornering the youth market, introduced "Woops," a postapocalyptic sitcom to their new lineup. "Woops" is standard sitcom fare except for the fact that the rest of the world is gone. This dilemma does not, of course, get in the way of the jokes.

2. It is not happenstance that the 1992 Clinton for President campaign used "Don't Stop" by Fleetwood Mac as its campaign song. Like a glad advocate of Norman Vincent Peale, the stirring chorus urges the blue listener not to give up on the future. As soon as Bill Clinton was elected, however, Democratic spin doctors worked to deflate any rash voter expectation that happy days would, in short order, be here again.

The Perot campaign used Patsy Cline's "Crazy" as its theme. If you really believed that Mr. Perot would deliver us from the Debt and restore prosperity to all, you had to be, as even the candidate himself admitted, "crazy."

3. See E. J. Dionne (1991) for the reasons behind mass apathy in regards to politics. In the same vein, see William Greider (1992) for a description of what the people already, at least intuitively, know.

4. The Modern Language Association has devoted many hours of conference time to the question of literary authority, the necessity, for some, to gut the canon and the death of the author. The phrase "nothing matters" comes from populist rocker John Cougar Mellencamp's album title *Nothing Matters & What if It Did*. Mellencamp, who projects himself as a stolid Hoosier with electric guitar talking common sense, has sold a lot of records concerned with the end of community.

5. Witness the impressive slate of books devoted to upbraiding the academy for failing to promote a universal curriculum. The response of most conservative critics to the dilemma of consensus over what constitutes a worthwhile university education is to argue that a standard curriculum should be enforced. See William J. Bennett (1984, 1992), Allen Bloom (1987), David Bromwich (1992), Lynne Cheney (1988), Dinesh D'Souza (1991), and Roger Kimball (1990).

6. For this reason, never take sides in a contemporary horror film. See *Candyman* (1992), wherein a plucky graduate student gamely fights both urban and supernatural predators to save her skin and soul. After surviving extraordinary assaults and winning our admiration, the "heroine" discovers, in the final moments of the film, that she is the true source of all evil.

7. Savage pleasure in destruction has even overtaken the game show. In *Trashed*, a new MTV show, contestants answer trivia questions in order to see their opponents' favorite possessions destroyed. College diplomas, concert memorabilia, special presents from Mom, and the like are blown up, chainsawed, blowtorched, and so forth as the players battle to win.

8. We need to believe, as physician and writer Thomas Seltzer does, that "the most beautiful sentence in the English language" is "There but for the grace of God go I" (quoted in Cheever, 1992).

9. The very practices that can no longer evoke strong feelings of security and optimism in the future, have been channeled into an arena of production where they are demonstrably effective. We can create convincing images of our demise with the selfsame technology that cannot inspire a future.

10. Think of the statement "I know it better than the back of my hand." That which we most completely understand, that which cannot be known more fully, we compare to the certain grasp we have of our own flesh.

11. See the *Hellraiser* films (1987, 1988, 1992). In this series, victims actively search out monsters who specialize in truly innovative, cutting-edge torture. Pinhead, the master of pain, a hero who knows how to creatively refashion weeping flesh, is now a favorite of horror fans.

12. Not surprising, it took a horror director (David Cronenberg) with a knack for filming the disintegration of flesh to bring William Burroughs's notoriously unfilmable *Naked Lunch* (1992) to the screen.

13. A Halloween episode of *The Cosby Show* dramatically made this point when Cliff brought home some goodies to entertain the kids. He circled the family around him and proceeded to dip into his bag of tricks. He eagerly brandished a rubber spider and other spooky items he had purchased for holiday fun and waited for his children to scream. They didn't do anything until Cliff began to unpack a power drill he had also purchased at the hardware store. Finally, he got a reaction from his previously blasé children. Even Cosby, perhaps the best television Dad of the past decade, understands that Jason's modus operandi matters when it comes to fright.

Cosby is not the only sitcom to use gore. *Roseanne* and *The Simpsons* both have annual Halloween shows that feature gore. Halloween is the favorite holiday of the Connors;

consequently, they go all out in their attempts to gross each other out with displays of graphic bloodletting that help promote family unity. The Simpsons also enjoy bloody mayhem and the destruction of the body. The 1993 Halloween show included an homage to *The Night of the Living Dead* in which all the citizens of Springfield, the Simpsons' hometown, were turned into flesh-eating zombies. Of course, the only way to kill the Springfield undead was to blow their diseased brains out of their animated heads. This was a task that Homer, the Simpsons patriarch, found particularly gratifying.

The Simpsons also includes, as a running commentary on the state of children's animation, the ultraviolent cartoon *The Itchy and Scratchy Show.* This parody of Tom and Jerry cartoons takes particular delight in showcasing the dismemberment of Scratchy the cat at every available opportunity.

14. According to Chuck Shepherd (1992), author of "News of the Weird," a weekly compendium of macabre news notes, we can now play serial murderer:

> In August, Tobias Allen of Seattle, Wash., a pen pal of convicted murderer John Wayne Gacy, released for sale his new board game Serial Killer (suggested price $49.95). The players make choices as to high-risk or low-risk killings (e.g., killing a politician or street person, respectively), and plastic babies are game pieces representing victims. The game is packaged in a body bag. (p. 5)

15. Even action films are no longer content to simply show their heroes emerge triumphant in exciting dustups. When an action hero battles the minions of evil today, justice must be administered to the body of the evildoer. In a discussion of Steven Seagal's work as a busy protagonist, Michael Sragow (1992) notes that

> what characterizes his combat scenes is an utter willingness to bend, fold, and mutilate the human body: eyes are thumbed back into the brain; knives and other utensils are shoved straight into the skull; limbs aren't just broken but shorn. Chekhov said that if you put a gun on the wall in the first act it has to go off in the third. In a Seagal movie, each act has the equivalent of the gun on the wall—the most gruesome one in *Under Siege* (1992) is a jigsaw—and you don't have to wait long for it to be used. (pp. 130-131; reprinted by permission, © 1992 Michael Sragow. Originally in *The New Yorker*)

16. I have opted to discuss Jason simply because he is exceedingly well known. There are, however, countless other shockers one could examine to reach similar conclusions about the nature of the contemporary horror film. In a recent, and admittedly incomplete, survey of recent horror releases, Anthony C. Ferrante (1992) listed over 100 gore films issued during the 1980s. He apologized for only offering a "brief overview" of the films making up the " '80's gore-renaissance" (p. 83).

Along with Jason the most popular monsters of the 1980s were Chucky (the slasher doll), dream invader and child molester Freddy, the chainsaw-wielding Leatherface, and Michael Meyers, who made Halloween something more than a time to dress up and collect free candy from friendly neighbors.

17. The nine films in the *The Friday the 13th* series are *Friday the 13th* (1980), *Friday the 13th, Part II* (1981), *Friday the 13th, Part III* (1983), *Friday the 13th: The Final Chapter* (1984), *Friday the 13th, Part V: A New Beginning* (1985), *Friday the 13th, Part VI: Jason Lives* (1988), *Friday the 13th, Part VII: The New Blood* (1988), *Friday the 13th, Part VIII: Jason Takes Manhattan* (1989), and *Jason Goes to Hell: The Final Friday* (1993).

18. Freddy, who is played by an identifiable actor (Robert Englund) is an exception. He gets some witty repartee in his films and must have his part realized by a competent performer. Most slashers lack Freddy's verbal skills and are content to go about their work anonymously. The usual slasher could be effectively realized by anyone, regardless of theatrical experience, up for the job.

19. For the Christmas 1989 buying season, Paramount Studios released an expensive sculpture of Jason (suitable for coffee tables and paneled dens) celebrating his 10 years in the business and demonstrating corporate support for his career in the 1990s. Jason's representation is also available for purchase by those who cannot manage to come up with the money for big-ticket collectibles. Nearly everyone can afford to run down to the mall and purchase his sensibly priced mask, knife, model, and poster.

Jason has also begun making the talk show rounds with "real" Hollywood personalities. On the *Arsenio Hall Show*, he was treated just like any other self-aggrandizing show-biz star and asked what new dynamic projects he had been involved in of late. Jason brandished his extra-large machete at a shrinking Arsenio by way of reply. It was a stupid question. Whatever Jason is, he is not an innovator. Any fan could tell you Jason makes no career moves. The future Jason will, like the Jason of old, only slash more teenagers. Stars basically do one or two things well, and this celebrity is no exception.

20. Traditionally, the full moon has preceded the Wolfman's transformation or more generally denoted the unwanted presence of spooky beings loose upon the land. While serving notice of evil, it always stood for a particularly mythic source of potential harm. It is now an old-fashioned tocsin. After the slasher, all earlier monsters are idle threats and the signifiers that went with them—full moon, castles, bats, and so forth—become so much ludicrous filigree.

21. Her last reprieve carries special overtones that distinguish it from the wisdom of the semi driver. It has long been a tradition of the older horror film, dating from the silents, that the touched were often gifted by God with second sight. Having been denied a normal mind, they were granted, in divine compensation, the ability to see beyond the parochial limits of ordinary vision.

If this had been a Universal film, Ralph would have initially been ridiculed for his hysterical pronouncements. Eventually, however, he would have won a grateful audience and been celebrated as a prophet. It does not immediately seem odd then that Ralph is not believed as he preaches blood and pain for the foolhardy who dare visit Camp Crystal Lake. What would never occur in older films does when even the oracle, the seer with God's blessings, possessor of a holy talent, is himself killed by Jason in *Friday the 13th, Part II* (1982). Oracles, the most farsighted people to engage the unnatural, will also perish in these difficult times.

22. To demonstrate this point, I attempted to count all the people killed in the entire *Friday the 13th* series. The bodies piled up so quickly that I could never get an accurate head count. Each time through the films I ended up with a different number. I thought of borrowing a click counter, the kind that ticket takers use at ballgames and concerts to accurately gauge how many people came through the turnstiles, and then realized that the fact that it was impossible to exactly total all the corpses without an inerrant adding machine made my point more effectively than a precise body count.

Recently, a commemorative magazine celebrating the latest Jason film has solved this problem. The largest type on the cover, bigger than the type announcing the release of the new film, promises a "Complete Body Count" for the entire series.

23. Jason fits with the fashionable bumper sticker "Shit Happens" that people are proud to display on their cars. "Shit Happens" is the perfect apothegm for the many who believe

life is just an undetermined sequence of chance over which they have no control. Jason is, in the end, nothing more than very bad shit.

24. Annie may have temporarily extended her short life by not hitchhiking to the camp; however, even if she had used a more conventional mode of transport she too would have eventually died. It does not matter, insofar as survival is concerned, whether or not a character uses her head. There are no measures one can use to guarantee personal safety.

25. In *Frisk* (1991), Dennis Cooper supplies a spot-on rendering of how contemporary horror fans enjoy the spectacle of death:

"Wh-wha-what's tha-that s-sou-sound?"

"Freddy Krueger just killed the girl's boyfriend," Joe said.

"H-how?"

"He sucked him into the bed and ripped his skin off or something," Joe said. "Then the mattress raised up and exploded like a volcano."

"G-gr-great." The kid smiled, shut his eyes. He looked dead. "I l-lo-love F-Fr-Fre-Fred-d-dy K-Kr-Krue-g-ge-ger." (p. 56)

26. One way to understand what the withholding of full titles from Jason's prey means is to compare how *Friday the 13th* uses or abuses personal tags to enhance the involvement between audience and text with a similar process used by the classic children's television program *Romper Room*. Both the film and the television show cemented their respective relationships with the audience through the common name.

The conclusion of *Romper Room* always had the earnest hostess reach for her magic mirror and accord hundreds of thousands of children in the audience, as well as more than a few parents, ersatz personal hellos while the show signed off for another broadcast day. It did not matter that she never called out to a particular child as no last names were ever used. There were real people somewhere in television land with such titles, and even though the names were soon lost among the masses, unless you were lucky enough to be personally noted, the illusion persisted that a dialogue between the show and the audience was ongoing.

27. It is also worth noting that we are also on a first-name basis with most contemporary monsters as well.

28. In *Friday the 13th, Part II* and *Jason Goes to Hell: The Final Friday*, anyone can become Jason. The same sort of unavoidable contagion, which assures us that we may all be monsters, animates *Body Parts* (1991) as well.

29. The same thing happens to Nancy, who makes it through Freddy's first adventure, *A Nightmare on Elm Street* (1985). When Nancy is killed in *A Nightmare on Elm Street III: Dream Warriors* (1987), her death is especially underlined to remind us that Nancy was once a "survivor."

7. AFTERWORD

There is everywhere in the civilized world a rapidly rising incidence of vice and crime, mental disorders, suicides and dope addictions, shattered homes, impudent children, violence, murder and despair. These are facts; I am not inventing them.

—Joseph Campbell (1972, p. 11)

The horror film now belongs, until it is once more revivified with a revamped set of novel conventions, to a tired genre. Of course, an occasional shocker is, now and again, given wide release. Jason has returned to the screen for his ninth appearance, Jack Nicholson sprouts a coat as the latest Wolfman, and there is a new *Faces of Death* film (IV) touring the midnight-movie-madness circuit, but in comparison to the number of films released at the end of the 1980s and the beginning of the 1990s, the flow of new product to the local cinema or video store has been stanched.

The exhaustion of the horror film does not, of course, mean that the vivid and cruel violence so closely identified with the contemporary horror film has also passed away. Violence has not disappeared with the waning popularity of the horror film. As the genre of destruction, *the* site for gore, fails to tantalize viewers, the spectacular violence at its center has not been similarly eclipsed by fresher distractions. In fact, the opposite is true. As the horror film returns less and less at the box office, excessive violence has fled its singular preserve and found a welcome home across a disparate number of popular venues. Gore is everywhere. And with the widespread dissemination of gore the body remains the central marker upon which we articulate the spectacular degradation of everyday life.

A proper account of all the sundry spaces where violence holds pride of place in the cultural mix is a task fit for only the most intrepid and tireless encyclopedist. A complete list, if it could ever be finalized, would have to rival one of de Sade's infinite tallies of variable abuse. And should such a list be finished it is unlikely that any reader could be found to bear the cost of actually reading the entire work. That said, it will suffice to quickly survey the scene and mark out symptomatic examples of the contemporary obsession with representations of endless violence.

A staple of journalism is the year-end wrap-up. In this review exercise, the most compelling reportage of the past year is reinterpreted in a holistic manner to create a coherent and defining portrait of the last 365 days. *The Village Voice*'s summation of the past year, titled "All the Rage 1993: A Year in a Variety of Random Acts," is a typical collection. All the 100-plus very short news items document random eruptions of violence across the nation. The central thrust of the essay is, quoting the succinct phrase of a professor of sociology and criminology cited in the story, that "violence is hip":

> "Society screwed me, and now it's payback time."—a man who walked into a Kenosha, Wisconsin McDonald's in August shot and killed two customers and himself, not even coming close to a record. . . . "So rarely does anyone do anything that so lyrically captures the spirit of the times."—Kate Roiphe, in the *Times*, on Lorena Bobbitt. . . . A TV crew from the Spanish-language program *It Happened Like This* filmed a North Lauderdale, Florida man confronting his ex-wife about their daughter's suicide at her graveside in January. The confrontation unexpectedly involved him shooting her 12 times. NBC aired the snuff footage, saying it wanted to "illustrate the horror of domestic violence." . . . "Yes."—Lyle Menendez's response, under oath, to the question, "When you put the shotgun up against her left cheek and pulled the trigger, did you love your mother?" . . . A 15 year old boy who "just seemed to want to make a name for himself" put a fully automatic Tec-9 pistol against the chest of a 35-year-old Chelsea woman and pulled the trigger. . . . The woman was returning from the hospital, having just been shot in the foot in a drive-by. (Doyle, 1994, pp. 28-36; reprinted by permission of the author and *The Village Voice*)

In scanning these depressing briefs, the reader must supply the narrative design or connective tissue between the violent vignettes. Outside of the fact that they all transpired over the past year and are now collected under one dark title, there is no readily apparent connection between the individual news items, None of the acts of violence were committed for similar reasons. The assorted victims are Black and White, men and women, straight and homosexual, young and old, affluent and poor. They really share nothing in common other than being hurt. The varied antagonists are also similarly well distributed across the demographic register.

Yet the meaning of this review, and the many other similar collages produced at year's end, is patently obvious despite the lack of a coherent pattern. The mere act of amassing these seemingly disparate events provides all the undergirding we need to fabricate a compelling narrative.[1] We can make sense of them; they do cohere in a meaningful fashion, not in spite of but because there is no tight connection between these wicked accounts. They make sense because violence is indiscriminate, senseless, an act of chance. To fashion an accurate sign of the times, to plumb the zeitgeist, simply string some acts of violence together, and common sense will take over.[2] Following the pattern most artfully explored by the present-day horror film, terrorizing an audience is most easily accomplished by subjecting the readership to an unmotivated succession of assaults.

The power of such accounts to shape commonsense perceptions of the way of the world is best exemplified by the "random acts of kindness" movement. Those who practice random kindness, the meek flipside to incomprehensible havoc, do so to "balance the ethos of suspicion, hostility and violence" that typifies our lives (O'Connell, 1994, p. 1E). We are urged to commit random acts of senseless kindness upon one another in the hope that such bizarre behaviors will have a restorative effect on the wild world we are forced to inhabit.

The move to remake ourselves as anti-Jasons and anodyne irrationals was started in 1982 by writer Anne Herbert. Ms. Herbert coined the phrase "practice random kindness and senseless acts of beauty" because she felt that "life seems to have many fine moments, but the cruelty level seems excessive" (O'Connell, 1994, p. E1). Over the past decade the expression has seeped into the mainstream and may be found on coffee mugs, T-shirts, bumper stickers, billboards, and other harbors for uplifting messages broadcast for the public good. In addition, three handbooks with helpful suggestions for "guerrilla kindness" have recently been published to aid the untrained or hesitant "smile maker" ("Stumped," 1994, p. E2).

Whether or not any one of us becomes a kind terrorist staging considerate spectacles on dangerous streets is really a moot point. What matters most about this program is that it exists at all, that there really is a call for the inexplicably good deed, and that the quixotic character of the movement is easily understood as an antidote to the equally unpredictable character of everyday violence.

More troubling, the drive to commit impetuous acts of good will is a radical departure from one of the most well known and commonsensical guides to good behavior—the Golden Rule. The Golden Rule works, for all but the most altruistic and saintly among us, on the basis of an implicit quid pro quo. It leads us to expect that we will receive from others that which we give of ourselves. Treat others right and you too will, most likely, be dealt with in a similar fashion. The Golden Rule is a rational calculus for determining how we should act toward one another.

In contrast, to act with unexpected kindness is "in a world of random violence . . . downright dangerous." This new ethic tells us to go ahead and be good to others even though doing so is crazy. It also fails, unlike the Golden Rule, to give us a clear sense of when we should behave well. The Golden Rule, if adopted, covers all behavior for all our waking hours. A commitment to practice random good acts means that we can never predict when and if we are going to exercise consideration for others. Goodness is just another arbitrary quantity and ethical decision making becomes solely a matter of chance. Still, all caveats aside, at least the random kindness movement allows us to expect that at least some of the time, if our luck is running well, we can hope to be treated humanely by strangers.

Although the call for erratic generosity to others is an apparent sign that the world remains a dangerous and unpredictable place, there are equally clear signs posted in other arenas that suggest that monstrous behavior continues unchecked. Recently, the National Death clock was hung in Times Square by the Gun Fighters of America (Barron, 1994, p. E2). The decision to mount the clock over Times Square and the throngs of wary pedestrians who scurry below it was not made capriciously. All public avenues eventually lead to the intersection of Broadway, Seventh Avenue, and 47th Street.

For decades, Times Square has represented the possibility of urban public space in the United States. When the year ends and we cast our wishes for good fortune onto the blank slate of the New Year, many of us do so while watching an illuminated ball fall over the assembled masses in Times Square. When civic leaders mourn the perilous decline of public space, Times Square serves as an ideal backdrop for picturing urban decay. Similarly, projects for urban renewal oftentimes spotlight Times Square as the ideal locale to begin restoring the common ground that belongs to us all. It is one of the places, even if we never set foot in Manhattan, where our paths cross.

Across this common plain, the National Death clock tells us the time. Here the hour is measured by ticking off the gunned down for the year and calculating the number of guns in American hands. The mere existence of such a clock, whose invention calls for the unwelcome merger of chronometry and pathology is, in and of itself, a terrible sign. Pay attention to the numbers and it gets worse. Every 14 minutes another falling body is counted as the death toll goes higher and the number of guns in our possession very nearly equals the entire population of the country.

The National Death clock, a technological and accounting marvel, is not, despite its high-profile location, the most notorious and commonplace measure of everyday terror. The most conspicuous and unavoidable account of urban violence is "gangsta" rap. Gangsta rap, unlike the Death clock, is mobile. No pedestrian or fellow driver has escaped hearing the rhythmic toll of gangsta rap as it thunders from cars and blasters stationed all across public space.[3] The Death clock more precisely gauges the numbers of dead, but gangsta rap offers a far more articulate and local vision of death and pain on American streets. And if everyday life is dangerous in America, it is most dangerous for African Americans.

Gangsta rap is young Black nihilism layered over a nervous collage of brutal noise, aggressive chants, appropriated sounds, and insistent beats. The work of Schooly D, Ice-Cube, Dr. Dre, N.W.A., Scarface, Snoop Doggy Dogg, Ice-T, The Geto Boys, Eazy-E, and an army of angry others gives us, in the words of Cornel West (1991), "the lived experience of coping with a life of horrifying meaninglessness, hopelessness, and (most important) lovelessness" (p. 223). Here, in music whose appeal is by no means limited to a Black audience, guns are fired, blood is splattered, and an endless parade of young men lead very short lives that are all but certain to end in a brutal finish.

Of late, this music has been intensely criticized for contributing to the oppressive conditions that have made the Black male a threatened species. Not coincidentally, as gangsta rap has drawn increasing censure, heavy metal, also frequently cited as an aural offender, is no longer, with one significant exception, attracting much attention for the antisocial character of its clangorous sound. The reason behind the shift in popular opprobrium is most likely a consequence of how differently violence is represented within each of these popular music genres.

Gangsta raps are first-person accounts, usually in the form of hyperbolic boasts, of urban terrorism. Outside of attacks on rap motivated by racism—and it should be noted that not all the criticism directed against gangsta rap is motivated by disdain for the color of the MCs—the most common complaint against the music is that it promotes even greater levels of urban violence by celebrating the unconscionable exploits of gang-bangers.[4] Critics of the genre also argue that the form too closely links the rapper with the deeds recounted in the rap. Impressionable listeners who admire the verbal gymnastics and macho braggadocio of gangsta rappers are then likely to be similarly enamored of the sociopathic violence engaged in by the rappers' protagonists.

This critique is similar to the problem many critics have with the subjective camera stalking the kill in the slasher film. Once a listener or theater patron assumes the point of view of a psychotic actor, he or she is then likely to identify rather too closely with the unwholesome desires of urban predators. Rappers who collapse the critical distance between themselves and the subjects of their work are guilty of criminal behavior, not because they speak of urban violence but because they fail to responsibly mediate between the singer and the song.[5]

In its first-person celebration of death and destruction, gangsta rap uses one of the signature formalisms of the slasher film. Yet rappers go the makers of contemporary horror films one better by emphatically asserting that, unlike other more fantastic representations of violence, their work has an undeniable basis in reality. As life on the streets gets tougher and tougher, the rhymes kick harder and harder.

It is this close, lived connection between gangsta rap and urban mayhem that allows Chuck D of Public Enemy to call rap "the Black CNN" (Nelson & Gonzales, 1991, p. 180). And given the terrible bulletins from the street, Chuck D is probably right to call rappers the news anchors of the disenfranchised.[6] Gangsta rap sounds like a field report, even if the news of the day comes via messengers who can't help but weave a bit of vainglorious swagger into the sound mix. In contrast, no horror film has ever come close to being mistakenly identified as an example of cinema verité.[7]

Unlike gangsta rap, heavy metal has failed to keep up with the terror of everyday life because, at least for most of the better known performers and groups in the genre, metal remains wedded to a now passé style of representing violence. Heavy metal is, in this regard, suffering the same fatigue that has struck the horror film, as both forms hold a somewhat dated affection for the highly stylized and overtly theatrical presentation of violence. The imagery common to both heavy metal and the latter-day horror film is still too thickly imbued with the odor of the supernatural to effectively capture the feel of everyday violence. This style now works to distance a knowing audience from the shock of violence. And, as hard as it may be to imagine, slasher violence is now on the verge of becoming as recherche as the imagery common to *Them!, Frankenstein,* and *Nosferatu.* For horrific imagery to succeed in scaring an audience, it must now resemble, more closely than ever, a terrifying news flash.

In this respect, gangsta rap remains threatening, as it feels closer to "real life" than does the stylistic overkill of metal and the shock film. For those unfamiliar with rap and heavy metal, these differences can be easily appreciated by comparing how extreme violence is represented in films with a rap sensibility, as in *Menace II Society* (1993) or *New Jack City* (1991), and how death is depicted in films with a heavy metal bent, as in *Jason Goes to Hell: The Final Friday* and *Shocker* (1990).[8]

As a consequence of remaining tied to a more overtly theatrical style seasoned with dated supernatural imagery, heavy metal is no longer the subject of widespread condemnation, even though, just a few years ago, the genre was very much in vogue as a pernicious influence. At least that was the case until Guns N' Roses put a Charles Manson track on its latest album, *The Spaghetti Incident*—the group's "roots" album. A roots album, composed of cover tunes, allows a band or performer to pay obeisance to those select performers who played a crucial role in shaping the artist's sensibility. In honoring Charles Manson as a formative influence, Guns N' Roses successfully renewed the moribund genre by replenishing its image repertoire. By naming Manson, a murderous leader, instead of Satan or some other demon spawn from Hell, to its own hall of fame, Guns N' Roses made the great leap forward and refired the metal debate.[9]

The high regard that Guns N' Roses has for Charles Manson is in consonance with the public's late appreciation for movies starring serial killers and relentless psychos instead of demonic slashers. Although slashers lead the way, we now seem to appreciate killers less obviously "horrific" and more "naturally" homicidal. In sum, this wrinkle in taste is best measured by the distance that lies between Hannibal the Cannibal and Elm Street Freddy. It is also an evolution in taste that parallels the shift in public concern from handwringing over heavy metal imagery to attacks on gangsta rap.

In films like *The Silence of the Lambs* (1991), *Pacific Heights* (1990), *Jennifer 8* (1992), *Rampage* (1992), *Blink* (1993), the *Relentless* films (1989, 1992, 1993), *Dead Calm* (1989), *Blue Steel* (1990), *Basic Instinct* (1992), *Sleeping With the Enemy* (1991), *Cape Fear* (1991), *Single White Female* (1992), *Unlawful Entry* (1992), and *The Hand That Rocks the Cradle* (1992) the slasher is remade as a canny, and always intriguing, serial killer or indefatigable psychostalker. Average hacks, those who commit just an ordinary murder or two, fail to command much attention at the cineplex. We need more; consequently, like the pioneering slasher film, each of these movies features spectacular scenes of destruction carried out on the flesh. These central set-pieces celebrate the handiwork of the killer in order to confirm for the audience that the multimurderer on view is a most talented specialist worthy of our undivided attention.

Mainstream films like the above have, however, made a slight departure from the "slice and dice" tradition. In a move toward showcasing greater opportunity for all, death is no longer limited to the young and dumb. The usual victims, witless teens, are gone. In abandoning teen victims, the mainstream film is now free to threaten a greater range of prey. Just as, on the day of assault, mass murderers take whoever happens to be in line to order a Whopper® or is riding the train, mainstream films have elected to offer death to a more demographically respectable range of victims.[10]

Mainstream violence is also bracketed within a more conventional narrative structure. There is a more "realistic" attitude toward unraveling the mystery behind the mayhem and apprehending the responsible party. Mainstream killers, like their slasher forebears, have distinct MOs, but the clues that reborn maniacs leave behind do lead to the successful capture or *mano a mano* destruction of the murderer. In addition, in a move that makes it easier for these films to be read as dramatic extrapolations from everyday threats, the killer is less obviously superhuman. Unlike the slasher, the mainstream killer's multiple talents (intelligence, endurance, cunning), while generally beyond the reach of most normal folks, are not so far advanced as to be outside the pale of human possibility. And, mercifully, given this demotion, once the killers are dead, they usually stay dead.

It should be made clear, however, that as we delineate the nature of popular violence in mainstream film, we are not discussing mere mysteries featuring a somewhat higher than normal body count. Simply because the mainstream film saps the power of the slasher and forces him, and sometimes even her, to kill within a more rational story arc does not mean that the heart of the slasher film has been entirely cut out. The focus of these films, as in the slasher film, remains centered on the figure of the killer and the bloody damage he can do.

Think of the most successful mainstream slasher film, *The Silence of the Lambs*, and imagine the sequel. What characters need to return for the next film in the series? Certainly, it would be good to see Jodie Foster back as FBI agent Clarice Starling, but if the film is to succeed it is absolutely imperative that Anthony Hopkins reprise his star turn as the popular gourmand and killer. He makes the movie, and no matter how much we would care to root for those who battle evil, it is the killer who carries our investment in the picture. So, while the mainstream claws abject horror back to respectability, leaving behind just a bit of the shocker's truly vulgar excess, when we pay our money at the ticket booth we are still anteing up to see death choreographed by a master.[11]

The mainstream has not been alone in responding to the trailblazing innovation of the slasher picture. Of late, there has also been a considerable interest in violence on the art house and festival circuit. Traditionally, these sites have been reserved for films made in opposition to the mainstream. Here, independent directors, difficult film grammars, and stories without commercial prospect are granted relief from the harsh demands of the bottom line.[12] Yet, as critic Lisa Kennedy (1992) makes obvious in her capsule summaries of a number of excessively violent art films, something has happened in the arena reserved for elite film:

> A manic, self-aggrandizing serial killer brings along a documentary TV crew on his appointed rounds—popping, stabbing, garroting a varied demographic of victims. A supersexy sociopath puts a '70s tune on the radio and takes a straight razor to his captive. A nun is tag-team raped on an altar. . . . It's hard to calculate the body count of this year's film festivals, but one thing is apparent: violence, even ultraviolence, is leaving its megabucks venues for artier digs. (p. 3; reprinted by permission of the author and *The Village Voice*)

Like the slasher film and the mainstream serial-kill picture, the art film has elected to embrace the spectacle of violence. Films as varied as *Reservoir Dogs* (1992), *The Cook, the Thief, His Wife, and Her Lover* (1990), *Swoon* (1991), *One False Move* (1992), *Romper Stomper* (1992),

Man Bites Dog (1993), *Bad Lieutenant* (1992), *Benny's Video* (1992), *Henry: Portrait of a Serial Killer* (1990), *Amongst Friends* (1993), *The Baby of Macon* (1994), and *Kika* (1994) all contain terrible moments of profane brutality.

In any other respect, these films have absolutely nothing in common. Yet the role that violence plays in each is so prominent that, even though they differ radically in other regards, they share a common center. Like countless meat movies, violence now makes many art films irredeemably memorable. See *Reservoir Dogs* and you remember the missing ear; watch *Man Bites Dog* and you won't forget the couple whose intercourse is interrupted; screen *One False Move* and Pluto will no longer immediately signify a dim mutt or distant planet.

Styles of representation once confined to a disreputable backwater have now emerged all across the pop spectrum. Few, if any, entertainments have neglected the lessons most successfully executed in the slasher film. Video games let you finish off your opponents by ripping their heart and spine out, local television news continues to make crime pay with endless clips of civic mayhem, "Court TV" devotes gavel-to-gavel coverage to the most lurid and violent crimes we commit, tabloid television continues to offer the finest in programming relentlessly fascinated with human brutality, a good deal of mystery fiction remains preoccupied with the cruel handiwork of the serial killer, and action heroes grow ever meaner, as ultraviolence consumes larger and larger portions of our leisure time. There no longer seem to be effective limits to either the location, as any genre or forum seems open to violence, or the amount of violence available.

In this taste revolution, wherein much of high and low culture grows ever more fascinated with the abuse of the flesh, violence signifies, in all its glorious splendor, an attempt to grasp the feel of the real. Nothing, for the moment, screams "this is real" better than skin and bone under assault.[13] Of course, such practices can camouflage "a state of siege"—everyday life—"as a thrill ride" (Hampton, 1993, p. 72). But unrestrained violence also signifies the groping attempt to construct a visual and verbal lexicon that has some faint chance of accurately capturing the true state of a cruel world. In this regard, the most flagrant excesses represent nothing less than a new form of apocalyptic realism. In the end, the truest images, and the most entertaining, are those pictures and words that make us hurt.

Notes

1. Local news programming does the same thing every evening with the daily parade of today's civic and domestic atrocities. If it bleeds, it leads. It also comes second, third, fourth, ad infinitum. So common and perhaps dangerous is this practice that a recent article in the Business section of *The Charlotte Observer*, titled "Yes, You Can Live Healthy on the Road," advised the business traveler to avoid the news on television if she or he wanted to stay fit (Kohn, 1994, p. D2).

2. Chilling crime reporting is an old staple of the newspaper. As Walter Kendrick (1991) notes, "By the 1860s, newspaper coverage of murders and other domestic mayhem had grown so thorough that playwrights and novelists could rely on their audiences' awareness that a tidy bourgeois surface might easily conceal the most appalling extremes of depravity" (pp. 140-141). It is quite possible that accounts such as these are really nothing new; however, older reports of violence do not read as if James Joyce had authored *A Clockwork Orange*. Crime reporting now uses near avant-garde writing practices to render a fit portrait of what it feels like to live in a dangerous world. In any other context such prose would be impenetrable for a lay audience, but when it comes to crime only the cut-up makes good sense.

3. Rap is not a uniform genre and all rap is not concerned with the daring misadventures of the gangsta. Multiple forms of the music are popular. Still, gangsta rap is currently the most popular and the most violent rap hybrid on the air.

4. Gangsta rappers are also frequently berated for lyrical stylings contemptuous of women and homosexuals. It is probably a mistake to single out the rhymes of gangsta rappers as misogynistic or homophobic. Given the lack of regard that gangsta rappers have for all but their very closest buddies, it is more accurate to simply condemn gangsta rap for its misanthropy.

5. Country singers have done the same thing in their work long before the Carter Family was first recorded early this century. Country music is, however, not generally subject to the same complaint as gangsta rap. There is, oftentimes, a thread of compensatory remorse running through country songs detailing the commission of evil deeds. When the singer rues what he or she has done, rural brutality is sanitized and the genre is exempted from the charge of promoting violence.

6. Marian Wright Edelman, president of the Children's Defense Fund, recently said, "Our worst nightmares are coming true. After years of epidemic poverty, joblessness, racial intolerance, family disintegration, domestic violence and drug and alcohol abuse, the crisis of children having children has been eclipsed by the greater crisis of children killing children." The occasion for these remarks was the release of the Fund's *1994 State of America's Children* report. According to the CDF, a "classroomful" of children are killed everyday and homicide is the third leading cause of death for elementary and middle-school children. In addition, arrests of juveniles for murder and serious cases of manslaughter rose 93% between 1982 and 1991 (Vobejda, 1994, p. 3A).

7. The recent Belgium film *Man Bites Dog* (1993) does offer the original possibility of proving this point wrong. *Man Bites Dog* is a vicious satire that intermingles the conventions of the documentary with those of the slasher film, as an increasingly loyal crew follows a serial killer through his busy days. The film is both funny and appalling as we learn just what it takes to succeed as an uncouth and bigoted multimurderer.

8. This difference extends even to the soundtracks for these films. Slasher films almost always feature heavy metal performers like Alice Cooper, Iron Maiden, and Judas Priest on their soundtracks. Films with a rap allegiance have, not surprising, used rappers. There is

at least one exception to this musical divide. Freddy Krueger has had his own rap album released, but then Freddy has always been the most loquacious of the slashers.

9. Those critical of the band's decision to cover a Manson tune seem to have been unaware that Manson's songs have been covered by many other groups of late. In recent years, Redd Kross, Psychic TV, and the Lemonheads have recorded Manson compositions. Of course, the fact that several performers feel the need to cover Manson's work is no defense against questionable taste; however, it is worth noting that, given his appearance on so many discs, Manson's influence does seem to be widespread.

10. We have not yet reached the point where all victims are equally well represented in serial kill pics. The most common targets are now dual-parent families and single women who are overwhelmingly White and upper middle class. Obviously, these victims do not represent all of us; still, the shift in victims does represent a significant move toward a more inclusive form of terrorism.

11. *The Silence of the Lambs* is an absolutely perfect compromise between the wild nihilism of the slasher flick and mainstream conventionality. To successfully bridge the space between these very different practices, the film gives us two killers. The relatively smart murderer, Buffalo Bill, is shot and killed, but the heart of the picture, the true center of the film, the extraordinary Hannibal Lecter, easily eludes the authorities and lives to kill again and again.

12. I do not wish to overrate the freedom given to filmmakers who practice their art without studio monies. Film is an expensive craft, and finances are always a concern for any filmmaker. Still, art houses and film festivals do offer the independent filmmaker some freedom from the harsh demands of the commercial bottom line.

13. Although try telling that to the unwilling star of the most often screened shocker ever—Rodney King. Yet, even as some members of the jury could not see the obvious and did not believe that Mr. King suffered under excessive force, the national debate over whether or not the Los Angeles police officers involved were just doing their job hung on whether or not you chose to believe your eyes.

REFERENCES

Altman, R. (1986). A semantic/syntactic approach to film genre. In B. K. Grant (Ed.), *Film genre reader* (pp. 26-40). Austin: University of Texas Press.

Aries, P. (1962). *Centuries of childhood: A social history of family life.* New York: Alfred A. Knopf.

Ausband, S. C. (1983). *Myth and meaning, myth and order.* Macon, GA: Mercer University Press.

Axis of fear. (1988, May). *Harper's,* p. 31.

Bakhtin, M. (1984). *Rabelais and his world* (H. Iswolsky, Trans.). Bloomington: Indiana University Press. (Original work published 1965)

Balun, C. (1987). *The gore score.* Albany, NY: Fantaco.

Barker, C. (1984). *Books of blood* (Vol. 1). Berkeley, CA: Berkeley Books.

Barron, J. (1994, January 30). Does anybody here know what time it is? *The New York Times,* p. E2.

Baudrillard, J. (1983, October). What are you doing after the orgy? *Artforum,* pp. 42-46.

Beck, J. (1987). Last workbooks. *Semiotext[e] U.S.A.* [journal].

Bell, D. (1992, July 26). Into the 21st century, bleakly. *The New York Times,* p. E17.

Bennett, W. J. (1984). *To reclaim a legacy: Report on the humanities in higher education.* Washington, DC: National Endowment for the Humanities.

Bennett, W. J. (1992). *The devaluing of America: The fight for our culture and our children.* New York: Summit Books.

Bevington, D. (Ed.). (1988). *The complete works of William Shakespeare* (Vol. 3). New York: Bantam Books.

Blackboard jungle, 1940-1982. (1985, March). *Harper's,* p. 25.

Bloom, A. (1987). *The closing of the American mind.* New York: Simon & Schuster.

Bowles, P. (1979). *Collected stories: 1939-1976.* Santa Barbara, CA: Black Sparrow Press.

Bromwich, D. (1992). *Politics by other means: Higher education and group thinking.* New Haven, CT: Yale University Press.

Burroughs, W. S. (1959). *Naked lunch.* New York: Grove.

Campbell, J. (1972). *Myths to live by.* New York: Viking.

Canby, V. (1990, September 19). A cold-eyed look at the mob's inner workings [Review of *Goodfellas*]. *The New York Times,* p. C1.

Carroll, N. (1982). Nightmare and the horror film: The symbolic biology of fantastic beings. *Film Quarterly, 36*(3), 16-24.

Carroll, N. (1990). *The philosophy of horror or paradoxes of the heart.* New York: Routledge.

Cawelti, J. G. (1985). The question of popular genres. *Journal of Popular Film and Television, 13*(2), 55-61.

Celine, L. F. (1960). *Journey to the end of the night* (J.H.P. Marks, Trans.). New York: New Directions.

Cheever, S. (1992, July 26). [Review of *Down From Troy* by Thomas Seltzer]. *The New York Times Book Review,* p. 1.

Cheney, L. (1988). *Humanities in America: A report to the President, the Congress and the American people.* Washington, DC: National Endowment for the Humanities.

Clover, C. J. (1992). *Men, women, and chainsaws: Gender in the modern horror film.* Princeton, NJ: Princeton University Press.

The Conservation Foundation. (1987). *State of the environment: A view toward the nineties.* Washington, DC: Author.

Cooper, D. (1991). *Frisk.* New York: Grove Wiedenfeld.

Costello, M., & Thurber, S. (1993). Bruised faces and broken hearts. *Safety & Health, 147*(5), 82-84.

Coupland, D. (1991). *Generation X: Tales for an accelerated culture.* New York: St. Martin's.

Coupland, D. (1992). *Shampoo planet.* New York: Pocket Books.

Creed, B. (1989). Horror and the monstrous-feminine: An imaginary abjection. In J. Donald (Ed.), *Fantasy and the cinema* (pp. 63-89). London: British Film Institute.

Daniels, L. (1975). *Living in fear: A history of horror in the mass media.* New York: Scribner.

de Coulteray, G. (1965). *Sadism in the movies* (S. Holt, Trans.). New York: Medical Press.

Deleuze, G. (1986). *Cinema 1: The movement-image* (H. Tomlinson & B. Habberjam, Trans.). Minneapolis: University of Minnesota Press. (Original work published 1983)

Deleuze, G., & Guattari, F. (1987). *A thousand plateaus: Capitalism and schizophrenia* (B. Massumi, Trans.). Minneapolis: University of Minnesota Press. (Original work published 1980)

De Montesquieu, Baron. (1949). *Spirit of the laws* (T. Nugent, Trans.). Riverside, NJ: Hafner.

Dickstein, M. (1984). The aesthetics of fright. In B. K. Grant (Ed.), *Planks of reason: Essays on the horror film* (pp. 65-78). Metuchen, NJ: Scarecrow Press.

Dionne, E. J. (1991). *The war against public life: Why Americans hate politics.* New York: Simon & Schuster.

Donnerstein, E., Linz, D., & Penrod, S. (1987). *The question of pornography: Research findings and policy implications.* New York: Free Press.

Doyle, L. (1994, January 11). All the rage: The year in a variety of random acts. *Village Voice,* pp. 25, 28, 30, 35, 36.

D'Souza, D. (1991). *Illiberal education: The politics of race and sex on campus.* New York: Free Press.

Dworkin, A. (1981). *Pornography: Men possessing women.* New York: Perigee.

Dyer, R. (1988). White. *Screen, 29*(4), 44-64.

Ebert, R. (1969, June). Just another horror movie—Or is it? *Readers Digest,* pp. 127-128.

Ebert, R. (1981). Why movie audiences aren't safe anymore. *American Film, 7*(5), 54-56.

Evans, W. (1984). Monster movies: A sexual theory. In B. K. Grant (Ed.), *Planks of reason: Essays on the horror film* (pp. 53-64). Metuchen, NJ: Scarecrow Press.

Ferrante, A. (1992, October). Hack 'em & slash 'em: The gore years in film. *Pulse,* p. 83.

Fieschi, J. A. (1980). F. W. Murnau (T. Milne, Trans.). In R. Roud (Ed.), *Cinema: A critical dictionary* (Vol. 2, pp. 704-720). Norwich, CT: Nationwide Book Services.

Fiorillo, C. M. (1987, May). [Review of *Lethal Weapon*]. *Films in Review,* pp. 299-300.

Freud, S. (1971). The Uncanny. In J. Strachey (Ed. & Trans.), *The standard edition of the complete psychological works of Sigmund Freud* (Vol. 17, pp. 217-252). London: Hogarth Press.

Gaines, D. (1991). *Teenage wasteland: Suburbia's dead end kids.* New York: Pantheon.

Gifford, D. (1983). *A pictorial history of horror* (rev. ed.). New York: Exeter.

Glut, D. F. (1973). *The Frankenstein legend: A tribute to Mary Shelley and Boris Karloff.* Metuchen, NJ: Scarecrow Press.

Gore, T. (1987). *Raising PG kids in an X-rated society.* Nashville, TN: Abingdon Press.

Gottfried von Herder, J. (1968). *Reflections on the philosophy of the history of mankind* (T. O. Churchill, Trans.). Chicago: University of Chicago Press. (Abridged by F. E. Manuel from 1784-1791 work)

Greenberg, C. (1985). Avant-garde and kitsch. In F. Frascina (Ed.), *Pollock and after* (pp. 1-34). New York: Harper & Row.

Greene, B. (1992, October 27). When chaos gets the green light. *Chicago Tribune,* p. T1.

Greider, W. (1992). *Who will tell the people? The betrayal of American democracy.* New York: Simon & Schuster.

Grossberg, L. (1992). *We gotta get out of this place: Popular conservatism and postmodern culture.* New York: Routledge.

Grosz, E. A. (1986). Language and the limits of the body: Kristeva and abjection. In E. A. Grosz, T. Threadgold, D. Kelly, A. Cholodenko, & E. Colless (Eds.), *Futur*Fall: Excursions into postmodernity* (pp. 106-117). Sydney: Power Institute of Fine Arts, University of Sydney and Futur*Fall.

Hampton, H. (1993, February). When in videodrome: Travels in the new flesh. *Artforum,* pp. 70-73, 113.

Hardy, P. (Ed.). (1986). *The encyclopedia of horror movies.* New York: Harper & Row.

Harper's index. (1985, June). *Harper's,* p. 13.

Hine, T. (1986). *Populuxe.* New York: Alfred A. Knopf.

Hogan, D. J. (1986). *Dark romance: Sexuality in the horror film.* Jefferson, NC: McFarland.

Holmes, R., & DeBurger, J. (1985). Profiles in terror: The serial murderer. *Federal Probation, 49*(4), pp. 29-34.

Jackson, R. (1981). *Fantasy: The literature of subversion.* New York: Methuen.

James, C. (1990, April 6). Peter Greenaway's elegant and brutal cook [Review of *The Cook, the Thief, His Wife and Her Lover*]. *The New York Times,* p. C12.

Kassiola, J. J. (1990). *The death of industrial civilization: The limits to economic growth and the repoliticization of advanced industrial society.* Albany: State University of New York Press.

Kemp, D. D. (1990). *Global environmental issues: A climatological approach.* London: Routledge.

Kendrick, W. (1991). *The thrill of fear: 250 years of scary entertainment.* New York: Grove Weidenfeld.

Kennedy, L. (1992, December 1). The kill: Eight critics talk about violence and the movies. *Village Voice Film Special,* pp. 2-6.

Kennedy, P. (1993). *Preparing for the twenty-first century.* New York: Random House.

Kidron, M., & Smith, D. (1991). *The new state of war and peace: An international atlas.* New York: Simon & Schuster.

Kimball, R. (1990). *Tenured radicals: How politics has corrupted our higher education.* New York: HarperCollins.

Kohn, B. (1994, February 7). Yes, you can live healthy on the road. *The Charlotte Observer,* p. D2.

Kristeva, J. (1979). Ellipsis on terror and the specular seduction. *Wide Angle, 3*(3), 42-47.

Kristeva, J. (1982). *Powers of horror: An essay on abjection* (L. Roudiez, Trans.). New York: Columbia University Press. (Original work published 1980)

Kroker, A., & Cook, D. (1986). *The postmodern scene: Excremental culture and hyper-aesthetics.* New York: St. Martin's.

Kroker, A., & Kroker, M. (1987). Panic sex in America. In A. Kroker & M. Kroker (Eds.), *Body invaders: Panic sex in America* (pp. 10-19). New York: St. Martin's.

Laplanche, L., & Pontalis, J. B. (1973). *The language of psycho-analysis* (D. Nicholson-Smith, Trans.). New York: Norton. (Original work published 1967)

Lederman, E. (1992, June). The best places to meet good men. *Cosmopolitan,* pp. 136-140, 144.

Lifton, R. J., & Strozier, C. B. (1990, August 12). Waiting for Armageddon. *The New York Times Book Review,* pp. 1, 24-25.

Lippman, W. (1946). *Public opinion.* New York: Pelican Books.

Loeb, P. (1986). *Nuclear culture: Living and worrying in the world's largest atomic complex.* Philadelphia: New Society.

Louvin Brothers. (1989). The great atomic power [lyrics]. On the album *Hillbilly Music . . . Thank God! Vol. 1.* Distributed through Capitol Records, Inc.

Lucanio, P. (1987). *Them or us: Archetypal interpretations of fifties alien invasion films.* Bloomington: Indiana University Press.

Lyotard, J.-F. (1984). *The post-modern condition: A report on knowledge* (G. Bennington & B. Massumi, Trans.). Minneapolis: University of Minnesota Press.

Marcus, G. (1992, August). Notes on the life and death and incandescent banality of rock 'n' roll. *Esquire,* 67-75.

Marcuse, P. (1992, May). Gimme shelter. *Artforum,* pp. 88-92.

Marriot, M. (1992, September 13). On meaner streets, the violent are more so. *The New York Times,* p. E4.

Maslin, J. (1990a, July 30). Attention, claims adjusters! Willis is back in "Die Hard II" [Review of *Die Hard II*]. *The New York Times,* p. C11.

Maslin, J. (1990b, December 2). Horror puts on its worst face: The human one. *The New York Times,* p. H19.

Masson, J. M. (1985). *The assault on truth: Freud's suppression of the seduction theory.* New York: Penguin.

McKinney, D. (1993). Violence: The strong and the weak. *Film Quarterly, 46*(4), 16-22.

McNaughton, C. (1994). *Making friends with Frankenstein: A book of monstrous poems and pictures.* Cambridge, MA: Candlewick Press.

Meltzer, R. (1987). *The aesthetics of rock* (rev. ed.). New York: Da Capo Press.

Meyers, R. (1983). *For one week only: The world of exploitation films.* Piscataway, NJ: New Century.

Modleski, T. (1986). The terror of pleasure: The contemporary horror film and postmodern theory. In T. Modleski (Ed.), *Studies in entertainment: Cultural approaches to mass culture* (pp. 155-166). Bloomington: Indiana University Press.

Monaco, J. (1980). Aaaiieeeaarrggh. *Sight and Sound, 49*(2), 80-82.

Naremore, J. (1988). *Acting in the cinema.* Berkeley: University of California Press.

Neale, S. (1980). *Genre.* London: British Film Institute.

Nelson, H., & Gonzales, M. A. (1991). *Bring the noise: A guide to rap music and hip-hop culture.* New York: Harmony Books.

Noriega, C. (1987). Godzilla and the Japanese nightmare: When *Them!* is U.S. *Cinema Journal, 27*(1), 63-77.

O'Boyle, T. F. (1992, September 15). Disgruntled workers intent on revenge increasingly harm colleagues and bosses. *The Wall Street Journal,* pp. 1B, 10B.

O'Connell, (1994, January 16). Passing it on. *The Charlotte Observer,* pp. E1-E2.

Oliver, M. B. (1993). Adolescents' enjoyment of graphic horror: Effects of viewers' attitudes and portrayals of victims. *Communication Research, 20*(1), 30-50.

References

O'Rourke, P. J. (1985, December 14). The year of living stupidly. *Rolling Stone*, pp. 91-96, 171.

Penley, C. (1989). *The future of an illusion: Film, feminism, and psychoanalysis*. Minneapolis: University of Minnesota Press.

Plagens, P., Miller, M., Foote, D., & Yoffe, E. (1991, April 1). Violence in our culture. *Newsweek*, pp. 46-52.

Prawer, S. S. (1980). *Caligari's children: The film as tale of terror*. Oxford: Oxford University Press.

Prince, S. (1988). Dread, taboo and *The Thing*: Toward a social theory of the horror film. *Wide Angle, 10*(3), 19-29.

Schatz, T. (1981). *Hollywood genres: Formulas, filmmaking and the studio system*. Philadelphia: Temple University Press.

Shaviro, S. (1993). *The cinematic body*. Minneapolis: University of Minnesota Press.

Shepherd, C. (1992, November 25). News of the weird. *Break*, p. 5.

Sloterdijk, P. (1987). *Critique of cynical reason* (M. Eldred, Trans.). Minneapolis: University of Minnesota Press. (Original work published 1983)

Sobchack, V. (1987). *Screening space: The American science fiction film*. New York: Ungar.

Sontag, S. (1979). The imagination of disaster. In G. Mast & M. Cohen (Eds.), *Film theory and criticism* (pp. 488-504). New York: Oxford University Press.

Sragow, M. (1992, November 16). Guns and lovers [Review of *Under Siege*]. *The New Yorker*, pp. 130-133.

Stone, J. (1983). The horrors of power: A critique of Kristeva. In F. Barker, P. Hulme, M. Iverson, & D. Loxley (Eds.), *The politics of theory* (pp. 38-48). Colchester, UK: University of Essex Press.

Stumped for smile-makers? Here are ideas. (1994, January 16). *The Charlotte Observer*, p. E2.

Thomas, L. (1983). *Late night thoughts on listening to Mahler's Ninth Symphony*. New York: Viking.

Todorov, T. (1975). *The fantastic: A structural approach to a literary genre* (R. Howard, Trans.). Ithaca, NY: Cornell University Press.

Tobin, R. (1990). *The expendable future: U.S. politics and the protection of biological diversity*. Durham, NC: Duke University Press.

Tudor, A. (1989). *Monsters and mad scientists: A cultural history of the horror movie*. Oxford: Basil Blackwell.

Turner, G. E., & Price, M. H. (1986). *Forgotten horrors: Early talkie chillers from poverty row*. Guernville, CA: Eclipse Books.

Twitchell, J. B. (1985). *Dreadful pleasures: An anatomy of modern horror*. New York: Oxford University Press.

Ventura, M. (1990, September-October). On kids and slasher movies. *Utne Reader*, pp. 119-121.

Vickery, J. B. (1966). *Myth and literature: Contemporary theory and practice*. Lincoln: University of Nebraska Press.

Virilio, P. (1986). *Speed and politics* (M. Polizotti, Trans.). New York: Semiotext[e]. (Original work published 1977)

Virilio, P., & Lotringer, S. (1983). *Pure war* (M. Polizotti, Trans.). New York: Semiotext[e].

Vobejda, B. (1994, January 21). New crisis: Children killing children. *The Charlotte Observer*, p. 3A.

Wagar, W. W. (1982). *Terminal visions: The literature of last things*. Bloomington: Indiana University Press.

Waller, G. A. (1986). *The living and the undead: From Stoker's Dracula to Romero's Dawn of the Dead*. Chicago: University of Illinois Press.

Weinstein, D. (1991). *Heavy metal: A cultural sociology.* Lexington, MA: Lexington Books.

West, C. (1991, Spring). Nihilism in Black America. *Dissent,* 221-226.

Williams, L. (1983). When the woman looks. In M. A. Doane, P. Mellencamp, & L. Williams (Eds.), *Re-vision: Essays in feminist film criticism* (pp. 83-99). Frederick, MD: University Publications of America.

Williams, L. (1989). *Hard core: Power, pleasure and the "frenzy of the visible."* Berkeley: University of California Press.

Willis, D. (1972-1984). *Horror and science fiction films* (Vols. 1-3). Metuchen, NJ: Scarecrow Press.

Wood, R. (1984). An introduction to the American horror film. In B. K. Grant (Ed.), *Planks of reason: Essays on the horror film* (pp. 164-200). Metuchen, NJ: Scarecrow Press.

Wood, R. (1987). Returning the look: Eyes of a Stranger. In G. A. Waller (Ed.), *American horrors: Essays on the modern American horror film* (pp. 81-85). Urbana: University of Illinois Press.

Wright, W. (1975). *Six-guns and society.* Berkeley: University of California Press.

INDEX

ABOUT THE AUTHOR

Jonathan Lake Crane was born in Hackensack, New Jersey, in 1959. He earned an A.B. in psychology from the University of Illinois in 1981 and later returned to pursue his doctorate in communication through the university's Institute for Communication Research. He received his Ph.D. in 1991. His work on the audience and Top 40 radio, the horror film, and music censorship has appeared in *Popular Music and Society, Communication,* and the *Journal of Communication Inquiry.* Presently, he is an Assistant Professor in the Department of Communication Studies at the University of North Carolina at Charlotte.